TECHNOLOGY, THE ECONOMY, AND SOCIETY
The American Experience

TECHNOLOGY, THE ECONOMY, AND SOCIETY

The American Experience

Edited by Joel Colton
and Stuart Bruchey

Columbia University Press
New York   1987

Library of Congress Cataloging-in-Publication Data

Technology, the economy, and society.

  Includes bibliographies.
  1. Technology—Economic aspects—United States.
2. Technology—Social aspects—United States.
I. Colton, Joel   . II. Bruchey, Stuart
T21.T427 1987   303.4′83′0973   86–24475
ISBN 0-231-05964-7

Columbia University Press
New York   Guildford, Surrey
Copyright © 1987 Columbia University Press
All rights reserved
Printed in the United States of America

Book design by Ken Venezio

Contents

Contributors

Stuart Bruchey, Allan Nevins Professor of American Economic History, Columbia University, received his Ph.D. at the Johns Hopkins University in 1955. He has served as president of the Economic History Association and has been awarded Guggenheim, Social Science Research Council, and National Endowment for the Humanities fellowships. He has been a member of the Institute for Advanced Study at Princeton and a fellow at the Center for Advanced Study in the Behavioral Sciences at Palo Alto. He is the author of *Robert Oliver: Merchant of Baltimore*, *The Colonial Merchant*, *Cotton and the Growth of the American Economy*, *Roots of American Economic Growth*, and *Growth of the Modern American Economy*, and of the forthcoming *The Wealth of the Nation: An Economic History of the United States*.

Derk Bruins, Associate Professor of Political Science at California State University, San Bernardino, received his Ph.D. at Columbia University in 1981. He has also taught at Occidental College and California State University, Fullerton.

Alfred D. Chandler, Jr., Straus Professor of Business History, Harvard Graduate School of Business Administration, received his Ph.D. degree at Harvard University in 1952. He has been awarded a Guggenheim fellowship and has received honorary degrees from the University of Leuven, the University of Antwerp, and Babson College. He is the author of *The Visible Hand: The Managerial Revolution in American Business*, which received the Newcomen, Bancroft, and Pulitzer prizes, and of *Strategy and Structure*, which received a Newcomen award. Co-author with Steven Salsbury of *Pierre S. du Pont and the*

Making of the Modern Corporation, he also is editor of *The Papers of Dwight David Eisenhower, 1941–1945,* published by Johns Hopkins Press in five volumes.

Geraldine Joncich Clifford, Professor of Education, University of California, Berkeley, received her Ed.D. at Columbia University in 1961. She has been awarded Guggenheim, Rockefeller, and Spencer Foundation fellowships and research grants. She is the author of *The Sane Positivist: A Biography of Edward L. Thorndike, The Shape of American Education,* and of a forthcoming historical study of women faculty in coeducational colleges and universities.

Joel Colton, Professor of History, and former Chairman, Department of History, Duke University, received his Ph.D. degree at Columbia University in 1950. On leave from Duke, he has also served as Director for Humanities at the Rockefeller Foundation. Currently he is a co-president of the International Commission on the History of Social Movements and Social Structures. He has been awarded Guggenheim, Rockefeller Foundation, and National Endowment for the Humanities fellowships, and has been elected a Fellow of the American Academy of Arts and Sciences. He is the author of *Compulsory Labor Arbitration in France, 1936–1939, Léon Blum: Humanist in Politics,* which received a Mayflower award, and *Twentieth Century* (a volume in the Time-Life Great Ages of Man series), and co–author with R. R. Palmer of *A History of the Modern World,,* now in its sixth edition.

Melvyn Dubofsky, Professor of History and Sociology, State University of New York at Binghamton, received his Ph.D. at the University of Rochester in 1960. He has been awarded fellowships and grants by the National Endowment for the Humanities, the American Council of Learned Societies, the American Philosophical Society, and the American Association for State and Local History. He is the author of *When Workers Organize: New York City in the Progressive Period, We shall Be All: A History of the IWW, John L. Lewis: A Biography,* and *Industry and the American Worker, 1865–1920,* now in its second edition.

David C. Hammack, Associate Professor of History, Case Western Reserve University, received his Ph.D. at Columbia University in 1974. He has also taught at Princeton University, has been a resident fellow at the Russell Sage Foundation, and has been awarded a Guggenheim fellowship for 1986–87. He is the author of *Power and Society: Greater New York at the Turn of the Century.*

Kenneth T. Jackson, Professor of History and of Urban Planning, Columbia University, received his Ph.D. at the University of Chicago in 1966. He has been awarded Guggenheim, American Council of Learned Societies, National Endowment for the Humanities, and Woodrow Wilson fellowships and a Fulbright lectureship, and is a Fellow of the Society of American Historians. He is the author of *The Ku Klux Klan in the City, 1915–1930* and *Crabgrass Frontier: The Suburbanization of the United States,* which, published in 1985, won both the Bancroft and Frances Parkman prize. He is also co-editor of *Cities in American History* and of *American Vistas.*

Martin E. Marty, Fairfax M. Cone Distinguished Service Professor, University of Chicago, received his Ph.D. at the University of Chicago in 1956. He has served as president of the American Society of Church History and of the American Catholic Historical Association, and is president-elect of the American Academy of Religion. A Fellow of the American Academy of Arts and Sciences, he is the author of, among other books, *Righteous Empire,* which won a National Book award, *A Nation of Behavers, Pilgrims in Their Own Land,* and most recently (1986), *Modern American Religion, Volume I: The Irony of It All.*

Morton Rothstein, Professor of History, University of California, Davis, received his Ph.D. degree at Cornell University in 1960. He has been awarded Social Science Research Council and National Endowment for the Humanities fellowships. Editor of *Agricultural History,* he has contributed articles and chapters to periodicals and collaborative volumes, and in 1983 won the Carstensen prize for one of his articles on agricultural history.

Harry N. Scheiber, Professor of Law, University of California, Berkeley, received his Ph.D. at Cornell University in 1961. He has been awarded National Endowment for the Humanities, Guggenheim, Rockefeller Foundation, and Fulbright fellowships, and has been a resident fellow at the Center for Advanced Studies in the Behavioral Sciences. He is the author of *The Wilson Administration and Civil Liberties, 1917–1921* and

Ohio Canal Era: A Case Study of Government and the Economy, co-author of *American Economic History,* co—editor with Lawrence M. Friedman of *American Law and the Constitutional Order: Historical Perspectives,* and contributor to *Ambivalent Legacy: A Legal History of the South.*

Harold G. Vatter, Professor of Economics Emeritus, Portland State University, received his Ph.D. at the University of California, Berkeley, in 1950. He has also taught at Carleton College, the University of Massachusetts, and Oregon State University, and has served as Lilly faculty fellow at the University of Chicago. He is the author of *The United States Economy in the 1950s, The Drive to Industrial Maturity, Some Aspects of the Problem of Small Enterprise,* and *The United States Economy in World War II.*

Preface

The essays in this volume grew out of an international research project sponsored by the International Commission on the History of Social Movements and Social Structures. The Commission, whose headquarters is in Paris, is an affiliate of the International Congress of Historical Sciences, the official coordinating body for historians and professional historical associations worldwide, which plans and convenes a historical congress every five years. For each of these congresses the commission chooses a theme on which to focus its historically oriented interdisciplinary research and enlists the support of research teams from a wide variety of countries in preparing individual national reports. In past years such themes have included labor in the Great Depression, peasant movements, migration, and small business enterprise. In 1980, the commission, meeting in Bucharest, resolved to explore globally the impact of technological innovation on changes in society from the eighteenth century to the present; social and economic aspects were to be examined as well as those cultural and psychological elements that have encouraged either resistance or adaptation to change. The results of that inquiry became available for the international congress that met in Stuttgart five years later.

The commission asked the editors of the present volume, both of whom serve as American representatives on the commission, to act as directors of the American research team, with wide latitude to choose the topics to be studied and to solicit the contributions of leading American scholars. To their deep satisfaction, the research directors received the support of some of the foremost scholars in the country in a wide range of fields and disciplines who have responded with insightful research papers in their specialties. How, they asked, has technological change affected such areas of American life as law, business, labor, the cities, agriculture, political parties, the military, education, religion, and other key sectors of the American economy and society?

In June 1984, under the auspices of the commission, the directors of the American team met in Salerno, Italy, for a three-day colloquium with the directors of the research teams from over twenty-five countries drawn from five continents. Many of the same scholars then met at the international congress in Stuttgart a year later. Both conferences examined the reports prepared by each national research team as well as composite syntheses designed to study the historical impact of technological innovation from a comparative and international perspective. At the two international meetings the synthesis presented on behalf of the American research team was so well received that the directors were encouraged to publish the essays by the American scholars in a separate volume and to make their contributions available to a wider audience both at home and abroad. It is hoped that the distinctive nature of the American experience, important in itself, will also help provide a basis for comparison with the impact of technological innovation in other parts of the world.

We should like to express our gratitude to the co–presidents of the commission during the period of this research for their active counsel and inspiration: the late Professor Werner Conze, of the University of Heidelberg; Professor Domenico Demarco, of the University of Naples; and Professor Jacques Droz, of the University of Paris. Above all, we owe special thanks to the secretary-general of the commission, Mme. Denise Fauvel-Rouif, who with unflagging enthusiasm, resourcefulness, and skill has administered the commission's affairs since its inception in 1953 and has been an unending source of support and encouragement for all involved in its work.

To our American collaborators on this volume, each and every one, we owe a special debt and thank them individually and collectively for their contributions. We are grateful also to Kate Wittenberg and her associates at Columbia University Press for their many services in seeing this manuscript through to publication and to Shirley B. Colton for her encouragement at every stage, including her presence at the international meetings and various editing contributions.

It was solely at the instance of one of the co-editors, and over the protest of the other, that violence has been done to the traditional alphabetical listing of co-editors. This disagreement, it may be recorded, has been the sole source of friction between them.

Joel Colton
Stuart Bruchey

TECHNOLOGY, THE ECONOMY, AND SOCIETY
The American Experience

1. Introduction

Joel Colton
Duke University

Stuart Bruchey
Columbia University

Technology, defined as the way in which we transform and use energy, is, in Fernand Braudel's formulation, the queen that changes the economy and hence changes the world. The French historian's epigram in some measure suggests the answer to a key question: how do technological, economic, and social changes interrelate? Although technological change is the source of economic development and growth, and a contributory factor to social change, it is not sufficient by itself, one may argue, for transforming society. Only when absorbed into the economy does technological change increase output, raise income, and have an important impact in numerous ways on the structural transformation of society.

There would probably be common agreement about the dozen or so prominent social changes in the United States over the last century that can be linked to technological and economic change. Beginning with the transformation from an agrarian to an urban society, the list would include demographic changes and the redistribution of population; rising living and health standards and consumption patterns; changes in the role of government and in the family, education, and religious institutions; an organizational revolution in business; the emergence and evolution of the labor movement; the changed composition of the work force and the pattern of job distribution; the changing status of women, blacks, young people, and the elderly; and the emergence of consumer and environmental movements. Not least would be the institutionalization of research and development, formalizing the process of technological innovation itself. With appropriate modifications, the same list could be projected for other countries and for contemporary society as a whole.

In the American experience, four major chronological periods of technological and economic development are discernible for our purposes: first, the years from the beginnings of the country to about 1870; second, the years 1870 (or 1890) to 1919; third, the years 1919–1945; and fourth, the contemporary era from 1945 to the present (with sharp changes emerging in the 1960s and 1970s– future historians may some day see here the opening of a fifth era).

From colonial times to about 1870 the foundations of an industrial society were successfully laid. The industrial revolution that began in England in the late eighteenth century was imported into the new American nation. By coincidence the American Declaration of Independence, Adam Smith's *Wealth of Nations,* and James Watt's steam engine all date from 1776. The new nation thrived on commerce and industry. The world of which the United States was a part was entering a new era of cumulative self-propelling advances in technology with broad repercussions for economic life and society. The use of energy derived from fossil fuels and its application as steam power gradually changed the world. By importing power-driven machinery and skilled immigrants from Europe, the United States created the basis for an industrial nation that grew rapidly in the decades from the 1820s on— except for the decade of the Civil War.

In the period after the Civil War the pace of industrial change quickened even more. A second industrial revolution took place with the expanded application of power, high-volume manufacturing, new industries, and new forms of transportation and communication. These years saw the inauguration of commercial electric power, so that as the twentieth century progressed the typical power unit would no longer be water or the steam engine but the turbogenerator. Only with modern energy forms could large-scale manufacturing and distribution take place; older forms of energy such as animal power, wind, and current were slow and unreliable. The expansion in manufacturing was accompanied by innovations in transportation and communications—the railroad, the steamship, the telegraph, the overseas cable. The late nineteenth century also witnessed an "organizational revolution"—new ways of organizing, managing, and coordinating workers, materials, and power-driven machinery into large integrated industrial units; without such organizational changes technological advances alone would not have been able to sustain mass-production and mass-distribution systems.

The organizational revolution of the 1890s cannot be overemphasized. Earlier, industrial enterprises were small and personally managed. Already in the 1850s and 1860s new management techniques helped coordinate the flow of goods on the railroads and helped oversee new mass retailing establishments such as department stores, mail order houses, and chain stores. After the 1890s the new managerial techniques, applied to industry, made possible the flow of goods and services through large-scale units of production and distribution; the decisive element was not input or industrial capacity alone but "throughput," the result of effective management—the "visible hand," in Alfred Chandler's apt formulation. In capital-intensive industries, production was increased not by adding more machinery and more workers but by improving and rearranging input, reorganizing production processes, and augmenting the importance of applied energy. New technology and new management together made possible large economies and impressive reductions in cost per unit. The culmination of the "organizational revolution" came with the mass production of the automobile. When Henry Ford's assembly line technique, perfected in 1913, reduced the time needed to manufacture a Model T from over twelve to one and a quarter hours, the entrepreneur cut the price of a car by about one half at the same time that he paid high wages ($5 a day) and amassed a personal fortune.

The new integrated large industrial enterprises went even further in the interests of economic efficiency. They succeeded in controlling raw and semifinished materials at one end and marketing operations at the other. They invested abroad, initially in marketing, and then in production. Among the large enterprises competition rarely occurred in price alone; product differentiation through retailing and advertising became important. The phenomenon of large industrial enterprises appeared not only in the United States but in Europe as well at much the same time and took root in clusters of industries with similar production and distribution patterns. In the United States the large enterprises were grouped around food, chemicals, petroleum, metals, and machinery. Here oligopolies developed in which a small number of firms competed for a market share; elsewhere similar monopolistic tendencies emerged. The stage was set for the emergence in our day of the multinational corporation and global oligopolies. Technological advances and corporate organization made large-scale reductions in production costs possible. Meanwhile increased per capita income led to increased demand for goods and services which motivated even further economic growth. Social problems of continuing contemporary importance had their origins in this age also; with large scale factory production came the fragmentation of tasks, a curtailment of the job satisfaction inherent in an older craftsmanship, labor alienation, and the growth of additional hierarchical levels of management. The proportion of white-collar workers and service employees, which would grow significantly over the long term, began to increase at this time.

The technological and economic changes underway after 1870 (and especially after 1890) intensified the shift from an agrarian to an urban society, the hallmark of the modern developed nation. Yet the change was a gradual one. Despite industrial advances in the years after 1870, the United States census reports indicate that until 1914 the urban population remained smaller than the rural population. Agriculture did not grow as spectacularly as industry and commerce in the years 1870–1914, and hence did not provide the foodstuffs that would have made possible a more rapid expansion of urban population. Although farm production as a whole increased, productivity, that is, yields per acre and output per farm worker, rose only moderately. Despite increased mechanization on the farm, there was as yet no great breakthrough in the application of science to agriculture. In the years 1870 to 1910 population grew at an annual rate of 2.12 per cent, but farm output rose only at an annual rate of 2.29 percent (the small surplus being exported).

Nonetheless the shift from an agrarian to an urban society in the years 1870 to 1914, even if incomplete, had a striking impact on American society in numerous ways. One effect of urbanization was a decline in the rate of population increase. The urban demographic growth rate turned out to be lower than the rural growth rate; smaller families were more common in the cities than on the farms. The growth rate declined even though advances in public health and medical care, more readily available in the cities, raised life expectancy and cut mortality rates. The urban family household differed from the rural in more ways than in size. The farm family was both a production and a consumer unit, home and work place were one and the same, and even education was in good measure confined to the home. (As late as 1870, the statistics reveal, the average American had only four years of schooling.) Men, women, and children worked cooperatively in long hours of arduous tasks on the farm, and an extended family, often of several generations, lived under the same roof. Whereas the more self-sufficient farm family made few demands on the outside world, the urban family sought amenities and domestic conveniences made possible by indoor water, gas, electric lighting, and eventually complete electrification. Families in the cities looked forward to educating their children in schools. The lightening of domestic household chores prepared the way for a long-run improvement in the lives of women and the opening of broader economic choices.

The new economic era created the modern city. Earlier, workers lived and worked in the same compact and densely concentrated urban areas; commerce and trade were intermixed with residential life, and industries, stores, offices, and homes were crowded together; there was a clear delineation between city and country. New forms of transportation created the modern city, a process that accelerated after the 1870s. The horsecar, steam-driven ferry, trolley, bus, and eventually the commuter railroad all contributed. It became possible for higher-income families to move to the periphery; commuting to work became a pattern. As early as the 1860s the inner urban core was losing population to the suburbs; commercial and residential life were in the process of separation. After the 1880s the electric streetcar linked residential areas to the heart of the cities.

The greatest impact on urban life came from the internal combustion engine, though in the early twentieth century, before 1914, it was not year clear how important the automobile would be. But by the 1920s, as the cost of the automobile fell, its future became clearer. One could now live, commute, and work without dependence on trolley-car tracks. Moreover, truck transportation replaced the horse-drawn wagon, and factories no longer had to cluster at the rail junctions of large cities. Industry freed itself from high land prices and municipal regulation, and moved away from the cities. In 1915 there were an estimated 158,000 trucks on the road; in 1950 there were 3.5 million. The electric trolley, the bus, the truck, and above all the private automobile changed urban life and work. Generalizations about the automobile and the internal combustion engine are many. The automobile, it has been said, has had "greater social and spatial impact on cities than any technological innovation since the development of the wheel." It has been compared in historical importance to "the clock, gunpowder, the printing press, and the steam engine." It made possible, for good or for ill, the metropolis, the suburb, the inner city, the freeway, and the urban cluster we call the megalopolis. It created not only ease of transportation but also traffic congestion and air pollution. No matter what its disadvantages, it made possible an unprecedented flexibility in living and work patterns and helped create an increasingly standardized urban homogeneity worldwide, an "automobile culture." The internal combustion engine, the diesel locomotive, and the airplane all transformed transportation, and hence created the modern world, shrinking distances and knitting the world together as never before.

The years 1919–1945 saw the consolidation and large-scale application of the technological and organizational changes of the earlier period. Electricity, motorized transportation, and new industries (including the chemical and petrochemical industries) made their mark even more visibly on the economy and society, as did the continued growth and power of corporate organization.

Between 1870 and 1914 the pattern was set for contemporary technological and economic growth, but it was the sixty years from 1920 to 1980, and especially the years after 1945, that brought spectacular breakthroughs in agriculture, accelerated the exodus from the farms, and completed the urbanization process. The application of science to agriculture had been foreshadowed in the nineteenth century by scattered agricultural experimental stations and by the Morrill Land Grant College Act of 1862, which paved the way for institutionalized agricultural research and training. In the interwar years in the twentieth century, continued mechanization—the wider use of the tractor, truck, and other power-driven machinery—was responsible for increased output, but the most dramatic change came with electrification, which transformed the rural countryside.

The critical developments took place in the 1930s with the Rural Electrification Act and the model for river valley development initiated by the Tennessee Valley Authority. Whereas only one-tenth of American farmers had electricity in 1930, the figure had risen to one-third by 1940. Even more significant changes in agriculture occurred after 1945. Mechanization and electrification were overshadowed by sensational scientific breakthroughs in biochemistry and agronomy. The new developments made possible hybrid seed for corn, improved wheat strains, resistant plant varieties, better animal breeds, and powerful commercial fertilizers. (The consumption of commercial fertilizers was two-thirds greater in the 1950s than in the previous decade.) Although the new agriculture depended on electrification and mechanization, and drew heavily on soil conservation and irrigation techniques of an earlier era, the great advances stemmed from scientific research. A new agricultural revolution was under way; agricultural performance was exceeding that of all other sectors.

The social effects were profound. Scientific agriculture and the large commercial market-oriented units called agribusiness, which made possible, and profited from, scientific agriculture, resulted in a dramatic exodus from the land and a sharp decline in the American farm population. The figures are startling. The farm population peaked in 1916 at 32.5 million and still counted 30.5 million in 1940 but dropped to 7.2 million in 1980 (or only 3.3 percent of the population). Simultaneously, the level of per capita income for the nation as a whole rose significantly, with vast implications for social change; until 1945 low farm income had held back overall per capita income.

On the negative side, the social costs of the new scientific agriculture were heavy; herbicides, pesticides, and artificial chemical fertilizers harmed the soil and polluted the nation's waterways. For the consumer an increased dependence on processed foods prepared by the agribusiness complex made foods more readily available (and with no seasonal limitations) but often had negative effects on nutrition, health, and sometimes taste.

How did the changes in production, distribution, and transportation we have been describing—mechanization, electrification, assembly line production, urbanization, the "organizational revolution," the rise of agribusiness, and eventually computerization—affect the other great factor of production, labor and the labor movement (including women, minorities, and the young)?

Technological change has always had an enormous impact on the American worker. From the earliest times it altered the lives of working people who had to accustom themselves to the unfamiliar discipline of the industrial workplace. With some exceptions, technological innovation has led to the gradual "deskilling" of labor, the weakening, dilution, and even disappearance of crafts and skills, and the loss of a sense of job autonomy. With technology, managerial supervision over the processes of production increased. Some labor historians have argued that the true motivation for close supervision has been to control labor independence, but it is more likely that the motivation has been simply to increase productivity and profits through the more efficient coordination of labor, materials, and technology. No matter what the motives, the reality remained a struggle for power, with labor seeking job autonomy and bargaining strength, and management seeking efficiency and maximum production.

The technological changes of the nineteenth century deeply affected the craft unions of skilled workers. Once powerful in the market place and not easily ignored, they lost their strategic role as mechanization and assembly line production took over (even if in pockets of the economy older production forms and skills for a long time continued to exist).

From the early 1800s to the 1870s machine production involved principally the textile industries and did not significantly spread to other sectors of the economy. In most trades the skilled workers, organized into craft unions, generally owned their tools, or even if they used tools and machinery provided by the employer, worked at their own pace with minimum supervision (even in the coal mines). There were no formal schooling or training programs; skills were passed on within the family, often under union-controlled apprenticeship programs. Employers even depended on local union hiring halls for their labor.

Sometime after the 1870s, as technology transformed the entire industrial scene, and as a national market widened with the building of the great transcontinental railroads with their accompanying telegraph lines, the revolutions in production, transportation, and communication we have been describing brought important changes for labor. Large numbers of workers were displaced and their skills rendered obsolete by the new automatic and semiautomatic machinery. The new production processes demanded a greater division of labor; everywhere there was a drive for rationalization of production.

The economic slump in the years 1873–1893—the Great Depression of its era—as well as intensified competition, led employers to cut production expenses, especially labor costs, to which the craft unions often presented a formidable obstacle. The larger corporations now hired unskilled workers for simple and repetitive tasks which could be learned quickly and easily. The corporations, as part of the "organizational revolution," curbed the authority of plant foremen, increased central managerial control, and instituted new hiring and personnel policies.

From the 1890s to the 1930s mass production, division of labor, and centralized managerial controls in the interests of efficiency and productivity transformed the world of labor. The period before and immediately following World War I was the heyday of Frederick Winslow Taylor's *Scientific Management*, which became as much a Bible abroad as it was in the United States. "Taylorism"—time and motion studies, job standardization, efficiency testing, the "one best way"— was seen as the path to maximum productivity. The Ford assembly line remained the model. There were, to be sure, exceptions to the general decline in the need for skilled workers; some ordinary laborers became semiskilled machine operators and new skilled workers appeared as technicians, machine makers, and maintenance personnel. But the "deskilling" of labor was the pattern.

The older unions, in an uphill struggle, could seek to contain the speed of change and to preserve jobs by reducing hours of work, but they were powerless to prevent mechanization. Facing the situation realistically, they did not fight innovation but sought principally to mitigate its consequences. Nonetheless the result was a weakening of the power of unions. In the 1920s union membership in the United States declined, falling from 5 million in 1921 to 3.5 million in 1929; in 1920 there were 500,000 dues-paying members in the United Mine Workers Union, in 1930 there were fewer than 100,000. The open shop prevailed and labor's only weapons were strikes and slowdowns. With mechanized technology, the specialization of labor, and the assembly line, labor still had considerable power through direct job action. Industry was vulnerable; a stoppage anywhere could halt production. But such action was no substitute for the bargaining power of strong trade unions.

The 1930s ushered in a new era. Ironically, in the years of deep depression and mass unemployment, the trade union movement enjoyed a rebirth and assumed a more central role in industrial relations than ever before. The new Congress of Industrial Organizations (CIO) and the reinvigorated American Federation of Labor successfully organized many of the technologically advanced, managerially integrated, mass-production basic industries, which they had been unable to do in earlier years. From 1933 to 1938 union membership in the automobile, steel, and electrical industries (all industrial unions bringing together skilled and unskilled workers) tripled in size. The vulnerability of management to labor in assembly line production was partially responsible, as was the militancy of the new organizations, but of even more importance was the fact that the federal government, under the New Deal, passed legislation that afforded legal protection to union organizing and collective bargaining, sheltering the efforts of the new unions.

World War II carried the process further, helped by the wartime labor shortage and large government defense contracts. To make possible the uninterrupted flow of wartime production the corporations needed the assistance of the unions to maintain job discipline in the workplace and thereby avoid wildcat strikes, lax work habits, and absenteeism. The corporations came to accept the new power of labor and the new order of industrial relations. By 1945, 35 percent of the labor force, or 15 million workers, were unionized, a figure that continued to grow, if more slowly, in the following years, before tapering off. Postwar industrial and labor relations continued to reflect this partnership. Management wooed union officials, offering rewards, high wages, job security, and unemployment benefits for industrial peace and increased productivity. Agreements to refrain from strikes for the duration of collective bargaining contracts became common. In return the unions refrained from interfering with management prerogatives in allocating capital, introducing new technology, and establishing work routines. With minimum union resistance, industry in the postwar years introduced new technology and increased the volume of production in an impressive demonstration of the vitality of American capitalism. The unions too grew in strength and wealth; they tended to bargain with management as equals and followed big business organizational policies and practices themselves.

New challenges lay ahead—for the economy as a whole, for management, and for labor. From the 1960s industry was caught up in profound new transformations in technology, comparable to and potentially more significant than the revolutionary changes of the years 1890 to 1930. The age of the electronics revolution and the computer had arrived. The new technology made possible increased productivity and reduced labor costs at a time when American industry faced serious external competition and shrinking profits. The large trade unions had no reasonable basis for opposing the new technology. Their own growth pattern, already eroded, was checked; since 1970 union membership has grown less rapidly than has the labor force, and in the years of recession and unemployment even fell in absolute terms. The American corporations have succeeded also in transferring overseas unskilled low-paying jobs, further depriving the unions of potential recruits. The multinational corporations increased in numbers and in economic strength. Their global operations were facilitated by the international mobility of capital and by the new technology; instantaneous transmission of data and management decisions was now possible.

With the new technology and a consumer-oriented society, jobs grew more rapidly in the so-called third sector, the service and clerical sector (where women, minorities, and the young found job opportunities—at lower pay). Workers in widely scattered retail service establishments and in capital-intensive computerized office settings proved relatively impervious to unionization. The impact of the new technology on labor relations continued to be dramatic; in a recent telephone strike the supervisory staff was able to operate the computerized equipment without the striking workers; striking American air traffic controllers were also quickly replaced. Labor relations were in a fluid stage. Industry accepted the stabilizing effects of collective bargaining and did not seek to uproot the unions. But what positive measures industry, organized labor, and government would take to mitigate the effects of structural unemployment and the displacement of labor by computerized technology was not resolved, nor was the related question of how the new technology ushered in by the electronics revolution would affect union strength and industrial relations in general.

The electronics revolution would not have been possible without another contemporary social phenomenon with wide ramifications— the emphasis on investment in research and development for the acquisition of new knowledge. Just as capital had once sought enhanced productivity through organization and rationalization, it now sought increased productivity through increased knowledge. Government, industry, universities, and other sources joined together to support scientific and technological research; the line between public and private funding tended to blur. The process of innovation—the "invention of invention"—become a matter of institutionalized teamwork; two of the most striking examples were the planning and development of the atomic bomb in wartime and the ventures into outer space in peacetime.

Here education has been closely involved. Even before 1900 the nation's public schools raised the educational level of the labor force, but as late as 1940 those who had four years of high school or more made up only 24.5 percent of the population, and those with college degrees 4.6 percent. The figures increased dramatically in the decades between 1940 and 1980, so that the proportion of high school graduates rose to 68.6 percent and college graduates to 17 percent. A technologically oriented society makes heavy demands on the schools at every educational level for necessary professional and vocational skills. That the schools, including colleges and universities, might become captives of a technological society was no idle threat and remained a pressing social and cultural challenge.

Many of the technological and economic changes we are describing had a significant impact on the status of women, who entered the contemporary American labor market in large numbers. In 1870, 15 percent of all gainfully employed workers in the United States were women; in 1921, 21 percent, and in 1980, over 50 percent were women. Women workers were still mainly confined to such lower paid "women's occupations" as clerical, secretarial , and library work, nursing, and elementary school teaching; their average wages were only three-fifths those of male workers. But the great social change made possible by an expanding economy opened up a range of choice; in 1980, 60 percent of working women were married but chose to work outside the household. Women's employment patterns reflected the overall change in the American occupational structure as a whole—an increase in the number of white-collar jobs and jobs requiring light physical effort, and a decline in blue-collar jobs, heavy labor, and agricultural work. Meanwhile, the growth in professional and technical opportunities created by the economy has stimulated the demand for women with advanced education. The feminist movement, various forms of government intervention, and other pressures further encouraged the entry of women into the labor force at all levels. Although grosser forms of discrimination were disappearing, grievances persisted over more subtle forms of unequal treatment.

Technological and economic changes affected America's ethnic minorities as well. The exodus from agriculture struck most sharply at rural blacks, who migrated to the cities in large numbers, so that by the 1980s there remained only 62,000 black farm households out of a former total of 1.84 million. Although the abandonment of the farms raised per capita income in the nation as a whole, the migration of blacks to the inner city, where they found low-paying jobs or no jobs at all, did not elevate their economic standing. Nor did the change in the American job structure in the economy help blacks; in the 1980s only 23 percent of blacks held white-collar jobs while 58 percent were in blue-collar, low-paying jobs. Their relative improvement in economic status during the prosperity of the 1960s was checked by the recession of the mid-1970s; the unemployment rate among young blacks was double that of whites. Similar observations might be made of the fastest growing minority in America, the Hispanic population. One can only conclude that the far-reaching legal and educational improvements in the status of American minorities were not yet accompanied by equivalent economic gains.

Meanwhile the American population as a whole continued to move and migrate to different parts of the nation, always a persistent phenomenon in American history. The "closing of the frontier" by 1880 did not stop continued mass migration, certainly not to the Pacific Coast. In the post-1945 years there was a continuing migration to the "Sun Belt" (broadly defined as the Southwest and Southeast). Although per capita income has long been lowest in the South, the new migration created the opportunity for moderating the disparities in average income for the nation as a whole.

Throughout American history technological innovation has called for the adaptation of the law to changing needs and circumstances. Over the years innovators and opponents of technological change have resorted to the courts, the legislatures, and the political forum. Resolution of disputes was often made more complex by American federalism. Although the states retained authority over most economic matters, the Constitution authorized federal power in many areas. Above all, it gave the federal government power "to promote the progress of science and useful arts" and authorized it to supervise copyrights and patents, standards of weights and measures, admiralty laws, and commerce among the states. With these powers the federal government over the years has regulated the issuance of patents, introduced tariffs to protect "infant" industries, encouraged the immigration of skilled workers, trained engineers, provided subsidies for the building of the railroads, and regulated navigation on inland waterways. Generally it has left to the states the protection of public safety. As early as the 1830s the courts ruled that corporations deserved special privileges and even constitutional protection and were to be treated as legal "persons". The post-Civil War Fourteenth Amendment, designed to protect the former slaves in their right to life, liberty, and property turned out, because of its interpretation by the courts, to be a powerful instrument for the protection of corporations.

Throughout the nineteenth century, the advance of technology had a significant impact on legal development. From the earliest times the courts showed a bias in favor of entrepreneurial interests, seeking to incorporate and apply new technology; the courts, in the words of one judge, were eager to accommodate to "the imperative demand made by the rapid progress of the age." Corporate officers were ruled to be immune from trespass suits or nuisance claims. Workers, however, did not fare equally well. In the case of industrial accidents the courts upheld the old common-law principle that an employer was not liable in any way for an injury. In labor relations the freedom-of-contract rule prevailed, that is, labor and employers were equal partners and the government had no right to violate the contract by intervening on the side of labor—even when the growing power of corporations had made a travesty of the rule's original intent.

Nor were the corporations as a whole subject to comprehensive supervision. Both the federal government and the states had long since limited themselves only to the regulation of enterprises and public utilities that were judged to have a quasi-public character, e.g., the railroads. By 1914, to be sure, the federal government was regulating many commercial practices through the Interstate Commerce Commission and the Federal Trade Commission, and the states were regulating electrical power and telegraph and telephone communications systems. On the other hand, the courts rejected many government efforts at industrial regulation; the attempt by the states to prohibit child labor was declared unconstitutional. Regulatory laws made a slow and belated appearance. By the 1920s most states had public utility controls, public health measures, some controls over child labor, and protection for consumers. Only gradually did the courts rule that public authorities, federal and state, should have the flexibility to meet technological and industrial changes, conceding that regulations once judged arbitrary and oppressive were necessary and valid.

Much of the judicial opposition to government controls disappeared as a result of the social and economic exigencies of the years of the Great Depression. The courts accepted federal intervention in many new areas. The result was a sweeping adaptation to the realities of twentieth-century industrial society, many years after such adaptation had taken place in other countries. Federal agencies now regulated the securities market, oversaw labor relations and collective bargaining, insured savings accounts, protected the consumer, operated a social security insurance system, and engaged in many other activities that in an earlier age would have been deemed excessive.

World War II carried federal authority even further when the government regulated wages and prices, rationed goods, controlled manpower, and allocated resources, but even with the end of wartime controls federal powers and activities expanded in the post-1945 era. Massive defense expenditures in peacetime—huge government contracts for arms, aerospace activities, and nuclear research—were a major aspect of this expansion. Directly or in collaboration with other agencies, the federal government actively encouraged technological innovation; it funded scientific research and often operated its own laboratories. Tax laws encouraged industrial expenditures on research and development. One unanticipated and unresolved dilemma arose: with science and technology serving as handmaidens of defense, conflicts inevitably arose between "national security" and "freedom of inquiry."

Despite the growth of regulatory powers under the New Deal and in World War II, for a long time there was still relatively little federal regulation affecting health and safety in a broad sense. Most matters having to do with occupational safety, pollution of resources, or consumer protection remained under the jurisdiction of the states, which were unable to cope with these vast problems, or indeed with the powerful corporations often responsible for them. Only slowly and gradually did the federal government begin to respond to the rising public demand for protection of the environment and other ecological issues. Public concerns were voiced about the effects of petrochemicals, pesticides, herbicides, and fertilizers, new drugs and pharmaceuticals appearing on the market, and the safety of new nuclear energy plants. Everywhere there was rising anxiety over the use and abuse of the nation's and the world's natural resources. Rachel Carson's book, *Silent Spring* (1962), which called attention to, among other things, the dangers of DDT, aroused widespread public fear about environmental and ecological damage. The automobile itself became an object of special attention; in the 1960s a vast national road construction program had been undertaken, and railroad transportation was neglected; cities became choked in engine exhaust and smog. Episodes in nuclear energy plants, as at Three Mile Island in Pennsylvania in 1979 or at Chernobyl in the Soviet Union in 1986, generated pressing new questions about the effectiveness of public safety measures. The most devastating nonnuclear industrial accident in history, at the Union Carbide plant in Bhopal, India, in 1984, aroused sensitivities and focused attention on issues of responsibility in the export of technology. On another front, impressive advances in medicine and pharmacology were being recorded, but new discoveries led to new problems; the birth defects in Europe resulting from the use of thalidomide shocked the world.

Observers in the 1970s and 80s were moved to raise a central question. Does technology inevitably mean progress? Must government and law accommodate uncritically to technological innovation and industrial and economic growth? Many accused industry of ignoring worker safety, consumer well-being, and the quality of the environment. A demand arose for closer surveillance and regulation— for technology assessment on a systematic basis. Pressure mounted to require the government to ask, in every instance of technological innovation, how the innovation would affect the total environment. In 1970 a federal Environmental Protection Agency came into being, and in 1972 an Office of Technology Assessment. Centralized monitoring of technology on an unprecedented scale was emerging in a country long associated with a hands-off approach to industry and technological change. Not least among many control measures, Congress required automobile manufacturers to modify engines to encourage the use of low lead or unleaded fuels and provide proper exhaust emission controls. Nuclear energy plants have been placed under closer supervision and on occasion have been closed until it was believed that safety regulations were met. From the mid-1960s the federal government, under strong pressure from special consumer and public litigation groups and public opinion as a whole, has taken seriously its new role in coping with environmental, consumer, and occupational protection.

There are many unanswered questions. The industrial corporations have understood the rising public pressure for government regulation of their activities, yet they also see such measures as a potential threat to investment, innovation, productivity, and competition. What impact will controls over technological innovation have on economic growth? How will the courts, in assessing environmental or health risks, be able to interpret complex and often contradictory scientific advice? There is an undeniable conflict between government regulation and traditional economic freedom, but there is also an awareness that citizens in a technologically advanced modern society are powerless otherwise to protect themselves, and that justice requires adjusting contemporary government and law to inescapable realities.

The "socialization" of technological innovation remains an overarching challenge. Environmentalists point to the exhaustion and pollution of the nation's natural resources as the price paid for economic growth. An antitechnology ideology has spread, epitomized in E. F. Schumacher's *Small is Beautiful* (1973). A nuclear arms control movement has emerged in response to the deadliest application of technology to war in all of history. There still seems to be no way of storing radioactive wastes even if environmental impact studies have become mandatory and national standards for safety and public health are the rule.

The far-reaching consequences of our complex contemporary technology demand continuing attention. Planned social effort, accompanied by the allocation of adequate resources for the study and control of the problems inherent in modern technology, is one recommendation. Late twentieth-century society has to ask itself whether technology can be permitted to advance autonomously, without social surveillance and proper safeguards. The same human and social intelligence that made possible the spectacular technological innovations of the contemporary era is called upon to exercise vigilance—for the sake of the planet and the survival of humanity itself. For our civilization to endure, society must remain the master of the technology it has created.

2. Technological Innovation and Social Change in the United States, 1870–1980

Harold G. Vatter
Portland State University

It should be more widely appreciated than it is that technological innovation is not only a major source of economic change but of social change as well. Indeed, the three areas—technology, economy, and society—are closely interrelated, with economic change serving as a connecting rod linking the other two. A moment's thought will make this clear: when technology increases productivity, per capita incomes go up and new product preferences emerge. But that is only the beginning of the matter. As we look back over the past it is clear that the satisfaction of new patterns of demand has required a transformation not only in the techniques of production but also in the forms of industrial enterprise. And the massive economic changes that followed in the composition of output, the location of industry, and occupational structure and consumption patterns have served to link technological progress to transformed social relationships.

If we view these interrelated changes against the backdrop of American history over the past century it becomes evident that it was the progress of technology, particularly in new manufacturing industries, steam power, and long-distance transportation, that from 1870 to World War I spurred the rise in per capita income and the speeding up of the historic shift from agrarian to urban society. Within the manufacturing sector the heart of the technological transformation lay in the establishment of great new steel equipment industries, the manufacture of machine tools and other stationary machinery, railroad rolling stock, furnaces, and rolling mills. And what were the social consequences of these economic changes? They were many and complex, but I will single out for my purposes the following prominent effects:

the shift from agrarian to urban society
occupational transformations
geographical mobility and the redistribution of population
the fall in the population growth rate
changes in the size and nature of the family
the "organizational revolution"
social movements
alterations in the status of women, blacks, and youth
changes in private consumption patterns and household amenities
changes in consumption patterns and government-community
    relations
improvements in health and living standards
increased longevity
educational changes
the socialization of technological progress

The ways in which these social transformations emerged as a result of technological and economic change during the last century is the subject of my discussion.

The Pre-World War I Epoch

In the era before the great twentieth-century union of science and technology, and before the knowledge revolution following World War II, the rise in productivity (taking into account all the factors of production) in the private nonfarm economy from 1870 to 1910 has been estimated to have been a rather substantial 1.63 percent per year.[1] The great new growth industry of that period, the railroad, considerably outperformed this general increase with an annual rise in productivity of 2.11 percent.[2] The increase in output per unit of labor, reflecting the contribution of the new technology to productivity and hence to per capita income, was an impressive 2 percent per year.[3] The affluent society was still a long way off, but the technological and social groundwork for it was well under way.

Urbanization and Agricultural Decline. The most momentous social transformation, not only in the United States but in all countries experiencing modern economic development, has of course been the relative
decline of farming and, with the help of farm-to-city migration, the
rise of nonfarm society dominated by the industrial and commercial
urban heartland. There can be no question that the inelasticity of the
demand for food in response to income change, within the context of
rising per capita income, is chiefly responsible for this metamorphosis.

Urban society (as defined by the United States Census) was the
minority segment of American society until World War I,[4] and its
growth was contingent upon the expansion of food production. The
comparative advantage of American agriculture in the production of
foodstuffs gave it a virtual monopoly in the home market. Yet with
some exceptions the American farmer's domination over the domestic
market was not sustained by any dramatic technological innovations
in the pre-World War I period. In general, farm production rose
because of more farms and farmers, longer hours worked, and more
land in use, including considerable increases in farm land cultivated
per individual farm worker. The practical results of the 1862 Morrill
Land Grant College Act and of the agricultural experiment stations
under the 1887 Hatch Act were not significant until after the turn of
the twentieth century.[5] While there was substantial advance in horse-
drawn mechanical technology, particularly in grain production in the
North and West, biology and chemistry were yet but poorly applied
to agriculture[6] and yields per acre and output per farm worker rose
only moderately. Between 1870 and 1910 the population of the country rose at an annual rate of 2.12 percent and farm output increased
at an annual rate of 2.29 percent,[7] the modest excess of output over
population growth being absorbed chiefly by exports. The number of
persons supplied by one farm worker increased only slightly until the
century's end; the record improved from 1900 to 1920 but still did
not compare with the dramatic post-World War II increases to come.[8]
Meanwhile the westward migration of farmers until about 1890 and
the success of American farm products in international markets also
helped slow the great urban transformation that was under way.[9]

The impact of technology in that era was being felt not on the farms
but in the nonfarm sector. As farming continued to suffer a relative
decline, the locus of power shifted inexorably to the enlarging urban
complex. In that sector the new technology and the invasion of man-

ufacturing and finance by the corporate form of business were contributing to the growth of giant enterprises. In consequence, a new duality appeared, with atomistic agriculture locked into market competition and political confrontation with the superior and growing power of the corporate nexus in rail transport, industry, finance, and trade. The prodigious corporate bureaucracies in transport, manufacturing, and marketing, which the socialist Eugene Debs believed to be the great revolutionary creation of his lifetime, were in considerable part an outgrowth of innovations in technology and production.

The Organizational Revolution. Rightly or wrongly, and for reasons that they no doubt often comprehended but dimly, farmers came to believe that the resultant market terms of trade were evolving adversely for them and were consequently yielding noncompetitively low rates of return on their investment and labor. Their countervailing response was the agrarian "revolt" against industrialism after the Civil War. The most rugged of individualists, the farmers, turned to collective organization to alleviate their economic distress. They tried to organize private power centers, such as cooperatives, to influence the market directly; when these efforts failed, they appealed to the government. While the appeal was not very effective, it nonetheless laid the groundwork for the more influential organizations of the farm bloc in the twentieth century.

The technology available to crop agriculture placed severe constraints upon the size of farms, which in turn contributed to the disadvantaged status of most of the agricultural population well into the twentieth century.[10] When the farmers, as a private business interest group suffering from a sluggishly advancing technology, called for government intervention to correct alleged market failures and power imbalances, they intended no attack upon private property as such; they sought only to rectify perceived imbalances caused by the uneven distribution of technological advances in the economy. Nevertheless, this appeal to government eroded laissez faire and helped politicize American economic and social life in the long run.

Other developments in agriculture foreshadowed later changes as well. The passage of the Morrill Land Grant College Act in 1862 and the spread of agricultural experiment stations in the late nineteenth century under the Hatch Act of 1887 anticipated the institutionalization of research that was to be a key development in the twentieth-century history of American agriculture.

Urban Growth. Although the typical metropolis that emerged from the urbanization process began as a transportation crossroads, it was not primarily as an entrepot or commercial complex that it made its mark but as an industrial center with accompanying residential activities. As such it illustrates well in its simplest form the connecting-rod phenomenon: technological change → economic change → societal change. Technological progress, concentrated in industry, power generation, and intercity transportation increased productivity and contributed to the rise in urban per capita income, the average level of which was always higher than in rural areas. The increased discretionary income available for the new products of technology and for the urban activities spun off from them, e.g., finance, trade, cultural activities and other services, further stimulated these highly elastic demands. The output of all urban sectors grew much more rapidly than agricultural output.

The physical concentration of production and population was further encouraged by the economies made possible by the large-scale production and volume of output related to capital-intensive technology. The growth of big business was often connected with technical changes in production because ever-larger plant and equipment investment (fixed capital) was required to keep average production costs for the enterprise to a minimum.[11] Such was the case in manufacturing, power generation, and railroading, where the use of coal to replace wood, the introduction of steam engines, machine tools, and, later, electricity, demanded increasingly larger fixed capital investment. The accompanying growth of the national and even the international market encouraged large-scale establishments as well as the emergence of incorporated firms with several plants and extensive marketing operations. These giant firms simultaneously provided opportunities for market controls to minimize the vagaries of unrestrained competition and the mobilization of resources to influence government policies. Large corporate commitments of fixed capital also stimulated the selling of corporate securities through urban-centered financial enterprises and capital markets.

For industrialization to be achieved, it was necessary to augment municipal government services and build a social infrastructure and adequate housing. Internal economies of scale for these services (but not for residential construction) were possible because of the long-term rise in population density.

In addition to corporations, other organizational innovations in this period included the labor union (an urban countervailing response of white male craft workers to the large corporation and a product of the concentration of workers in the city labor market), the business trade association, the beginnings of governmental regulatory agencies, the professional association, the institutionalization of engineering education, and the spread of financial enterprises. In the private and public spheres, organizations everywhere were trying to substitute administrative decision for the blind forces of the market and to advance their particular interests before those of the public or the government.

The confrontation between the individual and the large organization spread through every facet of urban life in the twentieth century. One result for the individual, despite ever higher consumption levels, was an increase in the amount of time required for the brute mechanics of living. This followed from the fact that every large organization, private or governmental, operated through intricate and impersonal processes requiring the client, customer, or citizen to fill out forms, wait, conform to procedures, shoulder the burden of administrative error, or resort to an elaborate appeals machinery.

The unfolding of the organizational revolution was a matter of twentieth-century technological diffusion. The bureaucratic evolution undoubtedly affected work motivation and interpersonal relationships. That mass-production technology completed the process of destroying craftsmanship and the "instinct of workmanship" is well known, as is Marx's emphasis upon such phenomena as tying the worker to the machine and to monotonous jobs, and at the same time separating the worker from any interest in the final product. Labor demoralization, apathy, and alienation resulted from the coercive managerial controls inaugurated under the factory system which stamped out craftsmanship, fragmented industrial tasks, and relegated labor to an inferior status.[12] It would appear that blind obedience to productivity and profit objectives in business (or to rigid bureaucratic procedures in public agencies) created over time counterproductive resistance by employees. The latter learned to shun responsibility and commitment, suppress information, and cultivate hostile attitudes toward the top echelons.[13] In the early 1980s these sociopsychological problems came under intensive examination by many administrators and American managers who were also looking inquisitively at their Japanese counterparts for possible solutions.

Population and the Family. The urban/industrial developments of the last quarter of the nineteenth century and the first two decades of the twentieth brought additional major social changes in a culture in which social effects were systematically excluded from the process of technological decision making.[14] Some of these changes, like the decline in the rate of natural population increase, had appeared to some extent prior to the Civil War, just as had industrialization and urbanization. Indeed, many of these changes applied to earlier decades, and there is no watershed for many of the processes discussed. Because of the higher birth rate in agricultural society, the farm-to-city migration itself lowered the overall natural rate of population increase. The lower urban birth rate was kept down by the inverse correlation between family size and the level of per capita income, but it was sustained by the advances in public health and medical care that cut the shocking premodern mortality rate and substantially raised life expectancy at birth.

The industrial city also transformed the family, which in turn further contributed to the declining rate of population growth. As the United States was transformed into a nation consisting predominantly of wage earners and employees, the American family changed in character. A glance at the occupational percentages of 1900 in table 2.1 reveals that at least two-thirds of the labor force were already wage and salary workers.

An urban family household dependent on wage or salary was strikingly different from a farm-owner or tenant-family household.[15] The large multigenerational farm family, like the artisan family, was not only a consuming unit but also a production unit, structurally and functionally integrated into the agrarian enterprise operating under the authority of the male head. Residence and place of work were the same, with even the education of the children confined largely to the home. Despite the gradual spread of compulsory public schooling, prompted by industry's need for technical literacy, the growth of cities, and the demands of democratic citizenship, as late as 1870 the average American received only four years of schooling,[16] and farm youth were at the lower end of the distribution.

For the urban wage-earning family, children tended to appear rather more of a responsibility than a valuable asset, although the shift in attitude was somewhat delayed during the decades of legally permissible child labor in industry prior to 1920. The farm family had viewed the child as a capital good yielding a stream of long-run investment income; in the new urban society the child-centered family made the child a durable consumption good calling for a stream of consumer satisfactions. The reduction in family size was facilitated, of course, by twenty-century innovations in family planning and birth control techniques.

The urban wage-earning household also became exclusively a consuming unit since work for wages was now physically and functionally separate from the place of residence. The spatial separation produced another social phenomenon—the daily commuter. Commuting, even before the advent of the automobile, produced a number of technological developments in metropolitan transit, including the electric trolley, early in the twentieth century. Concomitantly, business enterprise addressed itself to household needs and in consequence developed a wide spectrum of new products, including indoor water fixtures, gas, and later electric lighting.

Many of these developments in the urban household laid the basis for a long-run improvement in the lives of women. Men and women worked more or less cooperatively on the farm. With urban industrialism, work and workplace become separated. The woman could no longer help the man by working with him in the fields (and overworking herself in the ill-equipped household).[17] But with the twentieth-century development of household appliances, electrification, and reduced child care responsibilities, the married woman could help bring in more family income by entering the labor market.

Technological changed reduced the proportion of heavy common. labor in the total of economic activity (see table 2.1), and at the same time increased the proportion of white-collar and service employment. Such employment, sometimes described as "women's occupations," while low-paying and discriminatory in character,

Table 2.1. Percentage Distribution of Occupations, 1900 and 1980

Occupation Group	1900, Percent of Labor Force	1980, Percent of Employed
White Collar		
Total	17.0	52.5
Professional and technical	4.3	16.1
Managers, administrators, proprietors (nonfarm)	5.8	11.2
Clerical	3.0	18.6
Sales	3.9	6.3
Blue Collar		
Total	35.8	31.7
Skilled, incl. foremen	10.5	12.9
Semiskilled, incl. transport	12.8	14.2
Unskilled (nonfarm)	12.5	4.6
Service		
Total	9.0	13.3
Private household	5.4	1.1
Other services	3.6	12.3
Farm		
Total	37.6	2.8
Farmers and farm managers	19.9	1.2
Farm laborers and foremen	17.7	1.6

Sources: U.S. Bureau of the Census, *Historical Statistics of the United States, Colonial Times to 1970,* (Washington, D.C.: GPO, 1975), part 1, p. 139, series D182-198; U.S. Bureau of the Census, *Statistical Abstract of the United States, 1981,* (Washington, D.C.: U.S. Bureau of the Census), pp. 400, 401, tables 672, 673. Some percentages calculated.

nevertheless increased the participation of women in the labor market, a development that in the long run was a more favorable condition for emancipation than continued confinement to unpaid home management, subordination to male control, and the rearing of numerous offspring. As Roger Burlingame once said, referring to the sewing machine and certain other inventions, women experienced enough freedom "so that they could attack the sources of their misery."[18] The long-run increase in women's participation in the labor market was probably expedited by the benevolent activities of a growing stratum of urban middle-class women organized into clubs and associations designed to improve the lot of the new feminine proletariat.[19] The decision to have fewer children, which had roots reaching beyond technology alone, further contributed to women's emancipation, for they no longer had to spend almost all of the prime years of a short life span in bearing, nursing, and rearing a contingent of human capital units for the farm enterprise.

The cohesion and stability of the earlier agrarian extended family was badly corroded under the urban nuclear family relationships that evolved during the twentieth century. This corrosion was affected by the separation of the household from production, the reduction in the number of children, heightened middle-class consumption aspirations associated with the rise in family income, the gradual transfer of children's education to the schools (including the addition of peer-group influences), and the growing assertion of children's independence (personal, but not necessarily financial) from parental authority as well as the associated development of a youth culture. The increasing participation of married woman in the labor market in the later twentieth century, the greater accessibility to divorce, and the growing propensity to shunt the elderly onto either various social agencies or their own resources. also weakened family ties.

The elderly as a distinctive social group hardly existed before the twentieth century. But improvements in health, rising per capita income, and the decline of farm and extended family life combined to isolate an ever growing elderly population and exclude a substantial proportion of the elderly from the job market. At the same time, despite social security and retirement programs, a large proportion remained in poverty as a disadvantaged social stratum.

Some of the changes undermining the older family cohesion were the direct products of the spread of the new industrial technology in an urban society. Other changes were spinoffs from technology and the related rise in per capita income.[20] Still others were quite autonomously generated from the social changes themselves, while interaction clearly pervaded the whole complex set of transformations.

The Post-World War I Epoch

The epoch following the watershed of the pre-1914 years and World War I brought the completion of the urbanization process and with it the suburbanization of the metropolis, as well as the accelerated ousting of millions of people from farming.

The technological basis for these significant changes centered upon three production complexes: commercial electric power, the gasoline-fueled internal combustion engine, and the chemical and petrochemical industries. The material base of these industries still consisted mainly of steel and coal, but light metals, petroleum, and natural gas were added in this era. Of far-reaching significance was the fact that the electrical and chemical industries were the first to establish research in a systematic way.[21]

The urbanization process was fed by a veritable collapse in farming, which intensified in the years following World War II. The farm population peaked in 1916 at 32.5 million, then drifted gently downward to 30.5 million in 1940. What followed was the most spectacular technological breakthrough in modern agricultural history, based in large part on government research efforts—the monumental achievements of the agricultural experiment station system. In the forty years following 1940 the farm population plummeted to 7.2 million, a mere 3.3 percent of all Americans. The two-thirds drop in farm employment during those four decades was for the most part a case of technologically caused social displacement; not even the large decline in railroad employment in those same years approached it in magnitude.[22] Meanwhile, the ambiguously defined "rural nonfarm" population (many of whom should be categorized as urban) kept rising, and nearly doubled in the forty years after the onset of World War II.

Agricultural productivity had all along been much enhanced by the tractor and truck, together with other power-driven implements and machinery, just as farm household living had been made more attractive by the automobile, the telephone, and the radio. During the interwar decades, mechanization was responsible for such improvement in productivity as occurred, and those two decades brought the virtual demise of the horse-drawn, natural manure era. Electrification then entered to bolster productivity and improve farm home conditions, especially after the inauguration of the New Deal's Rural Electrification Administration in the mid-1930s. To be sure, there were intimations of the coming biological revolution, e.g., hog cholera serum, the hybrid seed transformation in the case of corn, improved wheat strains, and experimental work in the breeding of resistant plant varieties and improved animal strains. But these developments were only a foreshadowing of future achievements.

Despite mechanization and the beginnings of biological and chemical breakthroughs, farm productivity (and therefore the rate at which farm workers were becoming redundant) rose only modestly in the interwar years. Only about 10 percent of all farms had electricity as late as 1930, and about one-third by 1940. The great chemical revolution was not yet underway. The annual consumption of commercial fertilizers in 1935–39, for example, was only one-third of what it became in the 1950s. The true technological revolution in farming occurred after 1940; and revolution it was, for agricultural performance from the end of World War II to 1980 exceeded that of any other major sector of the economy. This postwar productivity revolution virtually expelled the agricultural population from the land and produced "deserted villages" as inexorably as did the eighteenth-century English enclosure movements—and in a strikingly shorter period of time.

The social impact of these changes on the population is demonstrated in both tables 2.1 and 2.2, which conceal, however, some vital aspects of the changes—the effect of the newer technology upon productivity and therefore per capita income, for example, which was the wellspring of major social change. The first four industries listed in table 2.2 are commodity-producing industries; the remainder may be thought of collectively as noncommodity or service-producing in the broadest sense. When *output* rather than labor in the commodity-producing sectors is brought into the picture, and they are compared with the service sectors as a group, it becomes clear that labor pro-

Table 2.2. Percentage Distribution of Persons Engaged in Production Selected Years, 1869–1980

Industry	1869	1899	1929	1980
Agriculture, forestry, and fisheries	48.3	36.9	21.2	3.6
Mining	1.3	2.5	2.2	1.0
Contract construction	4.9	4.9	5.0	6.2
Manufacturing	17.6	20.0	22.2	22.2
Transportation, communications, and public utilities	5.1	7.7	8.6	6.6
Wholesale and retail trade	7.8	10.8	16.9	20.3
Finance, insurance, and real estate	.4	1.2	3.3	6.0
Private services	11.1	11.9	13.9	18.4
Government services	3.5	4.1	6.7	16.7

Sources: U.S. Bureau of the Census, *Historical Statistics of the U.S., Colonial Times to 1970,* (Washington, D.C.: GPO, 1975), part 1, p. 240, series F250-F260 (Kendrick estimates); U.S. Bureau of the Census, *Statistical Abstract of the United States, 1981* (Washington, D.C.: U.S. Bureau of the Census), p. 390, table 658; *Economic Report of the President,* February 1983, p. 205, table B-37. Percentages partly calculated, the totals of which may be affected by rounding.

ductivity, with its attendant restraints upon the growth of jobs, increased faster in the former sectors. For example, as percentages of the national income per worker, labor income per worker in commodity production stood at .54 in 1870, whereas it was 2.7 times the national level in noncommodity production. As early as 1900, however, the relative income level per worker in commodity production had risen to 71 percent of the national average, while in services production it had fallen to 1.6 times the average national level.[23] Gallman and Howle comment as follows on this convergence: "In a broad sense this is the result one might have expected, since the commodity sectors were presumably the more directly, generally, and widely affected by the processes of technical change associated with industrialization."[24] The twentieth century evinced a similar pattern. Again reference is to income per worker as a percentage of national income per worker:[25]

	1869–1879	*1889–1899*	*1919–1940*	*1950–1955*
Agriculture	42	37	47	76
Manufacturing and Mining	93	128	120	123
All other	220	160	120	100

It seems clear that through the turn of the twentieth century productivity-raising technological innovation was strongly operative in manufacturing and mining, as it was in agriculture after World War II. Meanwhile, the rise in the percentage of persons in the noncommodity industries from 28 percent in 1869 to 68 percent in 1980 (table 2.2) seems to have been accompanied by a comparative decline in productivity. However, the "all other" sector (i.e., sectors apart from agriculture, manufacturing, and mining) included many activities in which technological progress was advancing rapidly. Within that group, railroad transportation and to a lesser extent public utilities[26] powerfully sustained the national productivity rise and slowed the drop in the group's comparative position even into the post-World War II period.[27] It was farming, until World War II, that was the drag upon the overall level of income per worker, and its later decline therefore helped lift the national average income per worker. Meanwhile, manufacturing created most of the convergence with noncommodity income per worker.[28]

The decimation of the family farm population and the desertion of much of rural nonfarm America[29] was the social product of the technological miracle in agriculture. While that miracle drew heavily upon continued mechanization, electricity, soil conservation, and irrigation, it was primarily due to the acceleration of interdisciplinary public and private research in the biological, entomological, and chemical sciences. The revolution in productivity may be observed in some selected indexes of farm production inputs (1967 = 100):[30]

	1950	1965	1980
Labor	217	110	65
Mechanical power and machinery	84	94	128
Agricultural chemicals	29	75	174
Feed, seed, and livestock purchases	63	93	106
Total index	104	98	106

The decrease in labor input and the increase in the use of chemicals dramatically reveal the technological transformation.

The soil and, in the long run, society itself paid a high price in the form of pollutants resulting from the use of nitrates, herbicides, and pesticides. The use of artificial and inorganic chemical fertilizers silently destroyed the soil, saturating it and adjacent waterways with substances that did not decompose into the earth.[31] Procedures for disposal of the enormous volume of agricultural wastes remained either outdated or ignored. Society also paid a price for the political power of the farm bloc's efforts to obtain a policy of government-supported cartelization. Meanwhile, technological marvels on the farm and in the food-processing "agribusiness" that sprang up were providing the rich, highly refined, potentially carcinogenic foods entering the diet of the affluent urban society. The per capita food production index drifted upwards from 83 in 1910 (1967 = 100) to 103 in 1970. However, food, excluding alcoholic beverages, as a percentage of all consumer expenditures fell from about one-fourth to less than one-fifth at the end of the 1970s.

The effect of technical progress in the production, processing, storage, transportation, and delivery of foodstuffs throughout the past one hundred years has been to close the time and space gap between farm and urban household, shift much food preparation from the kitchen to a growing agribusiness complex, and provide not only fresher foods but many additional processed and prepared, ready-to-cook, convenience items to the consumer. Certain major innovations stand out prominently in this remarkable evolution. They include the refrigerator car and other railroad freight car improvements, food shipment by air and truck, electrical refrigeration, the preparation of dressed meats and poultry, the rise of the food canning and soft drink industry, the processing of cereals, bakery bread, and oleomargarine, the mechanization of milk and other dairy production, the mass production of cigarettes, and the frozen food industry. The general effect of these and related developments was to increase the diversity of diets, conquer most of the seasonal limitations on food supplies, reduce food shopping time, and greatly diminish the amount and burden of home food processing and preparation.

Electricity and the Motor Vehicle. A complete shutdown of fossil-fueled commercial electric power would almost immediately stop all production and a major part of consumption in contemporary American society. The system of vehicular, airline, and dieselized railroad transport would cease to function as existing stocks of accessible gasoline and fuel oil were exhausted. Telephonic and electronic communication would stop. Society would promptly learn how far it had departed from the old world of the coal or wood fire, the steam engine, the horse, and the whale oil lamp. Even the intermediate world of a more primitive "alternative technology" advocated by some opponents of contemporary techniques would be unattainable.[32]

This doomsday scenario shows that electricity was the most vital, socially pervasive technological innovation in twentieth-century America. It became the supplier and activator of energy for all of the nation's activities in a high-energy, labor-saving economy. In addition to the direct delivery of electrical energy, commercial electric power was an indispensable factor in the utilization of all fossil fuels used for the generation of energy. The growth in electricity-connected energy use and its availability for businesses and households reduced human effort per unit of product, reshaped the quality of life, accelerated rising living standards, and spurred some technological unemployment.

The commercial electric industry originated in the 1870s, antedating the rise to importance of the motor vehicle by over a quarter century. The extent of society's dependence upon it increased rapidly even during the years of the industry's maturity, and as the twentieth century unfolded, it became virtually indispensable for human existence. The phenomenal post-World War II rise in electrical consumption provides dramatic evidence of this. Between 1960 and 1980, for example, real GNP rose 3.6 percent per year, but electric energy generation rose 5.7 percent per year. Over the same period, residential customers increased their average annual consumption from about 4,000 kilowatt hours to 9,000 kilowatt hours; the increase for commercial consumers was from 17,000 to almost 54,000 kilowatt hours.[33]

The American household and workplace revolved around electricity. The household could enjoy a large collection of effort-reducing middle-class amenities—light, heat, telephones, thermostats, radios, TVs, stoves, microwave ovens, washers, dryers, irons, dishwashers, garbage disposers, refrigerators, freezers, air conditioners. Electricity, and the technology based on it, permeated the very heart of middle- and upper-class levels of living. By activating the equipment for mass communication and transportation, it also contributed to the ever more hurried pace of life.

The social repercussions of the motor vehicle were also obvious. Its effects have been likened to those of the clock, gunpowder, the printing press, and the steam engine.[34] The passenger car also raised the level of living and increased contact between people, even as the highway network developed to serve it tended to disperse them physically. The passenger car and the motor truck created the motorized suburb, the blighted inner city, the freeway-centered society, and other variations in urban living patterns. Nevertheless, the automobile was without doubt the most flexible, swift, and adaptable means of individually controlled transportation ever invented.

The social significance of the motor vehicle has been well documented and widely recognized, and need not be reviewed here. Robert Heilbroner has suggested that, were the automobile to be put out of commission, the effect upon our society "would be as grave and as socially disastrous as a catastrophic famine in the Middle Ages."[35] Such an eventuality would undoubtedly cut off the supply of electric power also, for maintenance of the supply system for electric power would also be difficult under modern conditions without the motor truck; an even more complete economic shutdown could be anticipated. (Some benign effects of the disappearance of the automobile may be conceded and need not be dwelt upon.) On balance the prospect would be grim. The impact on our society of the automobile, the truck, the tractor, and the diesel locomotive are too well known to be spelled out in detail; they have created contemporary society.[36]

The Status of Women. A major social change of the post-World War II epoch was the improved status of women. This general improvement, compared to earlier times, accompanied the overall rise in productivity and in output per capita which affected most of the population, men and women. More significant was the relative improvement in the status of women vis-a-vis men. Here, increasing participation in the job market has been the most dramatic index of change. Women as a percentage of all gainful workers in the market rose steadily from about 15 percent in 1870 to 21 percent in 1920 and to over 50 percent in 1980; and women workers in the job market as a percentage of the female population from about 19 percent in 1890 to over 50 percent in 1980.[37] This enormous rise in the participation rate was conditioned, to be sure, by confinement to "women's occupations" (clerical, secretarial, nursing, etc.) and by the persistence of an average wage rate that is only three-fifths that of men. Also, millions of low- and moderate-income working women with families continued to bear the bulk of after-hours home responsibilities well into the twentieth century. Nevertheless, the rising participation rate demonstrated that women were exercising an ever larger range of choice. A female labor force that was overwhelmingly composed of single, widowed, or divorced women in the late nineteenth century needs to be contrasted with the contemporary situation in which 46 percent of working women in 1947, and 60 percent in 1980, were married.[38] Women's participation in the labor market helped them to confront continuing issues of occupational, wage, and household discrimination, and even mount a revolution in sexual values.

The connection between the opening up of job opportunities for women and the changing structure of the job market is important. Indeed, "women's occupations" became precisely those that witnessed the largest changes in the economy, an increased demand in white-collar jobs, jobs requiring light physical effort, and services (including government); a decline in demand in farming, blue-collar jobs, and common labor (see table 2.1).[39] It was rising per capita income and the shortening of the work week, the results of a changing technology, that laid the basis for women's opportunity to acquire the job training and earn the income prerequisite to economic independence. Thus an economic connecting rod again can be seen as providing the medium of transmission between technology and social change. Technology, demand patterns, and the wage and price structure determined the changes in the job structure.

There were additional gains concomitant with the new economic and social status of women. Prominent among these were greatly expanded sexual freedom, including the choice to have fewer children; with the gradual spread of improved contraceptive techniques, a reduction in the age-old fear of pregnancy; a greater autonomy in the choice of a life partner; latitude in life-style and dress; and easier availability of divorce which afforded one kind of escape from marital subordination and incompatibility. Women moved steadily toward the level of sexual freedom that historically had been enjoyed only by men.

The advent of electricity afforded a comparative release from drudgery for women, who were traditionally more absorbed in home management than men. Home electrification was only half completed by the mid-1920s; it was almost total thirty years later. Other household amenities also lightened domestic burdens with the availability of indoor water, flush toilets, bathing facilities, and central heating.

Household appliances, particularly the use of electricity for refrigeration, washing, drying, ironing, cleaning, cooking, and baking, likewise raised the general level of living for the population but also increased the productivity of housework and enhanced women's domestic status. This was true whether the woman entered the labor market or stayed in the home.

Higher education for women was a further gain which brought women much closer to achievement levels that were previously open primarily to men. Education is a social phenomenon also related to technological change. The ratio of the number of master's or second professional degrees conferred upon men to the number conferred upon women was 5.35 in 1895, but declined to 1.02 by 1980. In the case of bachelor's degrees the male/female ratio fell from 4.50 in 1895 to 1.10 in 1980, i.e., over the same eighty-five years.[40] There can be no question that the growth in certain professional and technical jobs (table 2.1) required for economic development, and in private services and government employment (table 2.2), stimulated the demand for educated women. In the case of M.D. degrees conferred, the male/ female ratio stood at 8.61 in 1950 but fell to 3.27 by 1980. For law school graduates the male-female ratio dropped from 27.4 in 1955 to 2.31 in 1980, a quarter of a century later. Women's entry into engineering, which took place in the 1970s, was even more impressive, only 191 engineering degrees were conferred upon women in 1950, but 7,669 were conferred in 1980; this was still only 9 percent of the total, however.[41]

The significant penetration of women into the professional, technical, and service fields was made possible by the technologically induced changes in the employment structure and by the stimulus of rising real wages. Not to be overlooked, however, was the accompanying spread of democratic activism, including the women's movement, one of the great social phenomena of the post-World War II era.[42]

The links between technological change, the economy, and social movements, such as the women's movement, the growth of participatory democracy, popular lobbies, political action committees, and public interest groups, are admittedly quite indirect and veiled. On the other hand, in many other instances such as the environmental/ ecological and nuclear arms control movements, the connections are more easily detected. It no doubt remains true that many important social or sociopolitical changes have been quasi-autonomous with respect to technology and the economy. Cases in point are the civil rights movement, the youth rebellion of the 1960's, the achievement of equality in voter participation by women in that same decade, the penetration of women into the ranks of the clergy, and similar phenomena.

The Status of Blacks. The advance in the status of women was an improvement largely for white women. Nevertheless, relative advances were also made by black females. With important exceptions the black woman moved from rural homemaker in 1870 to urban domestic worker in the first decades of the twentieth century, and then to low-level service employee in the later twentieth century.

What was the connection with technological change? The black woman, far more than the white, was driven out of agriculture by the same forces that reshaped the whole of the economy and society. The decline of agriculture struck the precariously tenured blacks, with their smaller, inferior, and less profitable farms, much more forcibly than it did whites. By 1981 this devastating American "enclosure movement" left only 62,000 black farm households out of a total of 1,841,000 in the United States.[43]

As late as 1920 almost half of all black women lived on farms. The proportion declined to 34 percent by the eve of World War II, and the urban pull of the war decade cut the figure to one-fifth. The dramatic changes in the quarter century of the technological revolution in agriculture following World War II cut the proportion to a mere 2 percent by the 1970s.[44] At the end of the 1970s, there were only 80,000 "black and other" farmers in the United States.[45] American blacks, men and women, were by 1970 among the most urban people on earth. Even in rural areas, the total of black females in 1970 was only 63 percent that at the turn of the twentieth century, while white rural females had increased to 134 percent of their 1900 numbers. The farm-to-city exodus brought other problems, and women bore the brunt of the accompanying burdens. A comparison with white families in 1978 illustrates one major aspect of the resultant instability.[46]

	Percent of total families in each racial group	
	black	*white*
Husband-wife families	56.1	85.9
Female head, no husband present	39.2	11.5

That families with a single, female head had a lower per capita income and a high degree of dependency on welfare support is widely recognized. The incidence of poverty for female-headed families with children under eighteen in 1981 was about 68 percent for blacks and 43 percent for whites; it was 67 percent for Hispanics.

Job distribution in the late 1970s indicated that, while the status of employed black women still contrasted sharply with that of employed white women, it nevertheless reflected long-run changing occupational patterns, and the contrasts were less severe than in the case of family structure. The distribution for each group appeared as follows in 1977:[47]

| | *Percent of total employed women in each racial group* | |
	black	*white*
White-collar workers	44	66
Clerical workers	25	36
Blue-collar workers	18	14
Service workers	37	19
Private household workers	10	2
Other	27	17

Almost no women, black or white, were classified as engaged in farming. The black-white contrast in private household service work remained stark; despite the decline in this type of work for the total labor force, 37 percent of all women engaged in it were black (black women represented 11 percent of all employed women). Nevertheless, the distribution of black women's occupations more or less matched, with a lag, the structural changes brought about by technological change.

The income of black women had almost caught up to that of white women by 1980; it was even reported that in 1960 median incomes were higher for nonwhite than for white women in several age and education groups. The black matriarchal home might have had something to do with this, for it apparently provided more vigorous support for female than for male education.[48]

The improvement in the status of black women seemed to point to an improved status for all blacks. However, the trends are uncertain, particularly because of the historical lag in the absorption of the black male into higher-paying jobs. The exodus from farming undoubtedly raised per capita income for black males, but in the context of ghettoization it did not by any means raise it relative to white.

In the two main occupational categories, white collar and blue collar, black males remained locked into the nineteenth-century pattern. Only 23 percent of all black men were employed in the expanding white-collar stratum in 1977 (see table 2.1). This may be contrasted with 42 percent for white males, 44 percent for black females, and 66 percent for white females. Meanwhile a huge 58 percent of all black men worked in blue-collar occupations, whereas 45 percent of white men were so engaged, and only 18 percent of black women and 14 percent of white women.[49] Black men were also the hard core of both the numerically reduced group of nonfarm laborers and the remnants of agricultural labor. These indicators confirm that the revolution in the American occupational structure tended to bypass black men. Nevertheless, the penetration of industry by the black male represented some expanded opportunities for the landless dispossessed, an opening enlarged by the manpower needs of World War II.

From the point of view of income, black men were concentrated in the low-paying blue-collar activities, just as black women were concentrated in the low-paying "women's occupations." Hence, it is not surprising that although black men's incomes averaged somewhat higher than black women's, the average of their combined incomes, when employed, fell well below the white average, similar to the average wage of all women in proportion to that of all men. However, the median household monetary income (in constant dollars) of blacks relative to whites did for a time move upward after World War II. It rose from about 52 percent of the income of whites in the immediate postwar years to about 61 percent at the end of the prosperous sixties; it was about 59 percent in 1979. A moderate relative overall improvement in income was taking place, although it now seems clear that the process of relative improvement was arrested in the decade of the 1970s.[50]

The relatively low income of blacks reflects in part a combination of technological and historical influences that deprived blacks of any significant property income. They were left propertyless after emancipation; and the discriminatory, low-productivity, sharecropping system of small farms kept them propertyless as long as they remained in agriculture. Hence, when blacks migrated out of agriculture into urban society they started a process of wealth accumulation from a base that was probably not much above one-fortieth of the average for whites in 1870.[51] Whites possessed at the outset a virtual monopoly of the material and human capital resources of modern technology. Nevertheless, blacks' rate of advance in the acquisition of material capital in the century following the Civil War was a remarkable 3.3 percent per year compared with the white acquisition rate of 1.1 percent per year. This relative improvement was striking despite the continued enormous discrepancy in average levels of wealth possessed.[52] However, black income did not rise as fast as black real investment; hence the market in that vital respect failed to advance blacks as it did whites. It would be no doubt be revealing to know the changing relative distribution of capital (including human capital) and consumer wealth between the two groups.

Appraisal of the human capital element in black compared to white wealth should proceed with recognition of the fact that the great shift in the nature of American technology in the twentieth century, as Edward Denison, John W. Kendrick, Theodore Schultz, and others have shown, was from material capital goods to investment in human capital, i.e., knowledge and training. The advance of knowledge, as distinguished from labor and material capital input, increasingly accounted for higher productivity. Science, scientific research, the laboratory, and business research and development played ever more vital roles in the progress of twentieth-century technology.[53] The organization of scientific inquiry, together with its growing interconnections with applied knowledge, heightened the importance of the organizational element in technology. The process of innovation became more rigorously a matter of institutionalized team work.[54] One important spillover was, as John Kenneth Galbraith termed it, the big business "technostructure"—the groups of managers, engineers, scientists, and technicians that made collective decisions for the business enterprise.[55]

The study of educational trends is one means, however inadequate, for getting at the comparative progress of blacks with regard to the enhancement of human capital. It is well known that the public school movement, a major social and economic development in itself, substantially advanced the educational level of the nation's labor force even before 1900. The rates listed below use as a crude criterion the percentage of school enrollment for the respective groups to measure this improvement.[56]

	White	*Black*
1860	59.6	1.9
1900	53.6	31.1
1920	65.7	53.5
1940	75.6	68.4
1970	88.3	85.3

By this criterion blacks steadily gained on whites from their original enormous disparity, although it took almost one hundred years to achieve approximate equality. The same general pattern of change obtained with respect to the reduction of illiteracy. A social revolution in education seems to have taken place. But the dramatic improvement in black status has to be understood against the historical background and shockingly disparate level initially.

The trends in years of schooling completed are also revealing. In 1910 only about 9 percent of all persons aged seventeen had graduated from high school, whereas by 1940 almost one-half, and by 1970 over three-fourths, had a high school education.[57] The following tabulation shows the percentages of all persons aged twenty-five years or over who had completed secondary school and college, the percentages of blacks, and a comparison of the two:[58]

	Four years high school or more		Four years college or more	
	1940	1980	1940	1980
All persons	24.5	68.6	4.6	17.0
Black persons	7.3	51.2	1.3	7.9
Ratio, black to all persons	.30	.75	.28	.47

These figures reveal a number of important facts. First, they indicate that the educational level of the labor force was not impressive on the eve of World War II, but that it progressed enormously in the ensuing four decades to meet the technological and cultural needs of a more technologically advanced society. Second, they show that the relative increase in college education of the over-twenty-five population, and therefore of the labor force, was greater than that for the general level (high school or more) of education. The G.I. Bill for the education of World War II veterans was partly responsible for this increase. Third, they show that the schooling level for blacks, again beginning at a very low level and at a late date, improved much more rapidly than for the population as a whole. Fourth, they indicate that black educational progress, measured in terms of total educational advances for the population as a whole, lagged behind the overall educational advance.

Many other social indicators buttress the conclusion that the comparative improvement of black status was one of the leading social developments in recent U.S. history. Blacks also became more urban than whites, and at a faster pace.[59] While advances in nutrition, public health, and medicine apparently failed to help blacks in the same proportion as they did the population as a whole, as illustrated by comparative infant and maternal death rates, there was nonetheless a noteworthy relative gain for blacks with respect to the significant overall health index: life expectancy at birth.[60]

The most distressing socioeconomic aspect of black status remained that of unemployment. In this socially significant respect urban black workers remained by far the most vulnerable group and unemployment rates for blacks, particularly black youths, have been chronically at least double those for whites. There was no trend toward improvement in this ratio during the decades after World War II. To what extent this phenomenon was due to lingering discrimination or to the discrepancy in educational levels is difficult to determine. In any case, disadvantages with respect to education, property, employment, health, income, and family stability made urban blacks the hard core of the permanent, propertyless underclass in a technologically complex world, just as they had been in an earlier, simpler, agrarian world. The crystallization of a distinguishable underclass of blacks (along with Hispanics and other minorities) provided a striking exception to the momentous shifts in social class lines in the post-World War II epoch, brought about by advanced technology and increased per capita income in general.[61]

The Environmental Movement. The post-World War II environmental, ecological, and conservation movements, as well as the spread of an antitechnology ideology, represented a social response to the highly developed complex material technology of the late twentieth century.[62] The nuclear arms control movement likewise was a social response to the "balance of terror" resulting from the greatest innovation in the history of military technology since the firearm.

The planning and teamwork that developed the atom bomb and the later ventures into outer space were the most striking illustrations of the socialization and institutionalization of technological advance in the twentieth century. Scientific and technological research by industry, universities, private foundations, and government, together with the widespread practice of project cooperation among these institutions, itself constituted a societal change revealing the vastly enlarged social character of the innovation process itself. At least three historic changes were responsible for this socialization of research and development effort: the increased sophistication of technology, the growth of large organizations and organizational expertise, and the material affluence that permitted the allocation of the necessary resources to such purpose.

However, while there was planning for individual projects, there was little planning in the overall allocation of resources devoted to technical progress, and in many cases very little orderly coordination of the methods whereby advanced technology was made publicly accessible.[63] The allocation of resources reflected a haphazard constellation of social and political consensus, and such consensus shaped the directions taken by technological advance.

The highly developed technology of the twentieth century not only produced advances in health, medicine, and drugs, it also created enormous volumes of noxious wastes that were damaging to humans.[64] With a new and heightened level of social response, the matter of environmental destructiveness, brought on by technology and by society's failure to apply protective measures, was finally elevated to a prime position on the social policy agenda.[65] The chief sources of the noxious wastes could easily be located as emanating from internal combustion engines, electricity generation and other fossil fuel burning, the giant chemical and petrochemical industries, radioactive waste (the result of a quarter-century of nuclear power generation for military and nonmilitary purposes), and nonbiodegradable agricultural and urban runoff. Of equal concern was the wasteful exploitation of natural resources and the indifferent material profligacy of consumers.

American society's large and growing GNP and its advanced technology was a two-headed monster with one head benevolent, the other sinister. The harmful element was not mere spillover, but was intrinsic to economic growth. It represented the whole production process of converting natural materials into manufactures and thereby creating hazardous byproducts. Which category was growing faster was unknown, but the volume and rate of growth of the harmful products were threateningly large. There was nothing "postindustrial" about the phenomenon. Certain major commodities were particularly destructive ecologically. As a consequence, society had to confront more insistently the question of the tradeoff between further technological progress and GNP growth versus ecological health.

By the 1980s only the most sanguine and cavalier could claim that technology would necessarily find solutions to environmental and human damage that would not in themselves involve new destruction. Both old and new technology were in most cases poorly if at all monitored and the ignorance of adverse effects was colossal. Private enterprise had a vested interest in concealment, much of the government's ecological effort merely "preserved illusions,"[66] and pragmatic Americans were noteworthy for attacking problems only after some particular crisis. Forty years after the dawn of the nuclear age no satisfactory method had yet been developed to store permanently the burgeoning volume of high-level radioactive wastes. The social and political response, until the early 1980s, to ecological deterioration, partly for the reasons just given, was thus belated and inadequate to the challenge.

Americans also suffered from the loss of smaller face-to-face community relationships and the decline in individual responsibility and social pressures for cooperation that had been characteristic of their earlier agrarian society. With urbanization and mass communication came a paradoxical combination of population concentration and growing individual alienation.[67] The advance of technology produced a growing social and economic interdependence, but interdependence also vitiated the individual's self-confidence and sense of social responsibility. The conviction that the individual could or should understand and effect social change atrophied. The sense that one was a mere cog in the machinery compounded the propensity to turn inward. The groundwork was laid for a flight from social responsibility.

Serious group responses failed to materialize even after such an episode as that in Donora, Pennsylvania, where in 1948 an eight-day temperature inversion caused a 400 percent increase in the death rate, an almost dead Lake Erie, and a Cuyahoga River that was a fire hazard.[68] Some responses began to materialize in the late 1950s, gained momentum with the publication of Rachel Carson's *Silent Spring* in 1962, and reached some sort of a peak with the passage of the National Environmental Policy Act and the establishment of the Environmental Protection Agency in 1970, the year that inaugurated the so-called "environmental decade." The federal government finally recognized environmental protection as a major responsibility, and environmental impact studies were widely introduced into public and private policy debate.

When viewed from another aspect, the high national income, even with its skewed distribution, probably produced sufficient leisure and education to arouse the compassion, concern, and fear necessary to attack the ecological effects of a threatening technology. With higher national income, public opinion could also accept the cost of arresting some of the main disamenities. Still, it is probably correct to say that "serious interest was restricted to a rather narrow high-income and highly educated segment of the population."[69]

Capital-Saving Technology. One of the more subtle yet far-reaching technological changes was the shift from capital-absorbing innovations embodied in fixed capital goods (plant and equipment) in the period between the Civil War and 1890 to capital-saving innovations after that time. The consequent rise, at about 1.2 percent per year, in output per unit of capital input in the private domestic economy over the period 1889 to 1953 can be demonstrated,[70] as well as the continuation of that trend at about one percent per year for the post-World War II period.[71] A constant dollar of capital stock, with the enhanced productivity brought about by applied knowledge in the twentieth century, carried increasingly greater capacity to produce. While that development attested to growth in productivity, it also contributed to the long-run decline of private fixed investment opportunities, since a given capacity increase required ever smaller net investment. The consequence of this was a tendency toward secular stagnation in aggregate demand—the Keynesian dilemma of a high-savings, capital-rich business economy with a secularly declining marginal efficiency of investment.

The gradual saturation of net fixed investment opportunities in the home economy, together with insufficient compensating offsets to saving through foreign capital exports, required the introduction of another large spending stream to substitute for the withering away of business investment spending if the economy were to continue to grow. That substitute became government purchases of goods and services. Thus the changes inaugurated by the New Deal may be seen as having their origin in a combination of insufficient private investment and the crystallization of a new consensus demanding a high, stable level of employment, and modern welfare services.[72] There is a close connection, it can be demonstrated, between the evolution of technological improvements in capital goods and the need for public spending, civilian and military. It may also be noted that the large growth of social welfare public transfer payments after World War II relieved poverty and subsidized the 20 percent of the population with the lowest income, thereby bolstering the "private" aggregate consumer spending stream. Expansion of demand in that category at approximately the GNP rate also proved essential for continued economic growth. The huge contemporary military spending directly reflected a technological race between the superpowers as well as the necessity to sustain demand for high employment. Finally, the variety of public expenditures on human resources may also be seen as a response to the growing technological need for rigorously mobilized knowledge.[73]

Migration and Technological Change. Reference was made earlier to the geographical distribution of economic activities as one main kind of connecting rod between technological change and social change. The mass geographical movement of people should be recalled as one of the remarkable characteristics of American society. The hundred years surveyed here saw the climax of westward migration and the closing of the frontier well before World War I.

We may select the growth of population in the Far West and on the Pacific Coast, particularly California, as examples of the continued migratory patterns of Americans far into the twentieth century. The spectacular population growth of that vast region was largely due to in-migration. The California population increases were extremely large and reflected waves of migration, with peaks in 1870–1880, 1900–1910, 1920–1930 (the decade of greatest increase), and in the decade of World War II. Thereafter the migration rate into the state and the population growth rate declined.

One indicator of the huge role played by migration is the number of white California residents born in other states compared with the number born in California. Calculating the comparison in percentages, the figures are:[74]

Year	Percent
1870	109
1900	60
1920	109
1930	145
1950	136

These percentages represent millions of people on the move; in 1920 whites born out of state totaled 1.3 million, and in 1950 over 5 million.[75]

The location of an industry in a new area, whether it produces an established or a new product (such as the motion picture industry), is a technological innovation with many consequences. So, too, was the transportation of oil and natural gas by pipeline, which slashed energy costs on the West Coast. In Schumpeter's terminology, that kind of process requires setting up a new "production function." Given an appropriate information network, new employment opportunities induce people living elsewhere to relinquish established life patterns and emigrate. The migrants to California, contributing to Gunnar Myrdal's process of "cumulative causation," in turn created a rising demand for housing and other consumer products and services, including governmental.

In the half century after the Civil War the state of California, destined to become the most populous, created fast-expanding industries out of its fields, mines, and forests—minerals, petroleum, citrus fruits, wine, wheat, and cotton. In the twentieth century, petroleum, ocean shipping, vegetables and processed foods, diversified manufacturing, aerospace, electronics, military goods, and the clustering of the nation's largest aggregation of scientists, engineers, and technicians were added to the record. The congregation of "knowledge" specialists was to an important extent due to the high federal spending on aerospace and military work. Many industries were made possible also by an effective truck transport network. An enormous expansion in private and public service activities followed. Persons engaged in service activities in the Far West (dominated by California) approached three-fourths of its total labor force by 1950.[76] There are few better illustrations of the power of technology to alter peoples' social existence than this dramatic history of migration in the building of the nation's most populous state. To be sure, all the migration cannot be attributed to industrial innovation. For example, thousands entered the state to enjoy its climatic amenities. But even these could not be enjoyed without the modern economic environment as an underpinning.

Other migration examples, such as in the Pacific Northwest, the Southwest, Florida, Texas, and, beginning with World War II, the Southeast, could be cited. They, too, would demonstrate the same connections between the advance of technology, the growth of industry, and Americans on the move. And they would also show why it was that in the long run regional per capita incomes converged, and regional industrial and occupational structures became increasingly similar.

The Future

The rate of technological advance and the interconnections between all the parts of what Jacques Ellul has called the "technological system" are surely increasing. The information revolution now adds additional thrust to a technology that thrives on the growth of knowledge more than on the accumulation of tangible capital and organization. Such technological growth will certainly generate unexpected social consequences and subject the process of social accommodation to even greater and more pervasive tensions. It will also further accelerate the pace of human life, with its attendant psychological and psychosomatic stress.

The continued development (and the global diffusion) of modern technology that generates environmental pollution is likely to produce unexpected crises for the human organism—new inexplicable diseases, nutritional deficiencies, degenerative body changes, and higher levels of physiological stress. At the same time, coping with these adverse health effects will require the allocation of unprecedentedly large resources and the establishment of appropriate new administrative structures. The mounting strains of adjustment, like the management of technological growth itself, will demand the further socialization of technical progress.

Some of the twentieth-century social changes described in the previous pages have nearly completed their pattern of evolution. Others will continue to develop as new technology continues to unfold. Adjustments in social groups and institutions, at present only beginning to appear on the public agenda, will become necessary as innovations, now in their infancy, require them.[77]

A few examples must suffice. The most urgent and world-shaking among such social adjustments will be the creation of institutions to prevent the use of nuclear weaponry on earth and in outer space. The lag in the development of international social controls over such weaponry illustrates the general tension between society's fast-moving, quasi-autonomous apparatus for technological innovation and its slow-moving, lagging, social constructs for coping with the results. In the specific case of nuclear weaponry, the lag is all the more frightening in view of the fact that the very survival of the human race is involved.

A similar example of that tension, although of a lesser order or social significance, is to be found in the building of nuclear-powered electric generating plants without giving serious consideration to the safe disposition of the radioactive spent fuel rods. This is only one extreme example of socially deficient procedures leading to the unconscionable dumping of hazardous wastes of all sorts. Such lags in social accommodation to new technology can hardly be explained as a more or less innocuous phenomenon of being caught by surprise; where the attendant, pervasive social damages, as in the case of spent fuel rod disposal, are so great, the lag comes to reflect either greed, criminality, or madness.

Somewhat more excusable is the failure to modernize the ways in which workers in the new regimen of industrial technology relate to their work conditions, their fellow employees, and their managerial bureaucracy. This will undoubtedly become an arena of significant change as computerization, robotics, "telework," information processing, and other indirect electronic control instrumentation spread through the industrial, commercial, financial, and public network. Electronic computerized office equipment will without doubt raise output and displace labor. But there is grave doubt that it will lighten the burden of input effort on the part of office personnel. Indeed it may well increase the intensity of office work for those still employed because it could unrealistically enhance management's expectations regarding the amount of employee effort required under the new, advanced techniques.

In the sphere of biotechnology, or genetic engineering, a revolution "of unprecedented scope of incalculable social effects" is taking place.[78] The innovations include microelectronic laboratory equipment, such products as interferon, the creation of new life forms, and genetic screening. It seems clear at this point that the chief issues involved fall in the area of ethics and social regulation. Any impact upon societal arrangements lies in the unforeseeable future.

In physics, chemistry, and space technology, it would be equally presumptuous to speculate about the social impact of lasers, photovoltaic cells, the superconducting collider (accelerator), new synthetic materials, continuous-beam electron accelerators, communications satellites, or manned space systems. The accelerator provides a striking example of the necessary socialization of the innovative process today. In April 1983 a multimillion dollar proposal was advanced for the construction of an advanced accelerator. Involved at the initial stage were twenty-two universities, a proposed National Electron Accelerator Laboratory, the U.S. Department of Energy, the Nuclear Science Advisory Committee, and the National Science Foundation. No one thought, however, of including the Office of Technology Assessment.

Some writers have viewed with appropriate alarm, and even defeatism, the difficulties of social and intellectual accommodation to, and management of, a technology that advances almost autonomously and at an increasingly faster pace. We may be wise to heed their warnings. On the other hand, if we approach the problem as one that warrants the allocation of substantial resources to it and requires planned social, rather than haphazard private, effort, it seems reasonable to expect that machinery for adequate adjustments can be created in time, and that there is no justification for total defeatism.

Notes

1. Calculated from John W. Kendrick, *Productivity Trends in the United States*, National Bureau of Economic Research (Princeton: Princeton University Press, 1961), pp. 338–339, table A-xxiii. The years referred to are 1874–1910; 1874 is an average for the 1870s, 1910 is a five-year average centered on that year.
2. Calculated from Albert Fishlow, "Productivity and Technological Change in the Railroad Sector, 1840–1910," in National Bureau of Economic Research, *Output, Employment, and Productivity in the United States After 1800* (New York: Columbia University Press, 1966).
3. Calculated from Kendrick, p. 338.
4. Of course, thousands of the residents of metropolitan suburbs were classified by the census as rural (or rural nonfarm), although they were urban in life style and attitude.
5. See Everett E. Edwards, "American Agriculture: The First 300 Years," in U.S. Department of Agriculture, *Farmers in a Changing World*, Yearbook of Agriculture 1940 (Washington, D.C.: GPO, 1940), pp. 250–256, *passim.*
6. William N. Parker and Judith L. V. Klein, "Productivity Growth in Grain Production in the United States, 1840–1860 and 1900–1910," in NBER, *Output, Employment and Productivity*, pp. 525–526.

7. Farm output calculated from Gene L. Swackhamer, "Agriculture and Technology," Federal Reserve Bank of Kansas City, *Monthly Review* (May–June 1967), p. 6, table 1.

8. U.S. Departmentf of Agriculture, *Changes in Farm Production and Efficiency*, Statistical Bulletin no. 233, June 1968, p. 16.

9. Jeffrey G. Williamson, *Late Nineteenth-Century American Development* (London: Cambridge University Press, 1974), pp. 177, 178, 180.

10. To invoke one crude measure of farm size, the average acreage per farm in 1870 was 153. In 1935, sixty-five years later, it was only 155. But in the following three decades, subsequent to the modern technological revolution in agriculture, acreage per farm had more than doubled. See U.S. Bureau of the Census, *Historical Statistics of the United States, Colonial Times to 1970*, part 1, (Washington, D.C.: GPO, 1975), series K7, p. 457.

11. For a recent attempt to quantify the importance in manufacturing of the new capital-intensive technology for optimal firm size, see John A. James, "Structural Change in American Manufacturing, 1850–1890," *Journal of Economic History* (June 1983), 43(2):433–459.

12. See Louis E. Davis, "Evolving Alternative Organization Designs," *Human Relations* (1977), 30(3):262–263.

13. See the excellent discussion of these issues in Chris Argyris, *On Organizations of the Future* (Beverly Hills, Calif.: Sage Publications, 1973).

14. Edwin T. Layton, Jr., ed., *Technology and Social Change in America* (New York: Harper and Row, 1973), p. 7.

15 I am indebted for a number of my comments on the transformation of the family to the informative discussion in Gerhard and Jean Lenski, *Human Societies*, 4th ed. (New York: McGraw-Hill, 1982), pp. 340–347, *passim*.

16. John A. Garraty, *The American Nation* (New York: Harper and Row, 1966), p. 570.

17. See Carl N. Degler, *At Odds: Women and the Family in America* (New York: Oxford University Press, 1980), pp. 407–408.

18. Roger Burlingame, *March of the Iron Men* (New York: Grosset and Dunlap, 1938), p. 379. For a related discussion with an interpretation in some respects different from that projected here, see Ruth Schwartz Cowan, "From Virginia Dare to Virginia Slims: Women and Technology in American Life," *Technology and Culture* (January 1979), 20(1):51–63. But see in the same issue, regarding the women's liberation movement, Nathan Rosenberg, "Technological Interdependence in the American Economy," p. 50.

19. Degler, pp. 321–323.

20. For a critique of the functionalist theory of the impact of industrial technology on the family that is relied upon here, but one limited to the middle-class family, see Ruth Schwartz Cowan, "The 'Industrial Revolution' in the Home: Household Technology and Social Change in the 20th Century," *Technology and Culture* (January 1976), 17(1):1–23.

21. See David F. Noble, *America by Design* (New York: Oxford University Press, 1977), pp. 111–118.

22. The railroad decline was caused in part by technological improvement but also, and to a much greater degree than in farming, by falling demand.

23. Robert E. Gallman and Edward S. Howle, "Trends in the Structure of the American Economy Since 1840," in Robert W. Fogel and Stanley L. Engerman, eds., *The Reinterpretation of American Economic History* (New York: Harper and Row, 1971), p. 29, table 4.

24. *Ibid.*

25. Robert E. Gallman, "The Pace and Pattern of American Economic Growth," in Lance E. Davis et al., *American Economic Growth* (New York: Harper and Row, 1972), p. 53, table 2.17.

26. It must be borne in mind that the service sector included the provision, for example, of electric current and telephonic communication, in which productivity rise, in the twentieth century particularly, was spectacular. Of course that rise was vitally dependent upon new equipment produced in the manufacturing sector. Both of these activities were preeminent in the development of basic scientific research, a hallmark of twentieth-century technological progress. For the earlier phase of the telephone industry, and a partial general bibliography, see Lillian Hoddeson, "The Emergence of Basic Research in the Bell Telephone System, 1875–1915," *Technology and Culture*, (July 1981), 22(3):512–544, especially the "set of three principles," p. 516. See also George Wise, "A New Role for Professional Scientists in Industry: Industrial Research at General Electric, 1900–1916," *Technology and Culture* (July 1980) 21(3):408–429.

27. For the years 1948–1976, see the average annual total factor productivity and output/labor growth rate estimates in John W. Kendrick and Elliot S. Grossman, *Productivity in the United States* (Baltimore: Johns Hopkins University Press, 1980), pp. 34, 37.

28. One of the most remarkable features of technological, occupational, and social changes over most of the last century was the failure of any of these to exert much effect upon the overall distribution of income emanating from the private market. Indeed, they failed to alter the basic socioeconomic system in any significant sense.

29. See "The Meaning of Rural—A Third of our Nation," in U.S. Department of Agriculture, *The Yearbook of Agriculture*, 1970, pp. 143–148. This volume has a number of chapters on the nation's large rural society. See also Economic Development Division, Economic Research Service, U.S. Department of Agriculture, *The Economic and Social Condition of Rural America in the 1970s*, prepared for the Committee on Government Operations, U.S. Senate, 92d Cong., 1st sess., Part 1, May 1971 (Washington, D.C.: GPO, 1971), pp. 29, 73, 120.

30. U.S. Bureau of the Census, *Statistical Abstract of the United States, 1981* (Washington, D.C.: U.S. Bureau of the Census), p. 680, no. 1207.

31. See Martin Jezer, "How Many Harvests Have We Left," in George E. Frakes and Curtis B. Solberg, eds., *Pollution Papers* (New York: Appleton-Century-Crofts, 1971), p. 144.

32. See Trevor I. Williams, "Technology and the Quality of Life," in Trevor I. Williams, ed., *A History of Technology* (Oxford: Clarendon Press, 1978), vol. 7, part 2, p. 1466.

33. *Statistical Abstract, 1981*, p. 591, no. 1018. These increases represent compound annual increase rates of over 4 percent for households and almost 6 percent for commercial customers.

34. See the review by James Foreman-Peck of James M. Laux et al., *The Automobile Revolution: The Impact of an Industry* (Chapel Hill: University of North Carolina Press, 1982), in *Journal of Economic History* (June 1983), 43(2):554–555.

35. Robert L. Heilbroner, *The Making of Economic Society*, 4th ed. (Englewood Cliffs, N.J.: Prentice-Hall, 1972), p. 102.

36. See, in this connection, S. C. Gilfillan, "Social Effects of Inventions," in U.S. National Resources Committee, *Technological Trends and National Policy* (Washington, D.C.: GPO, June 1937), pp. 28–29.

37. Calculated from data in *Historical Statistics*, pp. 129, 131, 132, Series D-26, D-28, D-36, D-37; and *Statistical Abstract, 1981*, p. 382, no. 638.

38. *Statistical Abstract, 1981*, p. 383, no. 640 (calculated).

39. However, the proportion of all women in service activities dropped drastically in the twentieth century.

40. Calculated from *Historical Statistics*, p. 385, Series H-758, H-759; and *Statistical Abstract, 1981*, p. 165, no. 283.

41. Degree data from *Statistical Abstract, 1981*, p. 167, no. 285.

42. Victor R. Fuchs argues that the climb in the participation rate of married mothers is due to the long-term wage rise, not the feminist movement. See the review of his *How We Live* by Alfred L. Malabre, Jr., *Wall Street Journal*, June 3, 1983, p. 20.

43. *Statistical Abstract, 1982–83*, p. 45, no. 64.

44. Calculated from *Historical Statistics*, series A79, part 1, pp. 12–13.

45. See *Historical Statistics*, series K84, p. 465, and *Statistical Abstract, 1981*, table 1146, p. 654.

46. U.S. Department of Commerce, Bureau of the Census, *The Social and Economic Status of the Black Population in the United States: An Historical View, 1790–1978*, Current Population Reports, Social Studies Series P-23, no. 80 (Washington, DC: GPO, n.d.), p. 175, table 125.

47. *Ibid.*, p.218, table 164.

48. See U.S. Bureau of the Census, *Changing Characteristics of the Negro Population*, 1960 Census Monograph by Daniel O. Price (Washington DC: GPO, 1969), pp. 188, 217. Note that education, which is both a technological and a social phenomenon, is directly related to income.

49. *Social and Economic Status of the Black Population*, p. 218, table 164.

50. *Ibid.*, p.31, table 14. Percentages are five-year averages (1947–51 and 1975–79) of the ratios. The latter average is calculated from the *Statistical Abstract, 1981*, p. 432, table 720. However, see the criticism of these data in University of Wisconsin-Madison, Institute for Research on Poverty, "Black Statistics: A Look at the Figures on Social Change," *Focus*, (Spring 1981) 4(3), esp. pp. 15–16. The black family income average, relative to the white, fell during the slow economic expansion years of the early 1980s (to 56 percent in 1981), partly because of the sharp jump in the number of black families headed by women. See U.S. Department of Commerce, Bureau of the Census, *America's Black Population, 1970 to 1982*, Special Publication P10/OPO-83–1 (Washington, DC: GPO, July 1983), p.4.

51. Lee Soltow, "Age and Color in a Century of Personal Wealth Accumulation," extracted in Harold G. Vatter and Thomas Palm, eds., *The Economics of Black America* (New York: Harcourt Brace Jovanovich, 1972), pp. 81–83.

52. *Ibid.*, pp. 83–84.

53. See John Rae, "The Application of Science to Industry," in Alexandra Oleson and John Voss, eds., *The Organization of Knowledge in Modern America, 1860–1920* (Baltimore: Johns Hopkins University Press, 1979), p. 249.

54. See E. Layton, "Condition of Technological Development," in Ina Spiegel-Roesing and Derek de Solla Price eds., *Science, Technology, and Society*, (Beverly Hills: Sage Publications, 1977), pp. 211–216, passim.

55. See also Sanford A. Lakoff, "Scientists, Technologists and Political Power," in Spiegel-Roesing and de Solla Price, esp. pp. 367–371.

56. Data from *Historical Statistics*, part 1, p. 370, series H-434, H-435.

57. *Historical Statistics*, part 1, p. 379, series H-599.

58. *Statistical Abstract, 1981*, p. 141, no. 229; ratios calculated.

59. See *Statistical Abstract, 1981*, p. 16, no. 19, and *Historical Statistics*, part 1, p. 40, series A-276–A-287.

60. See *Statistical Abstract, 1981,* p. 69, no. 105 and p. 73, no. 111. See also *Historical Statistics,* part 1, p. 56, series B-116–B-125, and p. 57, series B-136-B-147.

61. See A. N. J. Hollander, "Science, Technology, Modernization and Social Change," in UNESCO, *The Social Implications of the Scientific and Technological Revolution* (Paris: UNESCO, 1981), p. 304.

62. The study of ecology in the United States has been dated from the late 1880s, and "was the technological effort of scientists at the University of Nebraska, under the leadership of Charles Bessey, to control vegetational changes in the midwestern grasslands." Ronald Tobey, "Theoretical Science and Technology in American Ecology," *Technology and Culture,* (October 1976), 17(4): 719. As for the contemporary movement for environmental management, I would not wish to speak of origins much before the founding of the International Union for the Conservation of Nature in 1948. See Ernst B. Haas, Mary Pat Williams, and Don Babai, *Scientists and World Order* (Berkeley: University of California Press, 1977), ch. 8, pp. 179 *ff.*

63. See "Delivery of Health Services," in E. J. Piel and J. G. Truxal, *Man and his Technology* (New York: McGraw-Hill, 1973), pp. 53–88, *passim.*

64. The relationship between noxious wastes and the population increase has been pointed out by William J. Baumol, and is cited in Robert L. Heilbroner, *Understanding Microeconomics,* 2d ed. (Englewood Cliffs, NJ: Prentice-Hall, 1972), p. 139.

65. Social responses to particular pollution problems in cities, especially after the industrial revolution, naturally had a long history. For an English example, see Carlos Flick, "The Movement for Smoke Abatement in 19th-Century Britain," *Technology and Culture,* (January 1980), 21(1): 29–50.

66. The phrase "preserved illusions" is from "Resources for the Future," *Resources* (February 1983), p. 11, and has reference to a decade's experience with the 1972 federal Clean Water Act.

67. Paul W. Barkley and David W. Seckler, *Economic Growth and Environmental Decay* (New York: Harcourt Brace Jovanovich, 1972), p. 111.

68. See John C. Esposito, "The Threat to Human Life and Health," in Frakes and Solberg, *Pollution Papers,* p. 110.

69. Edwin S. Mills, *The Economics of Environmental Quality* (New York: Norton, 1978), p. 184.

70. See Kendrick, *Productivity Trends in the United States,* pp. 165–169.

71. See Harold G. Vatter, "The Atrophy of Net Investment and Some Consequences for the U.S. Mixed Economy," *Journal of Economic Issues,* (March 1982), 16(1): 237–253.

72. See Harold G. Vatter, "Perspectives on the Forty-Sixth Anniversary of the U.S. Mixed Economy," *Explorations in Economic History (1979), 16:297–330.*

73. George W. James, "The Technological Revolution," *Challenge,* vol. 2, no. 5 (February 1963), 2(5): 39.

74. Everett S. Lee et al., *Population Redistribution and Economic Growth, United States, 1870–1950* (Philadelphia: American Philosophical Society, 1957), p. 252.

75. *Ibid.,* p. 302.

76. Harvey S. Perloff et al., *Regions, Resources and Economic Growth* (Lincoln: University of Nebraska Press, 1960), p. 272.

77. For a representative recent discussion of major technological prospects, see Ernst Weber, Gordon K. Teal, and A. George Schillinger, *Technology Forecast for 1980* (New York: Van Nostrand Reinhold, 1971).

78. Dick Russell, "The Marketing of Genetic Science," *The Amicus Journal* (Summer 1983), 5(1):14.

3. TECHNOLOGY AND THE TRANSFORMATION OF INDUSTRIAL ORGANIZATION

Alfred D. Chandler, Jr.
Harvard University

The Nature of the Transformation

Although this chapter emphasizes the experience of the United States, it also reviews the transformation of the organization of production and distribution in several advanced industrial nations in the late nineteenth and twentieth centuries. It focuses not on the organization of the actual units of production and distribution—farms, mines, factories, shops, and offices—but rather on the organization of the flow of goods and services through these units from the extraction of the raw materials to the delivery of the finished product to the final consumer. It focuses, therefore, on the organization of the business enterprises that carried out these processes and on the organization or the structure of the industries in which the flow occurred. It argues that a basic transformation of industrial organization so defined occurred about a century ago and that this transformation was a response to basic innovations in the technology (that is, the "hardware") of production and distribution.

Until the last decade of the nineteenth century business enterprises were small and personally managed, and the industries in which they operated were fragmented. Many small units competed in national and international markets primarily on the basis of price. The rapid expansion of trade and markets in the eighteenth and early nineteenth centuries had brought specialization. By the mid-nineteenth century business enterprises in the more industrialized economies normally operated a single unit of production—a farm, mine, mill, or shop— or carried on a single unit of distribution. Distributors had become wholesalers or retailers, importers or exporters who specialized in a single line of goods—textiles, apparel, hardware, furniture, tobacco, drugs, jewelry, and the like. Owners managed these single-unit enterprises either as individual proprietors or partners. Where salaried managers were employed, they were few in number and worked directly with owners. A class of middle managers—salaried managers who managed junior managers and reported to senior ones—had not yet come into existence. As yet no business enterprises were administered through hierarchies of managers comparable to that depicted on chart 3.1. Because these small, personally managed enterprises had little control over the volume of supplies available or the finished goods produced for national and international markets, the flow of goods through the processes of production and distribution were coordinated by price—price that was set in a general way by the availability of goods and the demands for them.

During the last years of the nineteenth century these patterns of industrial organization began to be profoundly transformed. In some industries, but certainly not all, the small single-unit firms were rapidly replaced by large enterprises that operated many units of both production and distribution. In these industries the flow of materials through the processes of production and distribution now became coordinated but by the administrative decisions of middle and top managers who supervised the internalized operating units, that is by managerial hierarchies similar to the one illustrated by chart 3.1.

As the visible hand of such hierarchies began to replace what Adam Smith defined as the invisible hand of market forces as a coordinator of flow, the structure of the industries in which they operated also became transformed. These industries became concentrated. A small number of large firms quickly came to dominate. In such industries contractual agreements about prices, output, and marketing arrangements were much easier to reach, monitor, and enforce than in industries made up of a multitude of small unit enterprises. Nevertheless such agreements were still difficult to establish and even more difficult to enforce. Instead a new type of competition appeared. It rarely occurred on price alone; instead, the few large integrated firms competed functionally and strategically for market share and profit in ways that will be described below.

This transformation from single-unit and multi-unit enterprises, from market to administrative coordination, from fragmented to concentrated industry structure, and from price to functional and strategic competition was technologically engendered. It resulted primarily from the coming of new technologies of production and distribution that vastly increased the volume of output of which a single unit of production was capable and the volume of transactions that a single unit of distribution was able to handle. This profound transformation in industrial organization was not so much the result of what historians have called the First Industrial Revolution, which began in Great Britain at the end of the eighteenth century; that is, it was not the result of the initial application of the new source of energy—fossil fuel, coal—to the processes of production. It resulted much more from the coming of modern transportation and communication that made possible the so-called Second Industrial Revolution. The effective operation of the new technologies—the railroad, telegraph, steamship, and cable—demanded new forms of organizations. The new hardware with its new type of organization made possible the movement of goods, passengers, and messages in unprecedented volumes with unprecedented speed and regularity. The new forms of transportation and communication, in turn, made possible the new methods of mass distribution and brought into being new technologies of mass production. Effective exploitation of this new hardware of production, like that for transportation and distribution, demanded organizational innovation. Above all, it required the creation of teams or hierarchies of managers to assure a continuing high volume flow through the process of production and distribution. These needs transformed the organization of business enterprises and the industries in which they operated.

Thus the first such managerial hierarchies appeared during the 1850s and 1860s to coordinate the movements of trains and flow of goods over the new railroad networks, and messages over the new telegraph system. They then quickly came into use to manage the new mass retailing establishments—whose existence the railroad and the telegraph made possible. For example, by 1905 such an organization permitted Sears Roebuck's mail-order plant in Chicago to fill 100,000 orders in a single day—more than the average earlier American merchant filled in a lifetime.[1] These administrative hierarchies grew to a much greater size in industrial enterprises that, again on the basis of modern transportation and communication, integrated mass production and mass distribution within a single business enterprise.

These new integrated, industrial enterprises have had much in common whether they were American, European, or Japanese. They appeared at almost the same moment in history in the United States and Europe and a little later in Japan, only because Japan was later to industrialize. They clustered in industries whose hardware had similar characteristics. Moreover they grew in much the same manner. In nearly all cases they became large, first, by integrating forward, that is, investing in marketing and distribution facilities and personnel, then by moving backwards into purchasing and control of raw and semifinished materials; then, though much less often, they invested in research and development. In this way they created the multifunctional organization illustrated by chart 1. They soon became multinational by investing abroad, first in marketing and then in production. Finally, they continued to expand their activities by investing in product lines related to their existing businesses, thus creating the organization depicted in chart 3.2.

In all industrially advanced economies the great majority of the new large integrated firms first appeared and continued to be located in industries having similar characteristics in production and distribution. As table 3.1 indicates, the 200 largest enterprises in the United States in four different years were clustered in food, chemicals, petroleum, metals, and machinery. In 1917, 152 (76 percent) of the 200 were in these industries; in 1948, the figure was 156 (or 78 percent). By 1973 a few of these industrials had so widely diversified their product lines that they could not be listed in any one industry. If those conglomerates that cannot be so categorized are excluded, the percentage in these industries was 76.8 (139 out of 181). The large firms appeared in subcategories of other basic industrial groupings listed in table 3.1 that had characteristics similar to the major groups in which three-fourths of the firms clustered. They were in cigarettes in the tobacco group, tires in rubber, newsprint in paper, plate glass in stone, glass, and clay, cans and razor blades in fabricated metals, and mass-produced cameras in instruments. On the other hand, the total number of firms among the top 200 in apparel, textile, lumber, furniture, leather, publishing and printing, and miscellaneous groups in 1917 was only 18 (9 percent); by 1948 it dropped to 13 (6.5 percent) and by 1973 to 9 (or 5 percent of 181 when the conglomerates are excluded).

Tables 3.2–3.4 indicate roughly similar clustering among the top 200 firms in Britain, Germany, and Japan. The primary differences between the United States and the other three countries is that there are more textile and fewer petroleum companies. In all three countries the number of textile firms declined as the century passed, and the number of oil companies increased, as did the number of machinery firms.

The Transformation of Industrial Enterprises[2]

Why did this new form of enterprise—large, integrated, and administered by salaried managers—appear in some industries but rarely in others? And why did it appear at almost the same historical moment in the United States and Europe? Why did it grow in the same manner in different economies, first, by integrating forward into volume distribution, then by taking on other functions, then by becoming multinational and finally multiproduct?

Because these enterprises initially grew large by integrating mass production with volume distribution, answers to these critical questions require a careful look at both of these processes. Mass production is an attribute of specific technologies of production. In some industries the primary way to increase output was by adding more workers and machines; in others it was by improving and rearranging the inputs, by improving the machinery, furnaces, stills, and other equipment, by reorienting the process of production within the plant, by placing the several processes of production required for a finished product within a single works, and by increasing the application of energy (particularly fossil fuel energy). The first set of industries remained "labor intensive," the second set became "capital intensive." In this second set of industries the hardware of production permitted much larger economies of scale than was possible in the first. That is, it permitted much greater reduction in cost per unit of output as volume increased. So in these capital-intensive industries with large batch or continuous process technologies large plants, operating at minimum efficient scale (scale of operation that brought the lowest unit costs), had a much greater cost advantage over small plants than was true with labor-intensive technologies. Conversely, costs per unit rose much more rapidly when production fell below minimum efficient scale (say 80 to 90 percent of capacity) than was true in labor-intensive industries.

What is of basic importance for an understanding of the coming of the modern managerial industrial enterprise is that the cost advantage of the larger plants cannot be fully realized unless a constant flow of materials through the plant or factory is maintained. The decisive figure in determining costs and profits is, then, not rated capacity for a specified time period but throughput—that is, the amount actually processed in that time period. Throughput is, then, the proper economic measure of capacity utilization. In the capital-intensive industries the throughput needed to maintain minimum efficient scale requires careful coordination not only of flow through the processes of production but also flow of inputs from the suppliers and flow of outputs to the retailers and final consumers. Such coordination cannot happen automatically. It demands the constant attention of a managerial team or hierarchy. Thus, scale is only a technological characteristic. The economies of scale, measured by throughput, are organizational. Such economies depend on knowledge, skills, and teamwork—on the human organization essential to exploit the potential of technological hardware.

A well-known example illustrates these generalizations. In 1882 the Standard Oil "alliance" formed the Standard Oil Trust.[3] The purpose was not to obtain control over the industry. That alliance, a loose federation of forty companies, each with its own legal and administrative identity but tied to John D. Rockefeller's Standard Oil Company through interchange of stock and other financial devices, already controlled close to 90 percent of the American output of kerosene. Instead, the purpose was to provide a legal instrument to rationalize the industry and to exploit more fully economies of scale. The Trust provided the essential legal means to create a corporate or central office that could, first, reorganize the processes of production by shutting down some refineries, reshaping others, and building new ones and could, then, coordinate the flow of materials, not only through the several refineries but from the oil fields to the refineries and from the refineries to the consumers. The resulting rationalization made it possible to concentrate close to a quarter of the world's production of kerosene in three refineries, each with a 6,000 to 7,000 barrel daily throughput, with two-thirds of that product going to overseas markets. (At this time the refined petroleum products were by far the nation's largest nonagricultural export.) Imagine the diseconomies of scale that would result from placing close to one-fourth of the world's production of shoes, textiles, or lumber into three factories or mills!

This reorganization of the Trust's refining facilities brought a sharp reduction in average cost of production of a gallon of kerosene. Average cost dropped from 1.5 cents a gallon before reorganization to 0.54 cents in 1884 and 0.45 in 1885, with costs at the giant refineries being still lower, and far below those of any competitor. However, maintaining this cost advantage required these large refineries to have a continuing daily throughput of from 6,000 to 7,000 barrels or a three- to fourfold increase over the earlier daily flow of 1,500 to 2,000 barrels, with concomitant increases in transactions handled and in the complexity of coordinating the flow of materials through the process of production and distribution.

The Standard Oil story was by no means unique. In the 1880s and 1890s new mass production technologies—those of the Second Industrial Revolution—brought sharp reduction in costs as plants reached minimum efficient scale. In many industries the level of output was so high at that scale that a small number of plants were able to meet existing national and even global demand. The structure of these industries quickly became oligopolistic. Their few large enterprises competed worldwide. In many instances the first enterprises to build a plant with a high minimum efficient scale and to recruit the essential management team have remained until this day leaders in their industries. A brief review of the industries, listed in tables 3.1– 3.4, in which the large enterprises have always clustered illustrates this close relationship between scale economies, the size of enterprise, and industrial concentration.

In groups 20 and 21 of the tables—food, drink, and tobacco—new production processes in the refining of sugar and vegetable oils, the

Table 3.1. The Distribution of the 200 Largest Manufacturing Firms in the United States, by Industry

Standard Industrial Classification	1917	1930	1948	1973
20 Food	30	31	26	22
21 Tobacco	6	5	5	3
22 Textiles	5	3	6	3
23 Apparel	3	0	0	0
24 Lumber	3	4	1	4
25 Furniture	0	1	1	0
26 Paper	5	7	6	9
27 Printing and publishing	2	3	2	1
28 Chemical	20	18	24	27
29 Petroleum	22	26	24	22
30 Rubber	5	5	5	5
31 Leather	4	2	2	0
32 Stone, clay, and glass	5	9	5	7
33 Primary metal	29	25	24	19
34 Fabricated metal	8	10	7	5
35 Machinery	20	22	24	17
36 Electrical machinery	5	5	8	13
37 Transportation equipment	26	21	26	19
38 Instruments	1	2	3	4
39 Miscellaneous	1	1	1	1
Diversified/conglomerate	0	0	0	19
Total	200	200	200	200

Note: Firms ranked by assets.

milling of wheat and oats, and the making of cigarettes brought rapid reductions in costs. In cigarettes, for example, the invention of the Bonsak machine in the early 1880s permitted the first entrepreneurs to adopt the machine—James B. Duke in the United States and the Wills brothers in Britain—and to reduce labor costs sharply, in Wills' case from 4 shillings per thousand to 0.3 pence per thousand.[4] Understandably, Duke and Wills soon dominated and then divided the world market. In addition, most companies in group 20, and also those producing consumer chemicals such as soap, cosmetics, paints, and pills, pioneered in the use of new high-volume techniques for packaging their products in small units that could be placed directly on retailers' shelves. The most important of these was the "automatic-line" canning process, invented in the mid-1880s, which permitted

Table 3.2. The Distribution of the 200 Largest Industrial Enterprises in the United Kingdom, by Industry

Standard Industrial Classification	1919	1930	1948	1973
20 Food	63	64	52	33
21 Tobacco	3	4	6	4
22 Textiles	26	24	17	10
23 Apparel	1	3	2	0
24 Lumber	0	0	0	2
25 Furniture	0	0	0	0
26 Paper	4	5	6	7
27 Printing and publishing	5	10	6	7
28 Chemical	11	9	19	21
29 Petroleum	3	3	3	8
30 Rubber	3	3	2	6
31 Leather	0	0	1	3
32 Stone, clay, and glass	2	6	7	16
33 Primary metal	35	18	24	14
34 Fabricated metal	2	7	9	7
35 Machinery	8	7	10	26
36 Electrical machinery	11	18	12	14
37 Transportation equipment	20	14	20	16
38 Instruments	0	1	1	3
39 Miscellaneous	3	4	3	1
Diversified/conglomerate	0	0	0	2
Total	200	200	200	200

Note: Firms ranked by sales for 1973 and by market value of quoted capital for the other years.

the filling of 4,000 cans per hour. The names of these pioneers—Campbell Soup, Heinz, Bordens, Carnation, Nestle, Cadbury, Cross and Blackwell, Lever, Procter and Gamble, Colgate, and others are still well known today.

In chemicals—group 28—the new technologies brought even sharper reductions in industrial than in packaged consumer products. The mass production of synthetic dyes and synthetic alkalies began in the 1880s. It came a little later in synthetic nitrates, synthetic fibers, and plastics and film. The first three firms to produce the new synthetic blue dye—alizarine—dropped production costs from 200 marks per kilo in the 1870s to 9 marks by 1886. Those three firms—Bayer, BASF, and Hochst—are still a century later the three largest German chemical companies.[5]

Table 3.3. The Distribution of the 200 Largest Industrial Enterprises in Germany, by Industry

Standard Industrial Classification	1913	1928	1953	1973
20 Food	23	28	23	24
21 Tobacco	1	0	0	6
22 Textiles	13	15	19	4
23 Apparel	0	0	0	0
24 Lumber	1	1	2	0
25 Furniture	0	0	0	0
26 Paper	1	2	3	2
27 Printing and publishing	0	1	0	6
28 Chemical	26	27	32	30
29 Petroleum	5	5	3	8
30 Rubber	1	1	3	3
31 Leather	2	3	2	1
32 Stone, clay, and glass	10	9	9	15
33 Primary metal	49	47	45	19
34 Fabricated metal	8	7	8	14
35 Machinery	21	19	19	29
36 Electrical machinery	18	16	13	21
37 Transportation equipment	19	16	14	14
38 Instruments	1	2	4	2
39 Miscellaneous	1	1	1	1
Diversified/conglomerate	0	0	0	1
Total	200	200	200	200

Note: Firms ranked by sales for 1973 and by assets for the other three years.

Rubber production (group 30), like oil, benefited from scale economies, even more in the production of tires than rubber footwear and clothing.[6] Of the ten rubber companies listed on the 1973 table, nine built their first large factories between 1904 and 1908. Since then the Japanese company, Bridgestone, has been the only major new entrant into the global oligopoly.

In metals (group 33) the scale economies made possible by maintaining a high-volume throughput were also striking. Andrew Carnegie was able to reduce the cost of making steel rails by the new Bessemer steel process from $100 per ton in the early 1870s to $12 by the mid-1890s.[7] In the refining of nonferrous metals the electrolytic refining process invented in the 1880s brought even more impressive cost reductions, permitting the price of a kilo of aluminum to fall from 47.5 francs in 1889 to 19 francs in 1890 to 3.75 francs in 1895.[8]

Table 3.4. The Distribution of the 200 Largest Industrial Enterprises
in Japan, by Industry

Standard Industrial Classification	1918	1930	1954	1973
20 Food	31	30	26	18
21 Tobacco	1	1	0	0
22 Textiles	54	62	23	11
23 Apparel	2	2	1	0
24 Lumber	3	1	0	1
25 Furniture	0	0	0	0
26 Paper	12	6	12	10
27 Printing	1	1	0	2
28 Chemical	23	22	38	34
29 Petroleum	6	5	11	13
30 Rubber	0	1	1	5
31 Leather	4	1	0	0
32 Stone, clay, and glass	16	14	8	14
33 Primary metal	21	22	28	27
34 Fabricated metal	4	3	6	5
35 Machinery	4	4	10	16
36 Electrical machinery	7	12	15	18
37 Transportation equipment	9	11	18	20
38 Instruments	1	1	3	5
39 Miscellaneous	1	1	0	1
Diversified/conglomerate	0	0	0	0
Total	200	200	200	200

Note: Firms ranked by assets.

In the machinery-making industries (groups 35–37), new technologies based on the fabricating and assembling of interchangeable metal parts were perfected in the 1880s. By 1886, for example, Singer Sewing Machine had two plants—one in New Jersey and the other in Glasgow, each producing 8,000 machines a week.[9] To maintain their output, which satisfied three-fourths of the world demand, required an even more tightly scheduled coordination of the flow of materials into, through, and out of the plant than did the mass production of packaged goods, chemicals, and metals. By the 1890s a tiny number of enterprises using comparable plants supplied the world demand for typewriters, cash registers, adding machines, and other office equipment; for harvesters, reapers, and other agricultural machinery; and for the newly invented electrical and other volume-produced industrial machinery. The culmination of these processes came with the mass production of the automobile. By installing the moving assembly line in his Highland Park plant in 1913, Henry Ford reduced the labor time used in making a Model T from twelve hours and nine minutes to one hour and fifteen minutes.[10] This dramatic increase in throughput permitted Ford to drop the price of the touring car from $600 to $350, to pay the highest wages, and to acquire one of the world's largest fortunes in an astonishingly short time.

On the other hand, in the groups in tables 3.1–3.5 where very few large firms appeared, that is, in the older, technologically simple, labor-intensive industries such as apparel, textiles, leather, lumber, and publishing and printing, neither technological nor organizational innovation substantially increased minimum efficient scale. In these industries large plants did not offer significant cost advantages over small ones. In these industries the opportunities for cost reduction through managerial coordination of high-volume throughput by managerial teams remained limited.

The differentials in potential scale economies of different production technologies indicate not only why the large hierarchical firms appeared in some industries and not in others, but also why they appeared suddenly in the last decades of the nineteenth century. Only with the completion of the modern transportation and communication networks—those of the railroad, telegraph, steamship, and cable—could materials flow into a factory or processing plant and the finished goods move out at the speed and volume required to achieve substantial scale economies. Transportation that depended on the power of animals, wind, and current was too slow, too irregular, and too uncertain to maintain a level of throughput necessary to achieve modern economies of scale.

Nearly all of these new volume-producing enterprises created their own national, and often global, marketing and distribution networks. They did so for two reasons. First, they preferred to rely on a sales force of their own to market their goods rather than depend on the salesmen of wholesalers and other intermediaries who sold the products of many manufacturers, including those of their competitors. Second, and more important, mass distribution of these products very often required extensive investment in specialized, product-specific facilities and personnel. This was in large part because the products themselves were technologically new, requiring initial demonstration, careful installation and continuing after-sales service and repair if they were to perform properly. It was also because their distribution required new methods of transportation and storage. Because the existing wholesalers and mass retailers made their profits from handling related products of many manufacturers, they had little incentive to make large investments in facilities and personnel that could only be used for a handful of specialized products processed by a handful of producers. Moreover, if they did, they became dependent on those few large producers for the supplies essential to make this investment pay.

Of all the new mass producers those making packaged food products and consumer chemical products required the least in the way of product-specific distribution facilities and personnel. However, the new canning and packaging techniques did immediately eliminate one of the major functions of the wholesaler, that of converting large bulk shipments into small packages. The manufacturers now packaged; they, not the wholesaler, began to brand and to advertise on a national and global scale. Their sales forces now canvassed the retailers. But because mass sales of these branded, packaged products demanded little in the way of specialized facilities and personnel, their processors continued to use the wholesaler to distribute the goods for a fixed mark-up or commission until the processors' output became large enough to achieve scale economies in distribution.

All other industrial groupings in which the large firms clustered required major investments in either specialized distribution facilities or specialized personnel or, often, both. The producers of perishables—meat, beer, and dairy products, particularly those in the United States—made the massive investment required in refrigerated or temperature-controlled railroad cars, ships, and warehouses.[11] The processors of vegetable oil, like the petroleum refiners, made comparable investments in fleets of tank cars, ocean-going tankers, bulk storage stations, and, in the case of petroleum refiners, delivery facilities for kerosene and then gasoline.[12] The producers of industrial chemicals not only required specialized storage facilities for the volatile and temperature-sensitive products but also needed trained chemical engineers to show their customers how to use the new synthetics—the new dyes, fabrics, finishes, detergents, nitrates, and other specialized industrial products. The makers of the new mass-produced machines—the sewing machines, the typewriters, cash registers, and other office machinery, the reapers, harvesters, and other agricultural machinery—needed specialized sales forces to demonstrate the new equipment and provide after-sales repair, service, and consumer credit.[13] The marketing of industrial machinery, particularly the recently invented electrical equipment, called for highly trained mechanical and electrical engineers to demonstrate, install, and service their companies' products.

In these ways and for these reasons the large industrial firm that integrated mass production and mass distribution appeared in industries with two technologically defined characteristics. The first and most essential was a technology of production in which the realization of potential scale economies and maintenance of quality control demanded close and constant coordination and supervision of material flows by trained managerial teams. The second was the production of goods whose marketing and distribution in volume required investment in specialized, product-specific human and physical capital.

Where this was *not* the case, that is in industries where technologies did not have a potentially high minimum efficient scale, where coordination of production was not technically complex and where mass distribution did not require specialized skills and facilities, there was little incentive for the manufacturer to integrate forward into distribution. In such industries as publishing and printing, lumber, furniture, leather, apparel and textiles, and specialized instruments and machines, the large integrated firm had few competitive advantages. In these industries, the small, single-function firm continued to prosper and compete vigorously.

For the large integrated firm, the most critical entrepreneurial act of the founders was the creation of an administrative organization—first, the recruitment of a team to supervise the process of production, and then the building of a national and very often international sales network. Only then did the enterprise become multinational. Investment in production abroad followed, almost never preceded, the building of an overseas marketing network. So, too, in the technologically advanced industries, the investment in research and development followed the creation of a marketing network. In these firms, this linkage between trained sales engineers, production engineers, product designers, and the research laboratory became a major im-

petus for continuing innovation in the industries in which they operated. The result of such growth was an enterprise whose
organization is depicted in figure 3.1. The continuing growth of the

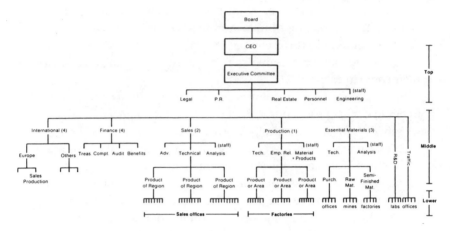

firm rested on the ability of its managers to transfer resources in
marketing, research and development, and production (usually those
that were not fully utilized) into a new and more profitable related
product line, a move that carried the organization of figure 3.1 to that
illustrated by figure 3.2. If the first step—that of integrating production

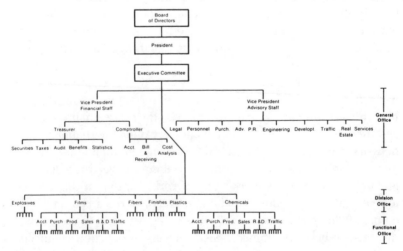

and distribution—was not taken, the rest did not follow. The firms remained small, personally managed production enterprises buying their materials and selling their products through intermediaries.

The Transformation of Industry Structure

The technologies of production and the specialized marketing and distribution facilities and skills that transformed industrial enterprises also transformed the structure of the industries in which they operated. These industries quickly became dominated by a small number of large, vertically integrated enterprises. The first enterprises to adopt a new technology for the construction of plants of minimum efficient scale, invest in product-specific facilities and skills in distribution (and also research), and create the managerial organization essential to coordinate these functional activities acquired powerful competitive advantages, or first mover advantages, to use an economist's term. To compete, rivals had to build plants of comparable capacity, make the necessary investment in distribution and, in technologically advanced industries, in research, and put together a comparable managerial hierarchy. However, the construction of a plant of the size needed to achieve comparable scale economies often meant that the total capacity of an industry exceeded existing demand. If newcomers were to maintain capacity utilization essential to assure competitive unit costs, they had to take customers from the pioneers.

This was a challenging task, as the new entrants' sales forces had to be recruited and trained while the experienced ones of the first comers continued to become more practiced in assuring prompt delivery, meeting customers' special needs, and providing the basic marketing services of demonstration, installation, after-sales repair and maintenance, and consumer credit. In the more technologically complex industries the first to install research laboratories and train technicians in very product-specific development skills had a comparable advantage. Finally, while the first comers were able to expand production and distribution facilities from retained earnings based on the initial cost reductions, the newcomers could enter the industry only by raising extensive funds in the capital markets to pay for the large plant and extensive distribution facilities. Given the competitive situation, this heavy instrument was in many ways even more risky than the initial investment in production and distribution made by the pioneers.

For these reasons, industries where new technologies of production permitted major scale economies in production and where the technological requirements of volume distribution necessitated product-specific investment in facilities and personnel became highly concentrated. A small number of large integrated enterprises easily met existing demand. The first comers soon came to dominate international as well as domestic markets. New entrants did appear at times of rapid market growth or when technological innovation created new markets. For example, the coming of the automobile in the early twentieth century, by creating demands for new products of the oil, rubber, metal, and glass industries, provided opportunities for newcomers to reach the size and achieve the competitive power of the pioneers. The number of new entrants, however, remained small; and there was little turnover among these industries' leaders. Thus, many of the first comers in the production of branded packaged food, tobacco, and consumer chemical products, industrial chemicals, oil, both ferrous and nonferrous metals, sewing, office, and agricultural machinery, appliances, automobiles, and other consumer durables remained the leaders of their industries for decades.

Although the technologically determined differences in the scale economies of volume production and the technologically based product-specific requirements of volume distribution explain why some industries became concentrated and others did not, the structure of these concentrated industries differed in different nations. In both the United States and Europe the new integrated enterprise had to obtain a sizeable share of the existing market if their production facilities were to operate at minimum efficient scale. A loss in market share by reducing throughput increased unit cost and so decreased profits. In Europe these industries became monopolistic. In some industries a single enterprise, usually the first to build a plant of minimum efficient scale for that production process, dominated the domestic industry. Where there was more than one, the small number maintained their market share through contractual agreements on price, output, and division of marketing territories.

In the United States the structure of these industries became more oligopolistic. The few dominant firms did not rely on contractual cooperation. Nor did they compete primarily by price, as did the firms in the fragmented industries. The largest (usually the oldest) became the price leader, basing his price on the relation of his and his competitors' plant capacities (that is their different minimum efficient scales) to existing demand. Instead of competing vigorously on price, the dominant firms competed for market share functionally and strategically.[14] In production they competed by improving processes and the coordination of processes to reduce costs, and increasing worker commitment and productivity. In marketing they relied on more effective advertising and providing better after-sales maintenance and repair, consumer credit, and other marketing services, as well as prompt deliveries on precise schedules. In purchasing they searched for new and more suitable sources of supply. Their research and development departments competed by not only improving the hardware of production but also improving existing products and developing new ones. Their financial offices sought cheaper short-term credit and more reliable long-term financing, and developed more accurate accounting and control systems. It is also important to note that these firms competed strategically by moving more quickly than their competitors into new and growing geographical and product markets and out of older and declining ones.

The reasons these concentrated industries became more oligopolistic in the United States and more monopolistic in Europe reflects differences in the size of domestic markets and in the laws affecting industrial competition and concentration. In the United States the completion of the basic railroad and telegraph network and the perfection during the 1870s of their operating techniques opened up the largest and fastest-growing domestic market in the world. The U.S. population, which already enjoyed the highest per capita income in the world, was equal to that of Britain in 1850, doubled it by 1900, and was three times its size in 1920.[15] This large and swiftly growing market permitted a number of plants in the new industries to operate at minimum efficient scale. Where new technologies were simultaneously adopted, as was the case in oil, mergers in the manner of the Standard Oil Trust first administratively centralized the many operating subsidiaries, then rationalized production facilities in order to exploit scale economies, and finally integrated forward into marketing and backwards into control of raw materials. Mergers that did not follow legal consolidation with centralization, rationalization, and integration were rarely able to compete with those that did.

Antitrust legislation encouraged this process. This legislation was, in turn, a response to the rapid transformation of industrial organization. The cost advantages of the new integrated mass producers brought political protests from the small manufacturers who were unable to compete with the new giants. Even stronger were the protests from the wholesalers, who were being displaced not only by the mass producers, as they integrated forward, but at the same time by the mass retailers—the department stores, mail-order houses, and chains—who began to buy directly from manufacturers. As the resulting antitrust legislation came to be administered by the executive branch of the federal government and interpreted by the federal courts, contractual cooperation in the form of trade associations, trusts, and even holding companies was nearly always condemned. On the other hand large, unified, centralized operating enterprises competing with a small number of comparable firms were only occasionally indicted. In the United States monopoly became illegal; oligopoly did not. In rare cases, such as in the production and distribution of cigarettes and aluminum, federal action transformed a monopoly into an oligopoly, or as in the case of oil enlarged the numbers in the oligopoly. However, there were few, if any, examples of such action transforming an oligopoly into a competitive industry where many firms competed primarily on price.

By the outbreak of World War I nearly all of the industries in which the large firms came to cluster during most of the twentieth century had become oligopolistic. The largest firms, usually those with the greatest capacity operating at minimum efficient scale, had become the industry's price leaders. This was true of the former Standard Oil companies that had integrated production and distribution after the break-up of the original company by the 1911 Supreme Court decision, of United States Steel and International Harvester in their industries, of DuPont in some chemicals and Allied Chemical and Union Carbide in others, of Armour and Swift in meat packing, and of the two largest makers of plate glass, the two largest companies in abrasives, the two giants in electrical equipment, and the three big automobile manufacturers.

The leaders in these and comparable industries attempted to maintain and increase profits by competing vigorously, functionally and strategically, for market share. Such competition brought significant changes in both market share and profit.[16] In oil, for example, the former Standard Oil companies lost share in their territories primarily to the integrated firms which had appeared in the first decade of the century in response to the opening of the Texas and California fields and the coming of the automobile. Indeed, even before the 1911 decision such competition had reduced Standard's share from 90 percent to 64 percent of the domestic market. In steel the United States Steel Corporation market share dropped from 62 percent at the time of its formation in 1901 to 40 percent by 1920. It continued to lose share during the 1920s. In automobiles such competition was particularly striking. Ford's share of the market fell from 55.7 percent in 1921 to 21.7 percent in 1937, while General Motors' rose from 12.7 percent to 41.8 percent in the same years. Chrysler, which in 1929 had only 8.2 percent of the market, had by 1937 surpassed Ford with 25.4 percent. For the decade from 1927 to 1937 Ford's losses totalled $94.1 million (with a $58.1 million drop in the surplus account). In the same decade General Motors' profits after sales stood at $1.9 billion.

In other nations whose domestic markets were smaller and growing more slowly than the American market and where there was less political pressure to pass new or to enforce existing legal sanctions against monopoly, such oligopolistic competition was much less common. Where the American market supported four or five large integrated enterprises, domestic markets in Europe only sustained one or two. In rubber, rayon, plate glass, explosives, synthetic alkalies, and phosporus, one firm dominated in each of the major economies. The number of major integrated oil companies outside of the United States was even smaller. By the coming of World War II only Royal Dutch Shell and Anglo-Iranian Oil (later British Petroleum) competed effectively with Standard Oil (New Jersey) and Standard Oil (New York) in the international markets. In industries that sustained two or more volume producers, the leaders cooperated more effectively and legally than did their counterparts in the United States. This was particularly true for volume producers of food and chemical branded packaged products in the United Kingdom and of industrial chemicals in Germany.

In Britain, makers of soap, starch, biscuits, chocolates, confectioneries, whiskey, and gin, as well as a smaller number of producers of industrial chemicals and machinery, quickly formed agreements on price, output, and marketing territories. When these agreements could not be effectively enforced in courts of law because British common law prohibited combinations in restraint of trade, these companies merged into a single holding company which permitted a central board to set and enforce agreements between subsidiaries. However, unlike their American counterparts, these legal consolidations did not take the next step of centralizing administration and rationalizing industrial production. They remained federations of family firms. They did not use mergers as the first step to exploit more fully the scale economies of new technologies.[17] For example, in the 1920s, Lever Brothers, the fourth largest British industrial enterprise in 1919 and the largest in 1930, included forty-one operating subsidiaries and thirty-nine different sales departments. The pattern was much the same for Imperial Tobacco and Distillers Ltd., as well as for mergers involving a small number of companies in sugar, chocolate, biscuits, confectioneries, and grain.

In Germany, where the large enterprises were fewer in number than in Britain and concentrated much more in the production of industrial rather than consumer goods, primarily metals, chemicals, and heavy machinery, and where cartel agreements were enforceable in the courts of law, industrial firms cooperated even more closely than in Britain. However, unlike the British, the Germans built large plants with high minimum efficient scale and invested extensively in worldwide marketing and distribution networks and even more than the Americans in research and development. Although they cooperated contractually at home, they quickly dominated global markets through administrative efficiency.

When the Germans, British, and Americans, as well as the French and nationals of other small industrial nations, began to compete in international markets, the patterns of competition reflected both the types of products produced and distributed and the ways of competition practiced in their home markets. In consumer goods, where American multinationals quickly achieved a strong position, the members of the global oligopoly competed, as did the Americans in the home market, functionally and strategically for market share. In industrial goods where the Germans were strong, contractual cooperation and cartelization became more the rule, but usually only after the leading firms had achieved their position through functional and strategic efficiency.

A brief review of global competition in the early twentieth century in the concentrated industries illustrates these differences. The makers of branded packaged food and consumer chemical products had first moved into international markets by establishing branch sales offices to plan and carry out local advertising and send out salesmen to take orders and check deliveries. Then American firms such as Heinz, Coca Cola, Quaker Oats, Corn Products, and Procter and Gamble built or bought plants in Britain and on the Continent; British companies, including Lever Brothers, Yardly, Crosse and Blackwell, Reckitts, Colman and Gilbey's Gin, and a very small number of German firms, including Stollwerck (chocolates), built their plants in the United States and in other countries. These competitors rarely attempted to achieve market power through contractual cooperation in international markets.

Oligopolistic competition remained the rule in oil and rubber. In the mass production of kerosene, gasoline, heating and fuel oil, rubber clothing, and tires, American companies competed vigorously with Europeans in Europe and the rest of the world, but the European companies made much less effort to compete in the United States. With the overproduction of crude oil after the opening of the East Texas fields in 1927 and 1928 the world's three largest oil companies, Standard Oil (New Jersey), Shell, and Anglo-Persian (later Anglo-Iranian) agreed to keep markets and outputs as they then existed.[18] in the 1930s the decline in demand resulting from the Great Depression led other leading American firms to join these agreements which were expanded to authorize the setting up of local committees to consult on price and output. However, few agreements on the specific prices were reached and even those failed to create effective enforcing agencies. In rubber there was no attempt to set up agreements between manufacturers. The only ones in the industry were between rubber-producing nations to restrict production of crude rubber; and these were opposed to the leading manufacturers who then felt forced to integrate backward by owning and operating rubber plantations.

In mass-produced light machinery, where the Americans continued to dominate international markets until well after World War II, there were even fewer attempts at contractual cooperation. American makers of sewing machines, office and agricultural machinery, washing machines, vacuum cleaners, stoves, and other appliances, and automobiles relied on their own extensive marketing organizations to demonstrate, install, service, repair, and provide consumer credit. Often they built and occasionally purchased plants abroad. When competition came, as it did in automobiles in Britain, it was usually because of the failure of the American home office to adjust to changing local market needs.

In industrial goods, however, the volume producers from different countries attempted much more regularly to collaborate in international markets. This may have been because of the small number of buyers and the specialized nature of the final products. In electrical equipment the four leaders of the global oligopoly, two American and two German, had a number of patent and licensing agreements with each other and with smaller companies in other nations. The same was true for German and American producers of storage batteries and allied products. Nevertheless, because the market for such equipment was until the 1930s growing rapidly, and technologies of process and product were advancing technologically, the smaller, although still quite large, British, Swiss, and Swedish firms were able to increase output and market share. They did so, however, only after they had developed production, distribution, and research facilities and skills comparable to those of the four leaders.

In metals and materials contractual cooperation by means of formal cartels was more prevalent than in the machinery trades. However, iron and steel firms were rarely successful even though they had the support of their national governments and the American producers had withdrawn from the European markets.[19] The number of firms may have been too numerous and the products too differentiated to enforce effectively the agreements reached. On the other hand, in nonferrous metals—copper, nickel, and aluminum—such contractual agreements were more successful and longer lived, because far fewer firms were involved. In addition, the enormous scale economies generated by electrolytic refining technologies provided the pioneers with the power to enforce agreements, for their costs were well below those of their somewhat smaller competitors. Comparable cartels of a small number of very large firms enjoying major scale economies were effective for the same reasons in glass, rayon, explosives, synthetic nitrates, dyes, pharmaceuticals, and films.[20] In chemicals, particularly, the Germans who had built the most efficient plants and created the most effective worldwide marketing organizations continued to have a major say in the drawing up of agreements and continued to have the economic power to enforce them. The Americans, because of the antitrust laws, only participated peripherally in these agreements and then did so primarily through patent and licensing agreements.

In the years following World War II monopoly gave way to oligopoly. Functional and strategic efficiency rather than contractual cooperation became the primary source of market power in international markets. In Europe a rapid growth in per capita income and sharp reductions of tariff and other trade barriers enlarged markets and increased the opportunity to exploit scale economies. New antimonopoly legislation, often on the American model and in Germany at the instigation of American authorities, made cartels and comparable agreements difficult to achieve and even more difficult to enforce. At the same time a transfer of technology softened the American edge in mass-produced power machinery and the German edge in industrial chemicals. A larger number of firms from a larger number of nations came to make up the global oligopolies in nearly all of the industries in which modern technology had brought the large integrated enterprise. Then, in the 1960s, the rapid transfer of technology to Japan (primarily in metals, chemicals, and mass-produced machinery and appliances) and the swift growth of per capita income, with the resulting increase of the domestic market, permitted that nation to adopt the new processes of production and distribution that had been the center of the Second Industrial Revolution in the West. The result was that Japanese enterprises quickly took their place in these global oligopolies.

The Transformation of Industrial Organization

Thus, as the twentieth century progressed, major industries—those at the commanding heights of all advanced industrial economies—became dominated by large integrated enterprises that competed at home and abroad in an oligopolistic manner. This transformation in the nature of enterprise and the structure of industry was basically technologically shaped. In the production and distribution of unprocessed commodities and of relatively simple products using relatively simple processes of production—such as textiles (from natural fibers), apparel, leather, lumber, furniture, and books and journals—industrial organization remained little changed. In many of these fragmented industries a multitude of small, often single-unit, single-function firms, continued to compete within their specific product markets largely on price.

But where new and increasingly complex high-volume hardware of production made possible a massive increase in output and with it a sharp decrease in unit costs, and where mass distribution of these products required specialized marketing services and facilities, the structure of the firm and that of the industry in which it operated were transformed. The effective use of the new technologies demanded the recruitment of one team of members to supervise the flow of materials through the plants, another to market and distribute the product, and then a set of middle and top managers to coordinate, monitor, and plan for the integrated enterprise as a whole. In such industries the new high-volume technologies thus brought concentration. A small number of large plants administered by an even smaller number of integrated enterprises were able to meet national and international demand. If markets expanded, the number of firms in the oligopoly might increase; but the industry remained concentrated. The patterns of competition remained the same. The firms competed for market share much more on functional and strategic efficiencies than on price. When markets declined, those who were able to control and adjust flows were able to maintain a continuing return on their operating facilities, even without explicit contractual cooperation with competitors. When such decline came, a number of these enterprises began to transfer their underutilized resources to new, often technologically more advanced processes and products.[21]

Thus, an understanding of the specific technologies of production and distribution is essential to understand the reasons underlying the transformation of industrial organization in the late nineteenth and early twentieth century. Different technologies brought different scale economies and distribution needs. These new high-volume technologies rested, in turn, on one fundamental innovation—the application of energy generated by fossil fuels to both the processes of production and distribution. Even more important than the application of this energy to production was its use in transportation. For only after the materials and goods were able to move through the economy at an historically unprecedented volume, speed, and regularity, was there either the need or opportunity to devise new technologies of mass production, with their potential for scale economies in processing and their specialized requirements in distribution that so transformed the organization of the industrial enterprise and the structure of the industries in which they operated.

Notes

1. Alfred D. Chandler, Jr., *The Visible Hand: The Managerial Revolution in American Business* (Cambridge, MA: Harvard University Press, 1977), pp. 230–232.
2. This section closely follows one in my "Emergence of Managerial Capitalism," in Alfred D. Chandler, Jr. and Richard Tedlow, eds., *The Coming of Managerial Capitalism: A Casebook in the History of American Economic Institutions* (Homewood, Ill.: Richard D. Irwin, 1985).
3. This story is told in more detail in Alfred D. Chandler, Jr., "The Standard Oil Company: Combination, Consolidation, and Integration," in Chandler and Tedlow, *The Coming of Managerial Capitalism.*
4. B. W. E. Alford, *W. D. & H. O. Wills and the Development of the U. K. Tobacco Industry*(London: Methuen, 1973), pp. 143–149. See also Chandler, *The Visible Hand*, pp. 249–258.
5. Sachio Kahu, "The Development and Structure of the German Coal-Tar Dyestuffs Firms," in Akio Okochi and Hoshimi Uchida, eds., *Development and Diffusion of Technology* (Tokyo: University of Tokyo Press, 1979), p. 78.
6. This statement is based on a review of histories and of internal reports and pamphlets by the leading rubber companies.
7. Harold Livesay, *Andrew Carnegie and the Rise of Big Business* (Boston: Little Brown, 1975), pp. 102–106, 155. When in 1873 Carnegie opened the first works directed entirely to producing rails by the Bessemer process he dropped cost to \$56.64 a ton. By 1889 with increase in sales the costs fell to \$25 a ton.
8. L. F. Haber, *The Chemical Industry During the Nineteenth Century* (Oxford: Oxford University Press, 1958), p. 92.
9. Chandler, *The Visible Hand*, pp.302–314.
10. Allan Nevins, *Ford: The Times, the Man, the Company* (New York: Scribner, 1954), chs. 18–20, esp. pp. 473, 389, 511. See also Alfred D. Chandler, Jr., ed., *Giant Enterprise: Ford, General Motors, and the Automobile Industry* (New York: Harcourt Brace and World, 1964), p.152.
11. Chandler, *The Visible Hand*, pp. 299–302, 391–402.
12. Standard Oil only began to make an extensive investment in distribution after the formation of the Trust and the resulting rationalization of production, and with it the great increase in throughput. See Harold F. Williamson and Arnold R. Daum,*The American Petroleum Industry: the Age of Illumination, 1859–1899* (Evanston, IL: North-

western University Press, 1959), pp. 687–701. For investment in gasoline pumps and service stations, see Harold F. Williamson et al., *The American Petroleum Industry: The Age of Energy, 1899–1959* (Evanston, Ill.: Northwestern University Press, 1963), pp. 217–230, 466–487, 675–685. For vegetable oil refiners, see Chandler, *The Visible Hand*, pp. 326–327.

13. Chandler, *The Visible Hand*, pp. 402–411.

14. The literature on functional and strategic competition is voluminous. After all, such competition has been central to courses in production, marketing, purchasing, control, and policy that have been taught in American business schools for decades. Michael E. Porter, *Competitive Strategy: Techniques for Analyzing Industries and Competitors* (New York: Free Press, 1980), provides an effective statement of the current thinking about functional and strategic competition. For European and American comparisons see Alfred D. Chandler, Jr., "The M-Form: Industrial Groups, American Style," *European Economic Review* (1983), 19:3–23.

15. W. S. and E. S. Woytinsky, *Trends and Outlooks in World Population and Production* (New York: Twentieth Century Fund, 1953), pp. 383–385.

16. Robert L. Heilbroner and Aaron Singer, *The Economic Transformation of America* (New York: Harcourt, Brace, 1984), p. 205, lists changing market share for five major industrial enterprises. Williamson et al., *The American Petroleum Industry*, pp. 502–503, 712 gives changes in market share of gasoline based on Federal Trade Commission reports. The information on market share and profits in the automobile industry, also taken from FTC reports, is given in Chandler, *Giant Enterprise*, pp. 3, 5–7.

17. Alfred D. Chandler, Jr., "The Development of Modern Management Structure in the U.S. and the U.K.," in Leslie Hannah, ed., *Management Structure and Business Development* (London: Macmillan, 1976), pp. 36–45. For Lever's organization see Charles H. Wilson, *History of Unilever* (London: Praeger, 1954), 2:302, 345.

18. Described in Mira Wilkins, *The Maturing of Multinational Enterprise* (Cambridge, Mass.: Harvard University Press, 1974), pp. 87–88, 233–234 for oil, and pp. 98–101, 196–197 for rubber.

19. J. C. Carr and W. Taplin, *A History of the British Steel Industry* (Oxford: Oxford University Press, 1962), ch. 44.

20. The operations of several of these cartels are described in William F. Reader, *Imperial Chemical Industries: A History* (London: Oxford University Press, 1969), vol. 2; George W. Stocking and Myron W. Watkins, *Cartels in Action* (New York: Twentieth Century Fund, 1946); and R. A. Brady, *The Rationalization Movement in German Industry* (Berkeley: University of California Press, 1933).

21. This strategy of continued growth of the industrial enterprise through product diversification brought a new chapter in the evolution of industrial enterprise and the industries in which it operated, one that is too extensive to be discussed here. The beginnings of this new chapter in the history of industrial organization are considered in Alfred D. Chandler, Jr., *Strategy and Structure: Chapters in the History of Industrial Enterprise* (Cambridge, Mass.: MIT Press, 1962) and Edith T. Penrose, *The Theory of the Growth of the Firm* (Oxford: Oxford University Press, 1959).

4. The Impact of Technology on American Legal Development, 1790–1985

Harry N. Scheiber
University of California, Berkeley

When the members of the Massachusetts state bar in 1861 addressed a tribute to Lemuel Shaw, the great chief justice of their Commonwealth's supreme court, they praised him as a judge who "molds the rule for the present and the future out of the principles and the precedents of the past." Judges who had gone before him, the bar address declared, had adapted the systems of common and commercial law to the needs of nineteenth century communities with different social and economic structures than those systems of law had originally been designed to serve; and Chief Justice Shaw had gone even further:

It was for you to adopt those systems to still newer and greater exigencies; to extend them and the solution of questions, which it required profound sagacity to foresee, and for which an intimate knowledge of law often enables you to provide, before they had even fully risen for judgement.

The Massachusetts court, under Shaw's leadership, had shaped law imaginatively to respond effectively to modern industrialization: "In your hands the law has met the demands of a period of unexampled activity and enterprise."[1]

What his fellow lawyers in Massachusetts found so praiseworthy in the career of this extraordinary judge was not, in fact, unique in the record of the American legal system in his day. Shaw had innovated brilliantly in doctrine, and the encomiums to his insight and foresight were indeed well merited.[2] Shaw's great achievement, however, was to provide American law with doctrinal formulations that won wide acceptance in both common-law decisions and constitutional law precisely because they reflected the prevailing trends and were consistent with dominant judicial thought. The Shaw court, in sum, captured the essence of how American law was responding in that day to the pressures, challenges, and dilemmas of a nascent— and, by the 1840s, accelerating—industrialization. Technological innovations, as well as the instrumentalities such as business corporations that were applying and diffusing innovations, demanded accommodations in the law. The interests that were "carriers of change" and the opposing interests that were threatened by or suffering palpable harm from the new technologies and their application carried their conflicts into legislative halls, the courts, and other political forums including state constitutional conventions. This was so in the day of the Shaw court and also afterward, to our own times.[3]

Fundamental changes in the fabric of American law resulted from the pressures of technological change and the clashes of social interests set in motion by innovation. This relationship between changing technology and the law produced a dualistic outcome: institutional durability, on the one hand, and, on the other, doctrinal adaptation in the face of changing social realities, power relationships, and beliefs.[4] It is this complex historical process, dating from the early part of the nineteenth century, that comprises the subject of this essay.

At the outset of the national government's operation, under the Constitution of 1787, both constitutional law and substantive public policy at the national level evinced some important specific concerns with technology. In the Constitution itself, of course, was a provision (art. 2, sec. 8) giving Congress the power "to promote the progress of science and useful arts, by securing for limited times to authors and inventors the exclusive right to their respective writings and discoveries." The same section of the Constitution empowered Congress also to establish the standards for weights and measures. Other provisions of the nation's basic law—especially those empowering Congress to frame admiralty laws and regulate commerce among the states—also provided the basis for the federal government to respond, both through legislation and through uses of the judiciary's power, to changes in technology and their effects upon economic and social life. Indeed, the essential idea of federalism underlying the structure of governance created in 1787—the diffusion of power by the vesting of powers at the national level, with other important powers remaining with the state governments—together with the constitutional foundation for judicial review, by which the federal Supreme Court would become supreme arbiter of state-national disputes, assured that responses of the law and public policy to changing technology would necessarily involve strategic interventions of major importance by the national government.[5]

The first Congress in 1790 implemented the patent power by enacting a law for vesting in inventors rights to the use of their ideas; but the law set up a system that was "administratively fantastic and impossible," requiring three of the government's highest-ranking officials—the secretary of state, the attorney general, and the secretary of war—to serve as a board to review and pass on applications.[6] This rather incredible arrangement quickly broke down in the face of several hundred applications annually, so that after 1793 all applications were approved and it was left to private suits in the courts to settle the issues of originality and use. Two significant principles emerged, however, in the policy for issuing patents—principles that would be enduringly important in this aspect of the legal system's relationship to technological innovation: first, that basic scientific ideas, as opposed to technological applications, were not patentable; and second, that it was an obligation of the government "to protect the public from unwarranted exclusiveness."[7]

The practical effect of the 1790 law was to inundate the courts with litigating and embroil inventors in costly, protracted, and often proliferating suits. For the legal system, and especially for federal judges who were seldom well qualified to deal with the technical issues, it was burdensome indeed; for the inventors and the process of invention, the results were ambiguous. That is to say, while the benefits of patent protection with their supposed incentives to inventive genius were often vitiated by costly litigation, derivative inventions and diffusion of even such critically important innovations as the reaper in grain agriculture doubtless were simulated by the absence of strong administrative restraints. Congress responded to criticism of its policy and to the rising numbers of patent applications by strengthening the administrative apparatus with the patent law of 1836, reforming the system and establishing structures that have endured to the present day. First, it established the Patent Office, to be headed by a commissioner of patents, with a modest staff under that official charged with exercising informed discretion on patent grants. Second, the reform legislation obligated the office to examine and test each invention, reasserting the requirements of usefulness and novelty before a patent might be issued.[8]

Despite the 1836 reforms in patent administration, the legal system has continued to process patent claims in ways that have encouraged litigation. The Patent Office characteristically has approved applications, with claimants left to litigate in order to obtain authoritative judgments on the matter of originality. Specialization within the professional bar and even the creation of special federal judicial bodies to hear patent claims have not materially changed this leading characteristic—the resort to litigation—of the way in which the legal system processes inventors' claims. Efficient judicial mechanisms can serve as a deterrent, perhaps, to spurious claims and piracy; but effectively the national government has institutionalized the litigative mode of dealing with rights to invention. Over time, there have been some landmark decisions by the Supreme Court: one line of cases has concerned the criteria for originality and usefulness, another the validity of requirements attached to the licensing of patents that affect the terms of competition (usually centering on conflict with the antitrust laws, a problem to which I return below).[9]

A second major concern with technology and its diffusion that was manifest in the new nation's earliest legislation was that affecting protective tariff and navigation policies. Insofar as the early republic had an "industrial policy," it consisted—in its large design—of encouraging the transfer from Great Britain and Europe of the extensive technological innovations associated with the Industrial Revolution, and simultaneously erecting a structure of protective tariff duties that would assist American manufactures as they adopted those innovations and went into competition for the domestic market which was formerly dominated by foreign producers. The role of the emigrant mechanic Samuel Slater in establishing textile milling with Arkwright machinery was emblematic of the way in which thousands of skilled immigrant workers carried new technology across the Atlantic—and bespoke the importance of the new nation's open immigration policies.[10] In civil engineering, textiles, metallurgy, woodworking, and the production of gunpowder, machine-tools, and shoes, the flow of skills and ideas from Europe brought techniques that were quickly adopted and refined by American entrepreneurs eager to substitute machine methods for relatively high-cost labor on this side of the Atlantic. Tariffs served both as stimuli for investment and barriers to competition, with the protective duties on manufactures complemented in the 1850s with rebates of duties on iron rails (to aid railroad construction) and a general policy of maintaining low or nil tariffs on certain basic raw materials.[11]

The federal government responded to opportunities to introduce or refine new techniques in the arms and transportation industries. In the nation's first decade, Eli Whitney won national contracts for arms production, promising to employ machine tooling at finer tolerances and interchangeable parts to a degree formerly unknown in American manufacturing. His success in mass production technology applied to arms making was further carried forward by direct governmental enterprise in the army's arsenals at Springfield, Massachusetts, and Harper's Ferry, Virginia.[12] A more far-ranging and diffused intervention by the national government characterized policy in the field of civil engineering and transportation. In 1818-19 the U.S. Military Academy at West Point became the focus of this effort, as Congress authorized the appointment of a first-rate faculty drawn from the French technical institutes and upgraded the curriculum to make West Point a leading source of academically trained engineers in the United States. Under the 1824 General Survey Act, the newly trained army engineers were loaned out during 1824–1838 to state and private engineering projects (canals, river improvements, railroads, bridge works) to aid in conducting preliminary surveys and drawing detailed specifications for construction. Under federal appropriations, moreover, the army conducted extensive river and harbor improvements specifically designed to facilitate the introduction and spread of steamboat transportation on the waters.[13] Later, in the 1860s, the surveys conducted by the army were of key importance to the planning and construction of the transcontinental railroads—themselves the objects of massive national subsidies in cash and land grants.[14]

To only a slight degree did the national government undertake to regulate—even in the interest of public safety—new technologies as they began to affect increasing numbers of the population. The only significant foray by the federal government into regulation of this sort was an 1838 act providing for an intensive investigation of steam-boiler technology and the causes of boiler explosions. More than three hundred lives were lost annually, at that time, in steamboat explosions alone. Against strong ideological countercurrents opposed to regulation—exemplified by a statement of the secretary of the treasury in 1825, in submitting data to Congress on steamer accidents, that "legislative enactments are calculated to do mischief, rather than prevent it"[15]—Congress responded to demands of commercial interests and passengers fearful of their safety. The 1838 law, which proved in fact to be poorly administered and lacking in effectiveness, did establish the principle of regulation: steam vessels were required to accept periodic inspection and certification, skilled engineers were mandatory on all steamboats, and safety equipment and procedures were specified. More effective enforcement was instituted under a revised regulatory program enacted in 1852.[16]

The swift rise in steamboat tonnage on internal rivers and the Great Lakes in the 1840s and 1850s forced a dramatic change in constitutional law with respect to admiralty jurisdiction. The traditional, long-accepted doctrine held that inland waterways that were beyond the ocean's ebb and flow were subject only to state, not federal, jurisdiction. Recognizing the new realities imposed by technological change and commercial innovation, Congress in 1845 extended federal maritime and admiralty jurisdiction to cover most navigation on inland waterways. This legislation, designed to impose legal uniformity upon the commercial system, eliminated the disparities in state laws that had prevailed, and specifically supplanted a Supreme Court decision of 1825 that had imposed the traditional "ebb-and-flow" tidal rule. In 1851, in the case of *Propeller Genesee Chief v. Fitzhugh*, the Supreme Court accepted the new legislation as constitutional.[17]

Another feature of new technology in communications, bridge construction, also demanded changes in national constitutional law. Suspension and iron truss bridges, capable of spanning great streams and harbors, came into use on waterways heavily used in commerce and travel. In 1851, the Supreme Court declared a bridge that spanned the Ohio River at Wheeling a public nuisance for its interference with steamer navigation. Immediately Congress moved to declare the bridge lawful, declaring it a postal road. In a reversal that was startling to many experts in the law, the Court yielded five years later (in *Pennsylvania v. Wheeling Bridge,* 1856), acknowledging that Congress could decide such matters affecting competing technologies and the interest-group conflicts they set in motion. The Court declared that the Constitution's commerce clause provided sufficient authority for Congress to act, thus significantly curbing the powers of state government. In a sense, the Wheeling Bridge decision complemented and carried forward an earlier waterways decision by the Court, the landmark ruling in *Gibbons v. Ogden* (1824), in which the exclusive power of Congress to regulate navigation on interstate waterways had been recognized. In that decision, attempts by New York and New Jersey to issue monopoly grants or open up navigation on the Hudson River, the waterway dividing the two states, had been declared unconstitutional.[18]

The power of the states to act in the transportation realm, as new technologies were applied by both public and private enterprise, was upheld, however, in other decisions by the Court with regard to *intrastate* bridges, turnpikes, and other structures. The most far-reaching and influential decision was that in the Charles River Bridge case of 1837, in which the Court upheld action by the state legislature in Massachusetts to authorize construction of a bridge over the Charles River that would charge no tolls and would thus compete with a long-established private corporation's nearby bridge; the latter would cease to produce revenue for its proprietors, so that the value of the franchise to them would be lost. The Court's decision in this great case was, as Willard Hurst has written, "the classic statement of policy in favor of freedom for creative change as against unyielding protection for existing commitments" and vested rights.[19] Its significance was twofold. First, the decision asserted the importance of rights enjoyed by the community as a whole, as against vested private rights—an essential underpinning of the police power for regulation. And second, the decision specifically addressed the issue of technological innovation and how the nation's constitutional law ought to accommodate it. So long as no reservation of rights or privileges had been explicitly promised by the state, declared Chief Justice Roger. B. Taney, the state remained free to "avail [itself] of the lights of modern science, and to partake of the benefit of those improvements which are now adding to the wealth and prosperity, and the convenience and comfort of every other part of the civilized world."[20]

Whereas the Charles River Bridge decision lent legitimacy to state action franchising corporations that would apply new technologies in communications, the 1848 decision of *West River Bridge v. Dix* was critical because it validated the states' authority to seize property outright in order to expedite the construction of new transportation lines—and without this power to expropriate, in the face of the Constitution's contract clause and the "due process" clauses designed to protect property rights that were included in state constitutions, it would have been practically impossible to build most canal or railroad lines, or to build bridges and (later) telegraph or other communications networks.[21] The court ruled that the power to expropriate, termed eminent-domain power, is an incident of state sovereignty and "is . . . paramount to all private rights under the government, and these last . . . must yield in every instance to its proper exercise."[22]

The Supreme Court thereby cleared the pathway for new enterprise; and the state legislatures and courts were given a virtually free hand in determining when rights of private property owners and franchised corporations had to give way to new technologies and enterprises. Swept aside, in this process, was the inherited common-law notion— which still had enough authoritative currency in 1815 that Chancellor James Kent of New York, a leading judge and commentator on the Constitution, then espoused it[23]—that once the state had granted a franchise, its "custom" (established business) could not be taken away, even indirectly, by state action such as Massachusetts would take so overtly in the Charles River Bridge situation.

The states, for their part, adopted an expansive view of the powers thus assured them. In addition to directly using the chartering and eminent-domain powers, the states also devolved upon private corporations that built transportation lines the privilege of taking land and other property through the expropriation procedures—requiring compensation, to be sure, but on terms highly favorable to the new enterprise—originally designed to support public (state) enterprise.

Such extraordinary privileges, as an Indiana court declared in 1838, were justified because "the advancement of the wealth, prosperity, and character of the state" were at stake.[24]

The pragmatism that characterized this view of legitimate state action was expressed in a much wider range of state law than that of the transportation field. I now undertake a consideration of legal responses, across this wider spectrum, to the pressures of changing technology and innovation in the field of subnational (state) law.

The work of state legislatures, courts, and constitutional conventions—and by the late nineteenth century, state administrative agencies as well—tells much of the story of how the fabric and institutions of American law were affected by technology. A focus on state law also provides insights that cannot be gained by looking only at national law, if we are to understand how law, in turn, shaped the diffusion of technology.

Mobilization of public resources through the legal system, in direct support of capital formation designed to apply new technologies, was one great area of action in the states. The great engine of change in this respect was innovation in communications, especially canals and railroads, complemented by the pressures from the developing economy for more elaborate banking and fiscal institutions. State legislation routinely extended the privileges and special immunities of incorporation, in the antebellum (pre-1861) period, to bridge, turnpike, canal, river improvement, and railroad companies; by the 1830s, manufacturing corporations—especially large-scale operations designed to function on a factory-organized basis—were also receiving corporate privileges on a broad front.[25] To be sure, corporation law indicated the tendency in the United States to leave the creation of new wealth and the application of emerging technologies to the private marketplace; the corporation was a "person," in legal parlance, vested with special privileges and status but otherwise a private actor.[26] But the states went further in mobilizing public resources than mere allocation of privilege. Capital formation and innovation were aided directly through the mechanism of direct subsidy, as loans, stock subscriptions, and tax exemptions were given to transportation enterprises. In addition, outright public enterprise—undertakings that were planned, financed, and operated by government itself, with the capital (and often operating) costs met through taxation and public loans—accounted for a large segment of the transport sector prior to the 1850s. Even in the railroad era, when the initiative and the major burden of financing fell to the private sector, the state governments and their subordinate municipal governments continued to subsidize directly through programs of cash grants, subscriptions, and bond guarantees. Legal challenges to such aid, on the grounds that it constituted unconstitutional "taking" from citizens for the benefit of purely private enterprises, were generally turned back by the state courts.[27] Tax-supported cash subsidies to manufacturing corporations were more controversial in the law, with some states' courts upholding such aid on the grounds that a great public interest was at stake, and courts in other states ruling that manufacturing firms (unlike transport firms) were not even "quasi-public" and so could not qualify for public aid.[28]

The states also made what may be termed "intangible contributions" to capital formation through innovations in legal doctrine and public law. Both legislators and judges were made sensitive, by interest-group pressures if nothing else, to the particular combinations of resources and available technology that determined the structure of economic opportunity in their respective states; they were made equally sensitive to how the law could be manipulated and invoked to establish priorities, protect or push aside vested interests, or encourage new technologies or enterprises, in those situations.[29] Generally these questions in policy and law addressed the issue of how natural resources were to be allocated, and by what priorities entrepreneurs or new technologies were to be given access to resources. Thus, in the early nineteenth century, courts in the East upheld statutes—some of them modeled on laws dating from the late colonial era—that authorized builders of milldams for waterpower purposes to use the eminent-domain power to take (on payment of compensation) the lands of adjoining agricultural proprietors, and then to flood those lands.[30] The courts shaped riparian law more generally to allocate priorities, among, for instance, the interests of fisheries, shoreline proprietors of land engaged in agriculture, industry , and navigation. The introduction of steamboats, the need to divert waters for canals, milldam technology and new construction, and—not least important—the use of very large-scale waterpower sites for factory production of textiles, beginning in New England in the 1820s, all led to significant doctrinal changes in riparian law. A pragmatic bias friendly to entrepreneurial interests employing new technologies often seemed to prevail; but the inherited common-law doctrines of private riparian rights, public trust, and rights of the sovereign and the community (doctrines *publici juris* and *privati juris*) also endured, shaping and channeling the process of doctrinal innovation and adjustment by courts.[31]

Later in the century, the development of new technology applied to agricultural drainage, to irrigation and reclamation, and to the use of hydraulic techniques for mineral extraction all put further pressure on inherited water law. In the Far West, beginning in 1850, individual territories and states adopted innovative rules of prior appropriation for water, or they adapted the inherited tradition of riparianism to the arid land conditions of their region.[32] In California and other mining boom states, the legislatures established regulations that abridged traditional property law to allow prospectors for minerals access to lands occupied already for agriculture. The courts upheld such legislation, on the whole, as they also upheld myriad local mining codes that became a source of robust, enduring "customary law" based on local practice and absorbed into the legal system of the states. Emblematic of how state law responded to the particular local resource endowments available for exploitation was a California statute of 1872 that authorized the exercise of eminent-domain powers by private interests who wanted to condemn private property for purposes of building "wharves, docks, piers, chutes, booms, ferries, bridges, toll roads" and other transport facilities, and also "canals, ditches, flumes, aqueducts, and pipes . . . supplying mines and farming neighborhoods with water, and draining and reclaiming lands, and for floating logs and lumber on streams not navigable."[33] Moreover, the state legislatures routinely granted franchises for log booms and lumber milling, often affecting large watersheds and effectively regulating commercial lumbering activity on major streams.[34]

This sort of intangible contribution to capital formation in regulating access to resources was more than matched in importance by the ways in which state judges refashioned critical features of the common law. They did so mainly in areas of law left untouched by the legislatures, though in some regards the judges interpreted statute law in ways that were of critical importance to relationships associated with technological innovation and diffusion. A classic case in point was the "fellow-servant doctrine" in the law of industry-labor relations. The fountainhead of the American doctrine was *Farwell v. Boston & Worcester Railroad,* decided by the Massachusetts court in 1842. Workers in the preindustrial world often suffered injury from working with large animals; ships were dangerous for sailors, as was notorious; and in crafts shops, workers were subject to accidents from fire, tools, or moving machinery, but generally they were working under direct personal supervision of the master. As the Farwell decision indicated, however, industrial accidents in the workplaces of modern technology were another matter altogether. Nothing exhibited the new dangers so radically as the railroads, whose workers—one of whom was plaintiff in the Farwell case—dealt with dangerous, massive moving machinery and with boilers subject to explosion and the resultant fires.[35]

In *Farwell,* the Massachusetts court ruled that employers could not be held liable for an employed worker's injury if another worker (a "fellow-servant") contributed to that injury through negligence or carelessness. The rule became nearly universal in American courts— not to be changed until workers' compensation legislation was enacted in the last decade of the nineteenth century—and it went far toward immunizing not only railroad companies but industrial employers against accident liability affecting their workers:

[T]he rule was, in its early stages, cleancut and brutally simple. The cost of industrial accidents was to be shifted from the entrepreneur to the workers themselves. Insofar as there was any responsibility toward destitute workers and their families, society as a whole, through its poor laws, would bear the burden, rather than leaving it to the most productive sector of the economy.[36]

The courts in many states also applied the old common-law rule that tort actions were personal, so that employee death as the result of accident eliminated all chance of recovery: the claim died with the victim.[37] By the last two decades of the nineteenth century, statutes softening the harsh effects of such common-law rules had begun to take effect. There is also some evidence that in at least a few states the courts held industrial interests to a negligence standard that indicated significant judicial sympathy for victims.[38] Nonetheless, it seems indisputable that the process of diffusing new technology in transportation—with all its far-reaching ramifications for development of the economy and its transforming social effects—was expedited and extensively subsidized by the common law.[39]

A similar subsidy effect flowed from nuisance doctrine and its application by courts in the states. The immunities extended to industrial and transportation enterprises were initially most visible in the communications sector. Carrying over from eminent-domain rulings that had given a privileged position to private transportation companies— and later, in many states, a similar position in the law to other types of enterprise, especially mining and irrigation or reclamation undertakings—was the concept that if an enterprise were in some special way "public" in its purposes, its officers could be rendered immune from trespass suits when conducting their business; and, more important from the subsidy standpoint, its operations could be immunized against nuisance claims carrying liability for damages from smoke, water pollution, noise, or other spillover effects.[40] "It is our duty to foster and promote such enterprises," a trial court declared in finding against nuisance claims that would have imposed damage costs on a railroad corporation: "We cannot and ought not to be indifferent to the imperative demand made by the rapid progress of the age,"[41] Similarly, a Kentucky court in 1839 justified abrogating traditional nuisance doctrine in the interest of leaving the state's railroads immune from damage suits by proprietors abutting the line who were seeking damages for disturbance to their homes and businesses: "The onward spirit of the age," the court declared, "must, to a reasonable extent have its way . . . [R]ailroads and locomotive steam cars—the offsprings, as they will also be the parents, of progressive improvement—should not, in themselves, be considered as nuisances."[42]

In this way the requirements of new technologies and the enterprises that applied them were canonized in the law: they became validating principles, in competition with inherited common-law traditions and against private claims or even claims advanced on behalf of the public itself. "The exigencies of the social state," as a New York court wrote in dealing with liability arising from a boiler explosion, had to come into the judicial calculus: "We must have factories, machinery, dams, canals, and railroads. They are demanded by the manifold wants of mankind."[43]

By such reasoning, the courts transferred to third parties and to the

public at large many of the spillover costs of technological innovation—just as they had transferred to workers much of the cost of
accidents. Partisans and foot soldiers on the side of new enterprise
and innovation, the courts maintained the posture of judicial neutrality: "It is so with everything, and always will be," as one state
court contended in extending immunity to a railroad corporation for
noise and other inconveniences imposed on private persons.[44]

The states also exercised a broad discretionary authority in establishing rules of property and contract, each of which conditioned the
spread of new technologies. It was the general practice for legislatures
and courts alike "to let technological changes have the fullest play"
through adjustments in both contract and property rules.[45] New techniques were introduced, and legal adaptation quickly followed, to
expedite innovation and maintain the flow of capital investment.
Hurst has summarized some of the changes—which, we are reminded,
were complementary to the continuing adaptation of corporation law
designed to accommodate new enterprise, new products, and expanding markets:

As new technologies fostered new areas and types of trade, businessmen
devised new contract devices to serve expanding transactions. The sale of
farm machinery on credit produced wider use of forms of chattel security.
Manufacturers who sold durable goods through extended networks of dealers
relied on the law of agency and turned to lawyers for new security devices
such as trust receipts on stocks of goods entrusted to intermediaries.[46]

Alongside such technical legal adjustments of doctrine and rules,
moreover, there emerged in the nineteenth century the "public utility" concept. Under its terms, certain types of enterprise were of such
overarching public importance that they would be subject to special
constraints and regulation—just as they had been privileged under
eminent-domain law and nuisance law to take property or were
immune from liabilities, on the grounds that they were of a quasi-
public character. The full flowering of administrative regulation would
come only in the twentieth century, to be sure; but rudimentary
regulation of railroad rates and operating practices had appeared in
the states in the 1850s, and by the 1870s the famous "Granger laws"
in the Midwestern states were imposing a developed form of administrative regulation of railroads.

The beginnings of national administrative law dated from late in the century—from 1887, when the Interstate Commerce Commission, the first of the national regulatory agencies, was founded—and not until establishment of the Federal Trade Commission in 1914 did the federal government have an agency specifically devoted to systematic monitoring of the competitive business order as it was affected by technology and market changes.[47]

Gradually, too, in the middle and late decades of the nineteenth century, both the states and the national government began developing technical expertise of their own. Small bureaucracies of experts in selected areas established the basis for a slow but palpable increase in the importance of scientific and technological capacity in the public sector. In mining, forestry, engineering, geology, fisheries, plant breeding and pathology, and animal disease, as well as in the general field of public health and sanitation, the bureaucracies had gained strong footholds by 1900.[48]

In the Progressive period that followed, many state governments established commissions that regulated not only railroads but also franchised electrical power and telegraphic and telephonic communications systems. As new communications technologies came into use, in other words, legislatures and courts recognized that "natural monopolies" (those providing a unique service, or a service of paramount importance to the community—those "affected with a public interest," as the law phrased it) required a higher degree of regulatory control than "ordinary" businesses.[49] At the same time, industrial commissions responsible for maintaining industry safety standards were formed in many states and armed with powers of varying scope. Their effectiveness depended, of course, upon the mobilization of technical expertise in their bureaucratic organizations. The growth of regulatory bureaucracies, the accrual of experience with public regulation and administrative law, and the development of technical expertise in the public sector all provided an indispensable foundation for modern regulatory and welfare-state development in the decades that followed.[50]

With dramatic intransigence, the federal and state courts alike resisted some of these changes. A great variety of state laws, together with some federal legislation such as child labor regulation, were found unconstitutional by the courts. Conservative judges held sway, and the new corporate order—struggling to adapt under pressures of successive new technological innovations, product substitution, and inter- and intraindustry competition, all intensified by a secular price deflation from 1873 to the mid-1890s—was not brought under the discipline of comprehensive regulation, let alone under uniform national regulation.[51] Yet there was a steady erosion of conservative constraints in the law: the great majority of state regulatory laws tested in the courts did, in fact, gain constitutional validation; and by the 1920s most states had established public utility regulation on a strong legal foundation, introduced public health and sanitation programs, successfully enacted some measure of regulation of working conditions and control over child labor, and advanced consumer protection legislation in fields such as food adulteration.[52]

As urban "spread" took place and industrial development altered the face of urban neighborhoods, moreover, some of the traditional laxity and beneficence toward industrial enterprise began to change. By the mid-1920s, the state and federal courts alike had validated land use regulations that imposed zoning restrictions. In the landmark Supreme Court decision of *Euclid v. Ambler* (1926), the justices rejected arguments that a zoning ordinance constituted an unconstitutional confiscation of property rights and values. Whereas in the nineteenth century, courts had tended to immunize innovative firms applying new technologies from traditional liabilities under the common law on the grounds that progress and change demanded that the law bend, now the Supreme Court stressed that the *public* authorities must have the flexibility to meet technological change. The court asserted that regulations which "even half a century ago, probably would have been rejected as arbitrary and oppressive" were now—in light of technological change—routinely found valid because their "wisdom, necessity, and validity" must be assessed "as applied to existing conditions."[53]

The state courts increasingly accepted the concept of an elastic police power which must be defined as sufficient to respond to new social realities—"in keeping with the growth of knowledge"—and as capable of dealing with modern conditions.[54] Against this tendency was posed the conservative legal doctrine of "freedom to contract" (the myth that the laborer and employer stood as equals in the marketplace, so that any state interference on labor's side constituted "class legislation" and was unconstitutional). Also posed against the growth of regulatory power were constitutional doctrines—mobilized by the conservative jurists from the mid-1880s until the New Deal years of the 1930s, based on the interstate commerce clause, the contract clause, and the Fourteenth Amendment—that were used to strike down state legislation and some national legislation as well.[55]

The walls of this conservative constitutional fortress were finally breached, however, in the midst of catastrophic economic conditions in the Great Depression of the 1930s. When the New Deal Congress, in Franklin D. Roosevelt's first term as president, enacted sweeping measures that brought agriculture and manufacturing under comprehensive national regulation, the Supreme Court responded by finding central elements of the program unconstitutional.[56] By 1935, however, as the Depression crisis continued to threaten the entire social fabric, and under intense political attack by the president, the Supreme Court did an abrupt about-face. Within two years, the Court had reversed itself to uphold the constitutionality of agricultural regulation and a broad discretionary power in the newly established National Labor Relations Board to regulate industrial-labor relations. Virtually plenary congressional power was upheld by the Court under terms of a now expansively interpreted commerce clause. State regulatory legislation concerning labor, mortgage relief, milkshed regulation, and other economic matters was upheld, as the contract clause and other constitutional doctrines were fundamentally revised. An ideology of "national needs" came to dominate constitutional law to an even greater degree than conservative doctrines had dominated previously.[57]

At the root of this judicial revolution and the transformation of national public policies to which judges were responding was a sweeping adaptation to the realities of twentieth-century technology and economic structure. The fundamental changes in the legal system— toward more centralized regulation of economic activities, a much larger proportion of national income captured through taxation for expenditure by the national government and the public sector generally, and a style of government intervention based upon wide discretion in administrative agencies—would endure into the post-Depression, postwar years. Indeed, the requirements of mobilizing for total war in the United States, in 1941–45, reinforced and solidified many of these tendencies. The protracted Cold War and periods of limited war after 1945 meant, moreover, that a large peacetime military establishment—something unknown in American history until then—would be kept in place, would be linked to massive aerospace, arms, and electronics industries that developed new technologies with public contract funding, and would more or less permanently augment the new prominence of the governmental sector in the national economy.[58] In this new regime of giantism in the public sector, especially with the acceleration of technological innovation that occurred after 1945, new tensions and challenges quickly emerged in the relationship between technology and the legal system.

The response of the legal system to accelerating technological change since 1945 has included three distinct types of innovation and adaptation. The first has been a set of positive governmental initiatives in support and promotion of new technologies. The second has embraced the regulation of technology through innovations in statute law and administrative law, leading to an expansion in the scope of centralized control. The last has involved the initiatives of the courts, as they have adapted common-law doctrines and interpreted statutes in light of new technological imperatives. Each of these strands in the recent history of American law will be treated briefly in what follows here.

Support and Promotion

The patent system, traditionally the principal legal mechanism for the encouragement of invention, has continued to play a central role in the relationship of law and technology. The Supreme Court has tended to apply stringent restrictive standards of "patentability," making it difficult on the whole to obtain final confirmation of patent claims. The complexity and expense of litigation, however, continue to be major factors in the patent process—one that favors, of course, the larger-scale firms. In very recent years, the legislatures and courts have had to confront difficult questions about the patentability (or, alternatively, extension of copyright protection) of such new forms of technology as genetic engineering, computer programming, and the like.[59]

The legal system also favors research and development through the functioning of the tax laws. Write-offs of long-term depreciation of new plant and other capital investment, together with full immediate write-offs of R&D, on corporate and individual income taxes are promotional in their effects. Until the tax reform proposals of 1986, moreover, successive revision of federal tax law have consistently favored accelerated depreciation write- offs.[60]

Directly sponsored government research, together with public funding of the research conducted by industry and nonprofit institutions, has assumed unprecedented importance in the United States since 1945. Government-operated laboratories in the fields of nuclear weaponry and civilian technology, military research (including both armaments and biological and chemical warfare), and space and aeronautics have played a critical part in the overall R&D effort of the last forty years. These new research efforts brought with them the "secrecy" classification of research and the loyalty and security screening of scientific personnel. These developments, in turn, gave rise in the 1950s and 1960s to a series of constitutional decisions concerning the proper reach of such regulation in the interests of national security, balanced against the values of freedom of scientific inquiry, on the one hand, and traditional individual liberties on the other. In 1982–84, the Reagan administration extended legal restraints further into basic (not applied) research than had been done for many years. The military orientation of research and development also became something of a pawn in the game of international diplomacy, moreover, with the extension of retaliatory travel limitations on Soviet visitors, keeping them from "sensitive" geographical areas in which both military and private high technology research and manufacturing were located.[61]

An important innovation in legal ordering of research and development efforts was the establishment of the National Science Foundation by Congress in 1950. The NSF quickly emerged as an agency devolving important supervisory and auditing responsibilities upon the scientific community outside government itself. Over the long run, however, the system of peer review of project proposals, together with the movement of scientists back and forth across both the "secrecy" classification line and the line separating government from the private sector, has tended to blur the traditional distinctions between government and private institutional structures.[62] Like the NSF, the National Institutes of Health—first founded in 1930—became important in the 1950s as a conduit for research funding in universities and other institutions. The NIH has also emerged as a government research organization at the leading edge of medical research.[63]

As we have seen, in the nineteenth century the legal system responded to new entrepreneurial needs with the development of the corporate form of business organization and with intangible contributions to capital formation. In a similar development, late twentieth-century American law has provided new structures to accommodate and channel the accelerating technological innovations in space and communications. Thus after a lengthy debate about the legal structuring of civilian participation in space technologies, a field created largely under aegis of the government in both national laboratories and sponsored university projects, Congress chartered COMSAT (the Communications Satellite Corporation), which is closely associated with the interests of the two dominant telephone corporations and has acted as the American partner after 1964 in the international agreement that created the INTELSTAT organization for the operation of a global communications satellite system. For nearly a decade COMSAT was the INTELSTAT system's manager for the consortium nations. In 1972, however, the Federal Communications Commission opened the field of *domestic* telecommunications satellite operation to any qualified entry, thus declaring a regime of competition in the United States market. It followed in 1980 with action to permit private competition under a new set of rules in the field of direct broadcasting from satellites.[64]

All of the foregoing measures in telecommunications law were intended to give impetus to new technological initiatives in the private sector, and they were part of the "deregulation" movement that was undertaken more generally—but in no sector more dramatically than in telecommunications and electronic computer communications— in the late 1970s and early 1980s. (A similar drastic movement away from strict regulation occurred with regard to the control of financial intermediaries. This development was virtually an extension of the computer-generated changes in technology in electronics and communications, as the nation's banks, stock brokerage firms, and other institutions merged operations and rendered obsolete many traditional distinctions in types of business and alignments of function and form.) Whether or not the deregulation process created new business and consumer uncertainties that might offset, through intensity of competition and business losses, the intended gains in technical innovation, the deregulation movement was intended as a stimulus for innovation and new investment through the manipulation of the legal system and its allocation of privileges, immunities, and subsidies.[65]

The Regulation of Technology

Despite the breadth and reach of New Deal regulatory innovations dating from the 1930s, the national government's regulatory functions until the mid-1960s remained focused mainly on market conditions and operations. This is to say, government regulated the terms of entry or terms of competition, and (in war emergencies such as the Korean War or Vietnam) actually administered directly both prices and wages, complementing the supervisory role played in labor-industry relations. Regulation of the *social consequences* of technology—such matters as occupational health and safety, pollution of common resources, resource depletion, and consumer protection—remained principally, though not exclusively, under the control of the state government[66]

Such decentralization of regulatory controls proved to be a weakness in the legal system, and it became a pressure point for far-reaching changes in the period after 1965. This weakness derived from the significant state-to-state variations in the terms and rigor of regulation. No minimum national standards for safety, environmental control, or public health prevailed; and there was often "competition in laxity," encouraged by the very structure of the system.[67] Moreover, even in states that did enact statutes for serious regulation of social consequences of technology, the enforcement agencies typically were understaffed and underfunded. In many respects, the states were outstripped and overmatched by the size and power of corporations with which they had to deal, by the complexity of the market forces that they sought to control, and by the accelerating pace of change in technology. Moreover, the political power of a particular industry, or even a single corporation employing a large proportion of a state's workers, could make it difficult for a particular state to impose effective regulation where it was most needed.[68]

Several forces in postwar science and technology placed in a new perspective the inadequacies of existing social regulation by the states. First was the revolutionary succession of changes in chemistry. They produced the changes in industrial and consumer materials associated with petrochemicals, the development of widely used new pesticides, herbicides, and fertilizers, and the extraordinary applications that led to the chemotherapeutic revolution in pharmacology. Second was the continued testing and development of nuclear weapons, together with the proliferation of nonmilitary applications of nuclear energy. Third was the rising pressure of commercial exploitation (and also pollution) upon natural resources—a pressure generated by the overall rise in industrial production, the intensified use of resources in new industrial processes, the exponential population increase in the world as a whole, and rising income and consumption levels in the developed nations. In the United States in particular, closely associated with population growth and new urban metropolitan concentrations, there was an astonishing rise in use of the automobile throughout the nation. The laws generally did nothing to discourage suburban spread, and from 1958 to 1970 Congress authorized a vast national road construction program; taken together with the neglect of public railroad transport, these components of the law in action did much to build an automobile culture that generated alarming problems of air pollution and the invasion of both urban and rural space by massive superhighways.[69]

Some catastrophic episodes affecting the environment and human life and health stimulated public fears about the possibilities of more pervasive, general dangers. Such catastrophes inspired widespread criticism of the adequacy of inherited legal institutions and prevailing regulations. Thus by 1960 there was extensive public discussion of the hazards of nuclear testing and power production. Converging with this concern was the impetus given to "environmentalism" (as a reform movement in politics) by Rachel Carson's book, *Silent Spring*, published in 1962. The book inspired searching scientific inquiries into the dangers of DDT—and also a highly organized and well-financed defense of DDT by the chemical industry. These inquiries led in 1971 and after to new state laws, federal court orders, and finally a federal ban against applications of DDT.[70] Tragedies in the United States resulting from the distribution of a dangerous polio vaccine and in Europe from the use of the drug thalidomide, which caused birth defects, raised widespread doubt about the adequacy—and also the probity—of procedures for testing by private laboratories in the pharmaceutical industry. The consequence was new federal legislation in 1972 strengthening the Food and Drug Administration's supervision of laboratory and field testing of drugs.[71]

The chemical industry's seeming insensitivity to humane concerns and its lack of accountability came once again to the forefront of public discussion when the banning of Agent Orange, the herbicide that eventually was proved to pose genetic and carcinogenic hazards, was debated in 1968–70. Like the earlier catastrophes, the Agent Orange debate contributed to directing public suspicion against not only the corporate developers of new technologies but also against the governmental regulators themselves. This suspicion of both big business and public regulatory agencies posed a direct challenge to the old presumptions that technological innovation meant "progress" and that law ought to accommodate such innovations as being in the public interest.[72] Reinforcing the challenge to the old presumptions were revelations of industrial firms' heedlessness of both worker safety and consumer health in the use and manufacture of asbestos and chemical products known by management to be dangerous.

Public concern also came to focus on such resource crises as the destruction of the California sardine fishery through ruthless commercial exploitation. Other species were endangered by the dumping of lethal pollutants such as mercury- and lead-bearing effluents as they had been by the use of DDT. A dramatic oil spill in Santa Barbara in 1969, lethal air pollution crises in the Los Angeles metropolitan area and some eastern cities, and extensive findings of dangerous pollution levels in waterways throughout the nation all gave additional force to public demands for more effective regulation. Indeed, the reforms that were advocated went beyond regulation of industrial interests to embrace more effective monitoring of government itself, including its regulatory agencies.[73]

Legal theorists and scientists alike called for technology assessment on a systematic basis, including institutionalization of the assessment effort in legal process. They were much influenced by the contemporary tendency in the sciences to move away from narrowly focused, specialized analysis of environmental phenomena and toward the study instead of "ecosystems." The need for this more comprehensive, systematic view of interrelated phenomena within complex systems had been indicated by such developments as the studies resulting in the ban on DDT use: the problem of residuals, passing through the food chain, and the ramifying systemic effects of the poison in all realms of the life cycles it penetrated offered a paradigm not only for science but also for law—at least if law were to respond effectively to the ethical and technical challenges posed by advancing applied science.[74] This paradigm required comprehensive appraisal of the systemic effects of technological innovations; the articulation, in light of new technologies, of relevant normative values, and hierarchical ranking of those values; and the long- term, as well as short-term, appraisal of costs and benefits to the society in light of those values. "The preservation of future options and the avoidance of irreversible consequences" was among the goals sought by the proponents of technology assessment. Another objective prominent in the literature of the early 1970s was the more effective direction and channeling of technological innovation and change, whether through modification of market incentives, institutional adjustments and reforms, or the "command model" of law operating to mandate the direction and content of research and discovery and technological diffusions and applications.[75] If law were thus to be mobilized, theorists further contended, then a prominent corollary issue that demanded attention was political in content: How could traditional constitutional values—personal liberty, social and political equality, and public participation in decision making—be preserved in the type of legal system sufficiently powerful to take significant control over technological change?

So compelling was the political appeal of the environmentalist campaign—reinforced by the contemporaneous Vietnam War protests, which also expressed a deep distrust of both government and the dominant political and economic structures—that in 1970 an essentially conservative, business-oriented Republican president, Richard Nixon, created by executive order the federal Environmental Protection Agency.[76] Indeed, public opinion polls of the time indicated that environmental issues were regarded by most voters as the most urgent domestic question; and there was a rapid proliferation of voluntary organizations and pressure groups, journals of opinion, and litigation groups dedicated to the environmental cause. "Earth Day," in April 1970, witnessed one of the greatest mass mobilizations of demonstrators and participants in the modern history of American politics.[77] Soon after, in 1972, Congress established the Office of Technology Assessment to provide scientific counsel on matters of public policy and law.

There followed a set of interrelated changes in public law which introduced a more centralized regulation of technology on a scale without precedent in the nation's history. The principal changes were (1) national legislation establishing or strengthening federal regulation in a broad range of policy areas, (2) the institution of goals and timetables for improvement of environmental standards, (3) the development of new legal requirements concerning activities of government itself and their impact on both populations and the environment, and (4) the emergence of a fundamentally new "litigative order," in which monitoring of technology, in both the public and the private sectors, was accomplished by pressure from public interest groups and their activities in the courts.

The first type of change, the introduction of new national controls, embraced such diverse goals as the protection of endangered wildlife, bird, and fish species and their habitats; the achievement of clean air and clean water; the protection of workers and consumers from industrial processes and materials and from product defects dangerous to human health and safety; and the introduction of more stringent controls over pharmaceuticals, pesticides, rodenticides, herbicides, and processes involving radioactive materials. In each of these policy areas, the federal government—acting both by statute and by executive action—effected during 1970–1981 sweeping administrative restructuring, the creation of new agencies and the merging or realignment of old ones, and the bestowal of new enforcement powers and responsibilities for monitoring on centralized agencies.[78] A drastic movement toward centralization of real power, in the American federal system of constitutional governance, was a key result of these new measures.

Moreover, unlike the scattered items of congressional legislation affecting safety and the environment prior to the 1960s, the new legislation tended "to cut across industry lines" and to apply wholesale to economic activity, including, in many cases, the enterprises of government itself.[79] In the view of some analysts, this tendency of legislation to transcend single-industry boundaries has had the effect of intensifying political conflict over control of technology and its impacts. The new laws are seen as leading to mobilization of strong national coalitions of business groups, often indeed in alliance as well with labor unions, to resist the wholesale application of more stringent federal standards seen as a threat to industrial investment, competitive freedom, and employment security. The result was ideological conflict and a higher intensity of opposition to new regulations.[80]

Substantively, these new laws established national minimum standards and goals. Many of the new statutes also required specific time-tables for the attainment of the goals. Thus, the 1973 Endangered Species Act[81] prohibited the taking of or trade in endangered species by private individuals or groups; it also imposed a positive obligation on all federal agencies to use their powers to preserve endangered species and their habitats. This act was interpreted by the Supreme Court in 1978 as indicating Congress' intent "to halt and reverse the trend toward species extinction, *whatever the cost.*"[82] Although subsequent legislation softened the language of the protective standard, the act has been the basis for court-ordered termination or modification of several major governmental projects; and the restrictive terms affecting private-sector activity have had a major impact. The same has been true of coastal controls and measures for marine mammal protection.[83]

The prohibitive approach was also embodied in new legislation concerning potentially toxic products and processes. Thus several laws—concerning pesticides and other agricultural chemicals, regarding consumer products, and affecting manufacturing processes that used raw materials or processes that were harmful to workers—imposed a prohibition that either limited or banned such materials and processes. In addition, the brace of new regulatory statutes in the 1970s established some degree of control over the export to foreign markets of products deemed hazardous and so subject to restrictions in U.S. domestic marketing. Two enforcement modes are specified in this new legislation: the first is across-the-board standards imposed on industries and products, providing a uniform basis for prohibition; the second is selective "culling," in which generalized standards and a consideration of risks versus benefits are applied by enforcement agencies on a case-by-case basis.[84]

In the case of air pollution environmental legislation (the Clean Air Act and amendments), the goal of healthy ambient standards has been pursued, however, by requiring through law the development and adoption of new technologies that will be consonant with pollution reduction. Thus Congress, mandated that automobile manufacturers alter the technology of engines for the use of low-lead or unleaded fuels, and also provide for exhaust emission control systems that would reduce polluting effects. An alternative approach has been the establishment by administrative agencies of specific technical requirements to meet such legislative mandates for ambient or equipment standards as "best available control technology"[85] or clean air,[86] with attendant legislative timetables for meeting such standards. At their most extreme, rules in this mode have provided for the closing down of plants or even entire industries that do not meet the standard at the specified times, or the withdrawal of financial assistance and the imposition of other sanctions against state and local governments that fail to meet the federally imposed ambient standards (for air or water purity) on schedule. Such drastic, or seemingly drastic, enforcement results actually have tended to blunt and modify the impact of the laws; although courts and agencies have, in fact, closed down plants and imposed severe sanctions in many situations, opposing pressures from industrial interests have led to the reconsideration of tough standards, long battles in court to prevent enforcement sanctions from being applied, and modification by Congress or the courts of the terms of regulation.[87]

Nonetheless, the imposition of such goals, standards, and timetables does amount to the use of law for what has been termed "technology forcing": the establishment of coercive sanctions and legal requirements, sometimes augmented by direct or indirect subsidies (including necessary research under government sponsorship), designed to channel technological innovation and diffusion in socially desirable ways, under close supervision of governmental authorities. It is regulation in a centralized mode, with many areas of policy "preempted" by the national government, displacing state authority. On the whole, such preemption and technology forcing were linked in the 1970s to produce a more stringent regulation of industry in the interest of environmental, consumer, and occupational protection. But in the hands of a pro-business regime ideologically opposed to stringent regulation as the Reagan Administration has been since 1981, the national regulatory agencies have often used the leverage of preemptive power to undermine and displace more stringent state regulations with less severe federal rules—or even none at all, which is termed the "no-standard national standard"—promulgated from the center.[88] Centralization, in other words, is a double-edged sword.

The third leading feature of the new regulatory order has been the introduction of new requirements affecting the operations of government itself. This feature reflects the fact that the political forces that produced much of the new legislation were based upon a distrust of government and not only upon a distrust of private interests.[89] Indeed, the centerpiece of the new regulatory regime, the Environmental Protection Act of 1970, has been termed a "policy-forcing" law because it recognized government itself as a force that generated environmental damage. The act required that prior to proceeding with any construction project or new program, a federal agency must undertake an economic impact statement assessing its environmental effects and costs. This requirement "opened virtually all government actions, regulatory and developmental, to legal challenge."[90] In the decade of the 1970s, about one-third of the cases in federal courts concerning environmental issues centered on action relating to the content and implications of environmental impact statements of government bodies. The EPA legislation was a widely emulated model in the 1970s for new state environmental laws and the creation of enforcement agencies in the state governments; the states, too, imposed environmental impact statement requirements on their own and local government operations.[91]

The fourth set of changes associated with the new regulatory order has been the emergence of a litigative process without substantial precedent in American history. The development of this was encouraged by such features of the new legislation as the environmental impact statement; it was also stimulated by the introduction into law of complex ramifying considerations of scientific fact-finding and interpretation. The new process has lent great prominence to new actors in lawmaking, enforcement, and adjudication. Several of the new congressional statutes granted citizens a broad right to sue for enforcement, for example, thus eliminating a major procedural barrier to suits.[92] A series of strategically important cases, in several areas of regulatory law, were conducted by public interest litigative organizations such as the Environmental Defense Fund; and they enjoyed a high degree of success in forcing governmental agencies to impose more stringent standards and curbing the practices of individual private firms or industries.[93] The dominant type of suit in the regulatory area has become more complex and involves more parties in court than in the older, classic type of litigation that pitted one private interest against another or a government agency against an alleged violator of the law:

Relaxation of standing requirements has led to multilateral judicial review proceedings, involving regulated firms, the [government] agency, and environmental and consumer advocates. Since agency proceedings form the basis for judicial review, they too have become multilateral, thereby increasing their complexity and length . . . Congress has sought to limit agency discretion by adopting more detailed statutory provisions and by imposing specific deadlines for implementing regulatory programs, thereby multiplying the grounds and occasions for judicial review.[94]

The courts, in turn, have done much to encourage this movement away from deference toward (if not even reverence of) administrative discretion, inherited from the New Deal era and its ideology of pursuit of "public interest" goals through the transfer of power to "disinterested experts" in the regulatory agencies. Even before statutes were enacted that confirmed the trend, the federal courts had expanded the concept of standing to permit public interest groups to sue. The courts had also shifted the burden of proof in ways that raised the federal regulatory standard in cases where suspected damage to public health or safety was concerned, and had forced federal agencies to recognize environmental values, as a matter of obligation, in dealing with the public and planning major projects.[95] As a prominent federal appellate judge declared in 1971, the courts "are increasingly asked to review administrative action that touches on fundamental personal interests in life, health, and liberty. These interests have always had a special claim to judicial protection, in comparison with the economic interests at stake in rate-making or licensing procedure."[96] Having differentiated occupational, environmental, and consumer protection from "mere" economic regulatory issues, the courts were instrumental in shaping the new legal regime of regulation.

One unresolved procedural issue—a continuing subject of controversy among legal scholars, jurists, and scientists—is the proper relationship of technological assessment to the judicial process. Some judges have stood ready to make bold judgments on substantive questions relating to technology and science; they have been willing to review the conflicting opinions of scientific experts and to declare one or another superior. Other judges have regarded this judicial style as inappropriate and fraught with danger. Again, the high stakes involved are cited. "We are dealing here," one jurist has asserted, "with all humanity's interest in life, health, and harmonious relationship with the elements of nature." Unwilling himself to pass judgment in an air pollution controversy over "dynanometer extrapolations, deterioration factor adjustments, and the like," or issues of statistical validity, he called for the courts to impose a *procedural* requirement for scientific assessment upon the agencies themselves.[97] In some instances, the courts have declared a bias in favor of agency discretion in the face of uncertainty. "Where a statute is precautionary in nature," for example, "the evidence difficult to come by, uncertain, or conflicting because it is on the frontiers of scientific knowledge," and public health is at stake, the agency will be permitted to impose new regulations.[98] The Supreme Court, however, has twice made substantive determinations of risk, in the face of conflicting scientific and medical assessments, in cases under occupational health and safety legislation. In one instance, it adopted a reading of the legislation that permitted stringent regulation; in the other instance, however, it curbed the regulatory initiative of the agency.[99]

The perplexities of assessing risk, whether as a matter of interpreting statutory requirements or simply as a matter scientific accuracy, continue to bedevil efforts at attaining objectivity in legal process. Those perplexities are also prominent in the contemporary debate concerning the impact (alleged to be mainly negative) of the new regulatory order upon technological innovation, productivity, and new investment in the American economy.[100]

New Judicial Initiatives

The last of the major trends in the legal system's response to technological change since 1945 pertains to the judiciary in its long-honored common-law role. Judges typically derive new rules, in the interstices left by statutes, from enduring principles of law; but when changing technology and social conditions seem to require it, they will also justify the reconsideration and revision of basic principles. As we have seen, the nineteenth-century courts, while they did uphold legislation that was regulatory in its focus, tended to reshape the common law in such areas as torts in order to accommodate and expedite both technological and entrepreneurial innovation.[101] In the 1960s, however, the state-level judiciary instituted changes in doctrine so sweeping that one of them—abandonment of the old rule that without fault there was no liability in torts—has been termed "the most rapid and altogether spectacular overturn of an established rule in the entire history of the law of torts."[102] What produced this great overturn was a series of state appellate decisions establishing "strict liability" in cases of product liability: no longer would elaborate rules about fault be applied, but instead the manufacturer would simply be held liable for any defects and resultant damages to consumers.

The California state supreme court, with Chief Justice Roger Traynor writing many of the key decisions, led in this overturn of established doctrine. Judge Traynor has been compared with Justice Shaw of the Massachusetts court in the nineteenth century; each of them boldly elevated broad social policy goals to the level of principle in times of rapid change and creatively reshaped the law to accommodate new social and technological realities.[103]

In a series of decisions handed down from 1963 to 1980, the California court declared that consumers in modern industrial society, with its giant industries and firms and a mass consumer market, were "powerless to protect themselves";[104] therefore the court stated that holding manufacturers strictly liable for injury from defective products was the only just rule. The California court extended strict liability to retailers and others in the chain of marketing. Culminating this series of California tort decisions was a 1980 case that imposed the principle of "industrywide liability" for harm to consumers where a generic product (DES, which was manufactured by two hundred drug firms and produced injury to children born of mothers to whom the drug was administered) was at issue. Since it was impossible to trace the particular manufacturer who had done the harm to a plaintiff, the court ruled, the industry as a whole was liable for damages. The loss could be spread among all the manufacturers; and they in turn could pass on the additional costs, if necessary, as a form of self-insurance. The court viewed these sweeping doctrinal changes as the only way to achieve justice in a modern industrial order that presented the consumer with problems standing in the way of redress in case of injury that simply were unknown and probably unimaginable in the earlier eras that had produced traditional tort rules.[105]

Other state courts besides California's, have contributed to the reconsideration of common-law doctrines. There has arisen what might be termed a new legal realism[106]—a reformist view of law, based on the notion that social justice and true, as opposed to merely nominal, judicial "neutrality" requires adjusting doctrine to social and economic realities. The organized legal profession has taken up the cause of legal reform, in this mode, and has concentrated its attention both upon procedural matters (especially scientific evidence) and substantive tort and liability rules affected by modern changes in economic organization and technology. Several institutions supported by the legal profession, most notably the American Law Institute and committees of the American Bar Association, have sponsored extensive studies and made specific recommendations for reform in tort law, rules of procedure and evidence, and other matters of substantive law. The ALI's "restatements" of law, as in torts, have sought both to survey and codify existing doctrine and to point the way towards reforms consonant with new technologies.

Other learned professions, acting both through national organizations and special research committees, have made similar contributions. Scientific and technical specialists, for example, have undertaken studies—sometimes complementing, sometimes in the absence of, similar efforts by the National Research Council or other government agencies—on specific new technologies. An example is a series of reports by the Acoustical Society of America that have influenced the rules governing admissibility of voiceprint identification evidence in trials.[107] Other such efforts of professional groups address more general questions. The American Psychiatric Association, for example, has sponsored task force studies on criminal responsibility and other aspects of behavior that go to the very heart of the criminal justice process. This organization's *Diagnostic and Statistical Manual of Mental Disorders*, an influential set of guidelines and principles now in its third edition, ranges over the whole conceptual landscape of psychiatry relevant to behavior in the legal system.[108]

These efforts by the professions have provided advisory guidelines for courts and legislatures to follow. Many of them have been controversial; but others have become law both through adoption by judges in procedural rule making and through the legislative process. Encouraged by innovative judges and by the learned professions' reformist initiatives, many courts and legislatures have adjusted rules of torts and procedure that go to the heart of the legal process in areas such as consumer and occupational health and safety, medical treatment and death, the oversight of the technological research process itself and other highly sensitive matters.

In dealing with occupational disease, for example, the courts have had to recognize and adjust to basic changes in etiology. Disorders caused by asbestos, radiation, coal, and metal poisoning may involve a delay of many years after initial exposure before the first overt symptoms appear. Hence both legislatures and courts have adopted new rules concerning time limitations for personal injury suits; they have applied concepts of "enterprise liability," as Judge Traynor's California court did in the DES case, when the origin of a harmful substance cannot be traced, and have attempted to formulate new standards of scientific diagnosis, causality, and risk prognosis in toxic tort suits.[109] In a highly controversial area of law in 1983–84, moreover, the question arose in the asbestos industry whether a manufacturing firm that confronted successful damage claims from workers who had suffered from asbestos exposure might escape from its responsibilities by declaring bankruptcy.[110] The allocations of political and legal responsibility for the handling of toxic materials has also been affected by federal law in the nuclear regulatory field, in effect setting national standards for damage claims that preempt state law and extending an umbrella of liability protection over the industry.[111]

The correct application of scientific standards and the use of expert testimony in criminal cases has long raised questions similar to those being confronted today in the area of toxic torts. Responding to the first introduction of polygraph testimony, federal courts adopted in 1923 a rule that became more generally applied in the federal courts and in many states as a concept governing the acceptance of expert testimony. Known as the *Frye* rule, it provided that expert testimony in scientific matters would be admitted as evidence in trials only when there was "general acceptance" of the relevant underlying theory bearing on the testimony in question in the scientific discipline(s) to which the theory belonged.[112] This standard in fact has proved difficult to render objective in specific instances: in the last analysis a judge must decide whether or not acceptance is demonstrably "general" in the relevant scientific community. Many forensic procedures that are widely used in criminal cases—blood analysis, ballistics, fingerprinting, voiceprinting, even photography—are life-and-death issues for some defendants, yet they are often subject to plausible expert challenge and serious differences of opinion. In light of accelerating research and the increase in scientific specialization, moreover, "not only are courts unable to determine the accuracy of the newest devices," as one commentator has written, "but many experts themselves are unable to keep abreast of all the developing techniques."[113]

The perplexities of rapidly advancing, increasingly complex, esoteric technologies create a similar type of problem affecting expert opinion in courts' reviews of both regulatory actions by government agencies and statutory language concerning risks. In some instances, as we have seen, the courts have thrown a heavy burden of proof on private interests or governmental agencies that seem to pose a threat to public life, health and safety.[114] More recently, however, the Supreme Court has cautioned that when a regulatory agency "is making predictions, within its area of special expertise, at the frontier of science . . . a reviewing court must generally be at its most deferential."[115] As a corollary, one federal circuit court has found that when an agency— in this case a federal regulatory body that had decided, over objections from state and local officials, to permit ground transport of radioactive waste materials through New York City—decides upon the mode of risk/benefit analysis to apply in establishing its rules, the courts should defer to it. In language that parallels the *Frye* rule in regard to scientific evidence, the court declared that: "As long as the agency's choice of methodology is justifiable *in light of current scientific thought*, a reviewing court must accept that choice."[116]

Whether such doctrines of judicial deference will significantly attenuate the force of the new litigative process, or instead will only inspire new efforts in Congress to specify in greater detail its regulatory goals and standards, may well be one of the major questions in American legal process in the years ahead.

Notes

1. Address of the Massachusetts Bar to Chief Justice Lemuel Shaw (1860), quoted in Charles Warren, *History of the American Bar* (Dover, N.H.: Longwood, 1980), p. 448.

2. See the full-scale study by Leonard W. Levy, *The Law of the Commonwealth and Chief Justice Shaw* (Cambridge, Mass.: Harvard University Press, 1954).

3. This constitutes a main theme of Lawrence M. Friedman, *A History of American Law* (New York: Simon and Schuster, 1973) and James Willard Hurst, *Law and the Conditions of Freedom in the Nineteenth-Century United States* (Ithaca: Cornell University Press, 1977), esp. ch. 3.

4. A deeply rooted scholarly controversy on the matter of winners and losers in this process marks recent discussion, for example, of the impact of private-law decisions by the antebellum judiciary in matters of property, contract, and tort law. See James Willard Hurst, *Law and Economic Growth* (Madison: University of Wisconsin Press, 1964); Morton Horwitz, *The Transformation of American Law, 1780–1860* (Cambridge: Cambridge University Press, 1977); Harry N. Scheiber, "Public Economic Policy and the American Legal System," *Wisconsin Law Review* (1980), pp. 1159*ff.*; Gary T. Schwartz, "Tort Law and the Economy in Nineteenth-Century America: A Reinterpretation," *Yale Law Journal* (1981), 90:1717*ff.*; and A. W. B. Simpson, "The Horwitz Thesis and the History of Contracts," *University of Chicago Law Review* (1979) 46:533*ff.*

5. See Stuart Bruchey, *The Roots of American Economic Growth, 1607–1861* (New York: Harper, 1965) and Harry N. Scheiber, "Federalism and the American Economic Order, 1789–1910," *Law and Society Review* (1975–76), 10:59*ff.*

6. A. Hunter Dupree, *Science in the Federal Government: A History of Policies and Activities to 1940* (New York: Harper and Row, 1957), pp. 11–13.

7. *Ibid.*, p. 12.

8. *Ibid.*, pp. 46–49. The number of patents issued rose from 426 granted in 1837 to 883 in 1850 and then 4,357 in 1860. U.S. Bureau of the Census, *Historical Statistics of the United States, Colonial Times to 1970* (Washington, D.C.: GPO, 1975), 2:959.

9. Merle Fainsod, Lincoln Gordon, and J. C. Palamountain, Jr., *Government and the American Economy*, 3rd ed. (New York: Norton, 1959), pp. 591*ff.*

10. H. J. Habakkuk, *American and British Technology in the Nineteenth Century* (Cambridge: Cambridge University Press, 1962), pp. 120–123. For an older, and useful, encyclopedic account, see Victor S. Clark, *History of Manufactures in the United States*, 3 vols. (Washington, D.C.: Carnegie Institution, 1929), 1:263–314.

11. Eugene Ferguson, "On the Origin and Development of American Mechanical 'Know-How,' " *Midcontinent American Studies Journal* (1962), 3:3–16; J. J. Pincus. "Tariffs," in Glenn Porter, ed., *Encyclopedia of American Economic History*, 3 vols. (New York: Scribners, 1980), 1:439–444. On the late nineteenth-century effects on manufacturing and technological innovation, see Gary R. Hawke, "The United States Tariff and Industrial Protection in the Late Nineteenth Century," *Economic History Review* (1975), 28:84–99.

12. Constance McL. Green, *Eli Whitney and the Birth of American Technology* (Boston: Little Brown, 1956); Merritt Roe Smith, "Military Entrepreneurship," in Otto Mayr and Robert Post, eds., *Yankee Enterprise: The Rise of the American System of Manufacturers* (Washington, D.C.: GPO, 1981), pp. 63–102.

13. Forest Hill, *Roads, Rails, and Waterways: The Army Engineers and Early Transportation* (Norman: University of Oklahoma Press, 1957); Louis C. Hunter, *Steamboats on*

the Western Rivers: An Economic and Technological History (Cambridge, Mass.: Harvard University Press, 1949); Erik F. Haites, James Mak, and G. M. Walton, *Western River Transportation: The Era of Early Internal Development, 1810–1860* (Baltimore: John Hopkins University Press, 1975).

14. See Paul Wallace Gates, *History of Public Land Law Development* (Washington, D.C.: U.S.G.P.O., 1968); Wallace Farnham, "The 'Weakened Spring of Government': A Study in Nineteenth-Century American History," *American Historical Review* (1963), no. 68, on the land grant policies and the legal process. An economic study recently published is Lloyd Mercer, *Railroads and Land Grant Policy: A Study of Government Intervention* (New York: Academic Press, 1982).

15. Quoted in Hunter, *Steamboats on the Western Rivers*, p. 527.

16. *Ibid.*, pp. 520–533. In 1852, responding to catastrophic steamer accidents in the first half of that year which resulted in nearly 600 deaths, Congress enacted stronger regulatory legislation. Engineers and pilots were subject to registration and licensing, and a corps of inspectors appointed on the Western rivers. See *ibid.*, pp. 533–546; and James Burke, "Bursting Boilers and the Federal Power," *Technology and Culture* (1966), 7:1–23.

17. The original ebb-and-tide boundaries of admiralty had been established in a decision of 1825, *The Steamboat Thomas Jefferson*. See Milton Conover, "The Abandonment of the 'Tidewater' Concept of Admiralty Jurisdiction in the U.S.," *Oregon Law Review* (1958), 38:46–48; and NOTE, "From Judicial Grant to Legislative Power: The Admiralty Clause in the 19th Century," *Harvard Law Review* (1954), 47:1221*ff.*

18. On the bridge cases, see Carl B. Swisher, *The Taney Period, 1836–1864, vol. 5 of History of the Supreme Court of the U.S.*, Paul Freund, ed. (New York: Macmillan, 1974); and H. N. Scheiber, "The Transportation Revolution and American Law: Constitutionalism and Public Policy," *Transportation and the Early Nation* (Indiana Historical Society, Indianapolis, 1982), pp. 1–29. On *Gibbons v. Ogden*, see the far-ranging analysis by W. Howard Mann, "The Marshall Court, Nationalization of Private Rights and Personal Liberty from the Authority of the Commerce Clause," *Indiana Law Journal* (1963), 38:117–238.

19. Hurst, *Law and the Conditions of Freedom*, p. 27.

20. 11 Pet. 420, 552–553 (U.S., 1837). The larger economic and political significance of this landmark case is considered in Stanley I. Kutler, *Privilege and Creative Destruction: The Charles River Bridge Case* (Philadelphia: W. W. Norton, 1971).

21. See Harry N. Scheiber, "Property Law, Expropriation, and Resource Allocation by Government, 1789–1910," *Journal of Economic History* (1973), 33:232–251, reprinted in Lawrence Friedman and Harry N. Scheiber, eds., *American Law and the Constitutional Order* (Cambridge, Mass.: Harvard University Press, 1978).

22. 6 Howard 507, at 531–32 (U.S., 1848). The opinion explicitly acknowledged the critical importance of the expropriation power, stating: "In fact, the whole policy of the country, relative to roads, mills, bridges, and canals, rests upon this single power . . . [without which] not one of the improvements mentioned could be constructed" (*ibid.*, at 533).

23. Kent's opinion is in *Croton Turnpike Co. v. Ryder*, 1 Johns. (chanc. 611 (N.Y., 1815). See generally Joseph Dorfman, "Chancellor Kent and the Developing American Economy," *Columbia Law Review* (1961), Vol. 61.

24. *Rubottom v. McClure*, 4 Blackford 505, at 507 (Indiana, 1838).

25. James Willard Hurst, *The Legitimacy of the Business Corporation in the Law of the United States, 1780–1970* (Charlottesville: University Press of Virginia, 1970), *passim;* Stephen Salsbury, "American Business Institutions Before the Railroad," in Porter, *Encyclopedia of American Economic History,* 2:601–618.

26. See Hurst, *Legitimacy of the Business Corporation,* p. 41.

27. Carter Goodrich, *Government Promotion of American Canals and Railroads, 1800–1890* (New York: Columbia University Press, 1960); Charles Fairman, *Reconstruction and Reunion, 1864–88,* part 1, vol. 6 of *History of the Supreme Court of the U.S.,* Paul Freund, ed., (New York: Macmillan, 1974), pp. 918–1116.

28. Harry N. Scheiber, "The Road to *Munn:* Eminent Domain and the Concept of Public Purpose in the State Courts," *Perspectives in American History* (1971), 5:329–331, 381–391.

29. The process of priorities ordering is illustrated in brilliant detail for one state in Hurst, *Law and Economic Growth,* on law and the lumber industry in Wisconsin.

30. The milldam acts are considered in Oscar Handlin and Mary F. Handlin, *Commonwealth: A Study of the Role of Government in the American Economy: Massachusetts, 1774–1860* (Cambridge, Mass.: Harvard University Press, 1947); and Horwitz, *Transformation of American Law.*

31. Scheiber, "Road to *Munn,*" pp. 334–355. Scheiber, "Public Rights and the Rule of Law in American Legal History," *California Law Review* (1984), 72:217–51.

32. Gordon R. Miller, "Shaping California Water Law," *Southern California Quarterly* (1973), 55:9–30; Robert Dunbar, "Significance of the Colorado Agricultural Frontier," *Agricultural History* (1960), 34:119–125; Donald Pisani, *From the Family Farm to Agribusiness: The Irrigation Crusade in California and the West, 1850–1931* (Berkeley: University of California Press, 1984).

33. Quoted in Harry N. Scheiber and Charles W. McCurdy, "Eminent-Domain Law and Western Agriculture, 1849–1900," *Agricultural History* (1975), 49:124. The California Context is etched more fully in McCurdy, "Stephen J. Field and Public Land Law Development in California, 1850–1866," *Law and Society Review* (1976), 10:235*ff.*, and intensive study of the early statehood years.

34. Hurst, *Law and Economic Growth;* Agnes M. Larson, *History of the White Pine Industry in Minnesota* (Minneapolis: University of Minnesota Press, 1949).

35. Levy, *Law of the Commonwealth,* pp. 166–182, presents a full analysis of the Farwell case (4 Metc. 49 [Mass., 1842]).

36. Friedman, *History of American Law,* p. 414.

37. *Ibid.,* pp. 414–418.

38. Schwartz, "Tort Law and the Economy," pp. 1717*ff.*

39. Morton Keller, *Affairs of State: Public Life in Late Nineteenth Century America* (Cambridge, Mass: Harvard University Press, 1977), pp. 401–404; Horwitz, *Transformation of American Law;* Harold M. Hyman and William M. Wiecek, *Equal Justice Under Law: Constitutional Development, 1835–1875* (New York: Harper and Row, 1982), pp. 36–40.

40. Scheiber, "Road to *Munn,*" pp. 366–367, 376–398; Paul M. Kurtz, "Nineteenth-Century Anti-Entrepreneurial Nuisance Injunctions: Avoiding the Chancellor," *William and Mary Law Review* (1976), 17:621–670.

41. *Matter of Cincinnati, etc., Railroad, Western Law Journal,* 6:352 (Court of Common Pleas, Hamilton County, Ohio, 1849). See, *inter alia,* Harry N. Scheiber, *Ohio Canal Era: A Case Study of Government and the Economy, 1820–1861* (Athens, Ohio, 1969);

and Scheiber, "Ohio's Transportation Revolution: Urban Dimensions, 1803–1870," in John Wunder, ed., *Toward an Urban Ohio* (Columbus: Ohio Historical Society, 1977), pp. 12–22.

42. *Lexington and Ohio Railroad v. Applegate,* 38 Kentucky 289 (1839), quoted in Kurtz, "Nuisance Injunctions," pp. 645–646.

43. *Losee v. Buchanan,* 51 New York 476 (1873). See Richard Abel, "A Critique of American Tort Law," *British Journal of Law and Society* (1981), 8:199*ff.* for a contemporary perspective on decisions in this mode.

44. *Hatch v. Central Vermont Railroad,* 25 Vermont 49 (1852).

45. James Willard Hurst, *Law and Social Order,* p. 187.

46. *Ibid.*

47. Hurst, *Law and the Conditions of Freedom,* pp. 87*ff.*; Thomas K. McCraw, "Regulatory Agencies," in Porter, *Encyclopedia of American Eonomic History,* 2:788–803.

48. Sidney Fine, *Laissez Faire and the General Welfare State: A Study of Conflict in American Thought, 1865–1901* (Ann Arbor: University of Michigan Press, 1956), pp. 352–372.

49. In *Nebbia v. New York,* 291 U.S. 502 (1934), the Supreme Court abandoned the "affectation" doctrine as a limit on the regulatory power, now denying that any businesses were per se not regulable.

50. See Keller, *Affairs of State.*

51. On competitive pressures on industry, see, *inter alia,* Edward Chase Kirland, *Industry Comes of Age: Business, Labor, and Public Policy, 1860–1897* (New York: Holt, Rinehart and Winston, 1961).

52. James Willard Hurst, *Law and Markets in U.S. History* (Madison: University of Wisconsin Press, 1982), p. 129; Keller, *Affairs of State,* pp. 368–369.

53. *Village of Euclid v. Ambler Realty Co.,* 272 U.S. 365 (1926). See Fred Bossleman et al., *The Taking Issue: A Study of the Constitutional Limits of Governmental Authority to Regulate the Use of Privately Owned Land* (Washington, D.C.: 1973).

54. *Miller v. Board of Public Works,* 195 Cal. 477 (1925).

55. Arnold M. Paul, *Conservative Crisis and the Rule of Law: Attitudes of Bar and Bench, 1887–1895* (Ithaca: Cornell University Press, 1960); William F. Swindler, *Court and Constitution in the Twentieth Century: The Old Legality, 1889–1932* (Indianapolis: Bobbs-Merrill, 1969).

56. William E. Leuchtenberg, *Franklin D. Roosevelt and the New Deal* (New York: Harper and Row, 1963).

57. *Ibid.*; and Arthur S. Miller, *The Supreme Court and American Capitalism* (New York: Free Press, 1968).

58. Grant McConnell, *Private Power and American Democracy* (New York: Random House, 1966); Otis Graham, *Toward a Planned Society: From Roosevelt to Nixon* (New York: Oxford University Press, 1976); Arthur S. Miller, *The Modern Corporate State: Private Governments and the American Constitution* (Westport, Conn.: Greenwood, 1976).

59. Martin Shapiro, *The Supreme Court and Administrative Agencies* (New York: Free Press, 1968), ch. 3; Fainsod et al., *Government and the American Economy,* pp. 591–603; American Bar Association, Section on Patent, Trademark, and Copyright Law, *Two Hundred Years of English and American Patent, Trademark and Copyright Law* (Chicago: American Bar Association, 1977).

60. Joseph Pechman, *Federal Tax Policy,* 4th ed. (Washington, D.C.: Brookings Institution, 1977).

61. Walter Gellhorn, *Security, Loyalty, and Science* (Ithaca: Cornell University Press, 1950); Paul Murphy, *The Constitution in Crisis Times, 1918–1969* (New York: Harper

and Row, 1972), pp. 299–316*ff.* On restriction of U.S. travel areas, see *New York Times,* November-December 1983, *passim.*

62. Daniel Greenberg, *The Politics of Pure Science* (New York: New American Library, 1967). See also Hurst, *Law and Social Order,* pp. 176–178.

63. See Greenberg, *Politics of Pure Science.*

64. NOTE, "Communications Satellite Act of 1962," *Harvard Law Review* (1982), p. 76; Nicolas M. Matte, *Aerospace Law: Telecommunications Satellites* (Toronto: University of Toronto Press, 1982), pp. 107–140, 165–169; U.S. House of Representatives, Subcommittee on Telecommunications, Consumer Protection and Finance, *Telecommunications in Transition: The Status of Competition in the Telecommunications Industry,* Committee Print 97–V, 1981; UCLA Communications Law Program and the International Bar Association, *International Satellite Television: Resource Manual for the Third Biennial Communications Law Symposium,* Charles M. Firestone, ed. (Los Angeles: UCLA, 1983).

65. "Deregulating America," *Business Week,* November 28, 1983, pp. 80–110; Donald Baker and Beverly Baker, "Antitrust and Communications Deregulation," *The Antitrust Bulletin* (Spring 1983), 28:1–38. On the effects of the divestiture of AT&T regional companies, see "Has the FCC Gone Too Far?" *Business Week,* Aug. 5, 1985, pp. 48–54.

66. The FDA was a major exception. Peter O. Steiner, "The Legalization of American Society: Economic Regulation," *Michigan Law Review* (1983), 81:1289–1290, 1297*ff.*; Thomas McCraw, "Regulatory Agencies," in Porter, *Encyclopedia of American Economic History,* 2:788-807.

67. David Vogel, "The 'New' Social Regulation in Historical and Comparative Perspective," in Thomas McCraw, ed., *Regulation in Perspective* (Cambridge, Mass.: Harvard University Press, 1981), 155–179. "Competition in laxity" was a phrase coined by Justice Brandeis, referring to the tendency of state governments to "bid down" their regulatory standards in order not to disadvantage business firms within their borders, when other states regulated less stringently. See William L. Cary, "Federalism and Corporate Law: Reflections upon Delaware," *Yale Law Journal* (1974), 83:663; and Roberta Romano, "Law as a Product: Some Pieces of the Incorporation Puzzle" (working paper, presented to Law and Society Association annual meeting, San Diego, 1985).

68. Scheiber, "Federalism and the American Economic Order," p. 71. See also Bruce Ackerman and William T. Hassler, "Beyond the New Deal: Coal and the Clean Air Act," *Yale Law Journal* (1980), 89:1471–1476, passim.

69. Donald Fleming, "Roots of the New Conservation Movement," *Perspectives in American History,* (1972), 6:7–94 (a highly critical but illuminating overview and analysis of environmentalism); Walter A. Rosenbaum, *The Politics of Environmental Concern* (New York: Holt, Rinehart, and Winston, 1973); Joel Primack and Frank von Hippel, *Advice and Dissent: Scientists in the Political Arena* (New York: National American Library, 1974); and Jane L. Scheiber, ed., *America and the Future of Man* (Del Mar, Calif.: CRM Books, 1973).

70. See John Harte and R. H. Socolow, eds., *Patient Earth* (New York: Holt, Rinehart, Winston, 1971); Fleming, "New Conservation Movement," pp. 41–43. For a perspective on modern industrial and environmental risk entirely different from my own, see Peter Huber, "Safety and the Second Best," *Columbia Law Review* (1985), 85:277–377. Huber strictly differentiates "private risk" (harm to an individual or group resulting from voluntary action in which a degree of possible damage is understood, e.g., cigarette smoking, or motorcycling without a helmet) from "public risk" (potential harms to which the population as a whole or seg-

ments of the population are exposed). Huber's argument rests upon a doctrinaire optimism that "inexorably and swiftly progressive *reduction* of public risk has characterized modern industrial development" (*ibid.*, p. 298).

71. James Harvey Young, *The Medical Messiahs: A Social History of Health Quackery in Twentieth-Century America* (Princeton: Princeton University Press, 1967), pp. 260–281, 408-422.

72. A. W. Galson, "Warfare with Herbicides in Vietnam," in Harte and Socolow, *Patient Earth,* pp. 136–150; Primack and von Hippel, *Advice and Dissent,* pp. 74–86; Fleming, "New Conservation Movement," pp. 62–63.

73. Orie Loucks, "The Trial of DDT in Wisconsin," in Harte and Socolow, *Patient Earth,* pp. 88–111; Robert and Leona Rienow, *Moment in the Sun: A Report on the Deteriorating Quality of the American Environment* (New York: Dial, 1967), esp. ch. 16; James Krier and Edmund Ursin, *Pollution and Policy: A Case Essay on California and Federal Experience with Motor Vehicle Air Pollution, 1940–1975* (Berkeley and Los Angeles: University of California Pess, 1977); and, for examples of prominent episodes in contemporary discussion, Garrett de Bell, ed., *The Environmental Handbook* (New York: Ballantine, 1970). The concern about a population explosion contributed further, of course, to the critical mood of the day concerning economic structures, government policy and pressure on resources. See Paul Ehrlich and Anne Ehrlich, *Population, Resources, and Environment: Issues in Human Ecology* (San Francisco: Freeman, 1970). On the California sardine depletion crisis, see Arthur McEvoy and Harry N. Scheiber, "Scientists, Entrepreneurs, and Public Policy," *Journal of Economic History* (1984), no. 44.

74. See, e.g., S. D. Ripley and H. K. Buechner, "Ecosystem Science as a Point of Synthesis," *Daedalus* (Fall 1967), 96 (4):1192–1199. See also the influential polemic by Barry Commoner, *The Closing Circle* (New York: Bantam, 1971); and Charles Myers, "An Introduction to Environmental Thought: Some Sources and Some Criticisms," *Indiana Law Journal* (1975), 50:426–453.

75. Laurence Tribe, *Channeling Technology Through Law* (Chicago: University of Chicago Press, 1973), pp. 49, 52 et passim: see also Richard B. Stewart, "Regulation, Innovation, and Administrative Law: A Conceptual Framework," *California Law Review* (1981), 69:1256–1377; Charles A. Reich, "The Law of the Planned Society," *Yale Law Journal* (1965), 75:1227–1270.

76. Alfred Marcus, "Environmental Protection Agency," in James Q. Wilson, ed., *Regulation in America* (New York: Basic Books, 1980), pp. 267–277.

77. U.S. Council on Environmental Quality, *Second Annual Report* (Washington, D.C.: GPO, 1971), pp. 89–93.

78. Harry N. Scheiber, "American Federalism and the Diffusion of Power: Historical and Contemporary Perspectives," *University of Toledo Law Review* (1978), 9:659–676.

79. Vogel, "The 'New' Social Regulation," pp. 162–163; McCraw, "Regulatory Agencies," pp. 803–806.

80. Marcus, "Environmental Protection Agency," pp. 271–272; James Q. Wilson, "The Politics of Regulation," in James W. McKie, ed., *Social Responsibility and the Business Predicament* (Washington, D.C.: Brookings Institution, 1974). See also Samuel P. Hays, "Political Choice in Regulatory Administration," in McCraw, ed., *Regulation in Perspective*, pp. 124–154.

81. Pub. L. No. 93–205, 87 Stat, 884.

82. Italics added. *T.V.A. v. Hill,* 437 U.S. 153, 184 (1978). See discussion in Jack R. Nelson, "Palila v. Hawaii Dept. of Land and Natural Resources: State Governments Fall Prey to the Endangered Species Act 1973," *Ecology Law Quarterly* (1982). 10:281, 283–288.

83. Eric Erdheim, book review, *Ecology Law Quarterly* (1982), 10:319 (on ESA enforcement); Biliana Cincin-Sain, "Managing the Ocean Commons: U.S. Marine Programs in the Seventies and Eighties," *Marine Technology Society Journal* (1982), 16:6–18.

84. Stewart, "Regulation, Innovation, and Administrative Law," pp. 1267–1277. On export controls—and their very great limitations with respect to protecting foreign persons consuming American products or at risk from manufacturing processes under U.S. firms' control—see Nicholas Ashford and C. Ayers, "Policy Issues for Consideration in Transferring Technology to Developing Countries," *Ecology Law Quarterly* (1985), 12:896–898.

85. Clean Air Act, 42 U.S.C. sec. 7475 (a) (Supp. IV, 1980). See Jerome Ostrov, "Visibility Protection Under the Clean Air Act," *Ecology Law Quarterly* (1982), 10:397–454.

86. This was the objective of the 1970 act that mandated the promulgation of ambient standards, based solely on health criteria. See Marcus, "Environmental Protection Administration," pp. 280–284.

87. *Ibid.*, pp. 278–303; Stewart, "Regulation, Innovation and Administrative Law," pp. 1271–1272; Wilson, *Regulation in America.*

88. Susan Bartlett Foote, "Administrative Preemption: An Experiment in Federalism," *Virginia Law Review* (1985), 70:1429*ff*; Harry N. Scheiber, "Some Realism about Federalism," *Emerging Issues in American Federalism* (Washington, D.C.: U.S. Advisory Commission on Intergovernmental Relations, 1985), pp. 56–58.

89. See text at note 72.

90. Lettie M. Wenner, *The Environmental Decade in Court* (Bloomington: Indiana University Press, 1982), pp. 10–11.

91. *Ibid.*, pp. 11–12; Nicholas C. Yost, "NEPA's Progeny: State Environmental Policy Acts," *Environmental Law Reporter* (1974), 3:500–590.

92. See, e.g., NOTE, "The Federal Water Pollution Control Act Amendments of 1972," *Wisconsin Law Review* (1973), pp. 893–902.

93. See Wenner, *Environmental Decade;* Karen Orren, "Standing to Sue: Interest Group Conflict in Federal Courts," *American Political Science Review* (1976), 70:723–741.

94. Stewart, "Regulation, Innovation, and Administrative Law," pp. 1276–1277; Abram Chayes, "The Role of the Judge in Public Law Litigation," *Harvard Law Review* (1976), 89:1281; Ackerman and Hassler, "Beyond the New Deal."

95. Angus McIntyre,, "Administrative Initiative and Theories of Implementation: Federal Pesticide Policy, 1970–76," *Public Policy Studies: A Multivolume Treatise,* vol. 7 (forthcoming).

96. *EDF v. Ruckelshaus,* 439 F. 2d 584, 597–598 (D.C. Cir. Ct., 1971) (S. Wright, J.).

97. *International Harvester Co. v. Ruckelshaus,* 478 F. 2d 615 (D.C. Cir. Ct., 1973) (Bazelon, J., *conc.*).

98. *Ethyl Corp. v. EPA,* 541 F. 2d 1, 28 (D.C. Cir.), cert. den., 426 U.S. 941 (1976). Compare an appellate court's view that when a statute (in this instance the Water Pollution Control Act, with 1972 amendments) contained language expressing the legislature's intent to protect public health, and there was absence of *definitive*

scientific knowledge as to precise levels of risk from a carcinogenic substance (asbestos), the court would validate agency action to curb industrial discharges of that substance. *Reserve Mining Co. v. EPA*, 514 F. 2d 492, 520–529 (8th Cir., 1975).

99. The mixed signals from the Supreme Court are in interpretation of the standards of worker safety and health established in the Occupational Safety and Health Act. See Industrial Union Department, *AFL-CIO v. American Petroleum Institute*, 448 U.S. 607 (1980) (the benzene case); and *American Textile Manufacturers Institute v. Donovan*, 452 U.S. 490 (1981) (the cotton dust case).

100. See Steiner, "Legalization of American Society," pp. 1286–1289. Another issue, forced upon American consciousness by the Union Carbide disaster in Bhopal, India, in December 1984, is the extent to which exported technology and overseas manufacturing leaves foreign nations at peril. An ironic aftermath was the similar, smaller scale accident in 1985 in West Virginia, for which Union Carbide was subjected to penalties for gross violation of U.S. safety standards.

101. See text at notes 25–46.

102. William L. Prosser, *Handbook of the Law of Torts*, sec. 97, at 654 (4th ed., 1971), quoted in Edmund Ursin, "Judicial Creativity and Tort Law," *George Washington Law Review* (1981), 49:303. See also G. Edward White, *Tort Law in America: An Intellectual History* (New York: Oxford University Press, 1980), 169–171; and John G. Fleming, "Is There a Future for Tort Law," *Louisiana Law Review* (1984), 44:1193–1212.

103. Ursin, "Creativity and Tort Law." On Shaw, see the opening section of the present essay.

104. *Greenman v. Yuba Power Products, Inc.*, 59 Cal. 2d 57, 63 (1963).

105. *Sindell v. Abbott Laboratories, Inc.*, 26 Cal. 3d 588 (1980), cert. den. 101 S. Ct. 285 (1980). For a full discussion, see Ursin, "Creativity and Tort Law," pp. 299–303.

106. This new legal realism is a variant, that is, of the legal realism of the 1930s, a movement in legal scholarship that sought to analyze the law, and especially the decisions of courts, as an expression of material and social interests rather than as an abstract system of doctrine.

107. See, e.g., papers in Association of Trial Lawyers of America, *Industrial and Toxic Torts: A Transcript of Proceedings, Boston, Mass., Nov. 9, 1979* (New York, processed, n.d.); and Richard Lempert and Stephen Saltsburg, *A Modern Approach to Evidence* 2d ed. (St. Paul: West, 1977), ch. 10.

108. Charles M. Culver and Bernard Gert, *Philosophy in Medicine: Conceptual and Ethical Issues in Medicine and Psychiatry* (New York: Oxford University Press, 1982), pp. 86–108.

109. Stanley J. Levy, "Product Liability Disease Litigation," *Industrial and Toxic Torts*, pp. 155–170; NOTE, "The Fairness and Constitutionality of Statutes of Limitations for Toxic Tort Suits," *Harvard Law Review* (1983), 96:1683–1695. The stringency of emerging product liability law in many states, together with the patchwork character of law resulting from state-to-state variations, has led to a strong movement since 1982 by an alliance of American business firms to obtain uniform national legislation that would preempt the field from the states. See *Business Week*, May 31, 1982, p. 34.

110. Reference is to the Johns-Mansville litigation. The asbestos suits also became the vehicle for settling important questions about class action, as the courts permitted a small number of workers who had suffered harm to sue on behalf of all fellow workers similarly situated.

111. The 1954 Atomic Energy Act had made all "radiation hazards" the exclusive responsibility of the federal government. Subsequent legislation limited the money damages that might be obtained in suits in event of nuclear damages. In *Silkwood v. Kerr-McGee,* 464 U.S. 238 (1984), 465 U.S. 1074 (1984).

    On larger questions of science and the law, especially the responsibilities of courts in dealing with issues on which there is a difference of expert opinion, see Joel Yellin, "High Technology and the Courts: Nuclear Power and the Need for Institutional Reform," *Harvard Law Review* (1981), 90:489*ff.* and Judge David Bazelon, "Science and Uncertainty: A Jurist's View," *Harvard Environmental Law Review* (1981), 5:209*ff.* Peter Huber, "Safety and the Second Best," makes an argument, which seems to me founded on poorly supported premises, that the courts should uniformly give deference to the expertise and decisions of the regulatory agencies; Huber would be unwilling even to credit testimony of independent expert witnesses. See, *inter alia,* Symposium, "Federal Regulation of the Chemical Industry," *Law and Contemporary Problems* (1983), vol. 46.

112. *Frye v. U.S.,* 293 F. 1013 (D.C. Cir., 1923). See the discussion in Lempert and Saltsburg, *Modern Approach to Evidence,* pp. 859–862 *et passim;* see also Eric Warner, "Sex Typing of Dried Blood: Science in the Courtroom?" *Criminal Law Bulletin* (1980), 16:325–357.

113. NOTE, "Evolving Methods of Scientific Proof," *New York Law Forum* (1967), 13:684. See also J. I. Thornton, "Criminalistics: Past, Present, and Future," *Lex Et Scientia* (1975), 11:1–44.

114. See text at notes 92–99.

115. *Baltimore Gas & Electric Co. v. National Resources Defense Council,* 103 S. Ct. at 2256 (1983).

116. *City of N.Y. v. U.S. Dept. of Transportation,* 715 F. 2d 732, 751 (1983). Italics added.

5. Technology and the Transformation of the American Party System

David C. Hammack
Case Western Reserve University

A succession of two-party systems has dominated political life in the United States since early in the nineteenth century. As a number of distinguished historians and political scientists have shown, these political systems have organized communications among political leaders and between leaders, interest groups, and the citizens at large. We know a great deal about the justifications for and the origins, evolution, and changing internal arrangements of these systems. We know much less, however, about the impact on them of technological change. This essay addresses that question, arguing that key changes in the technologies of communication and transportation have played a significant role in the evolution of America's political parties.

In the 1820s and 1830s, new technologies made possible the creation of the world's first stable party system based on a very large electorate. More recently, the new and more widely diffused technologies of transportation, communication, and information management of the 1960s and 1970s have contributed significantly to the contemporary decline of the two-party pattern. On reflection, it is not surprising to find that new transportation and communications technologies shaped the party systems. The role of the parties and of the overall party systems, after all, is to organize political communications. New technologies that enable people to communicate more cheaply and more frequently, or in new ways altogether, inevitably have an impact on the institutions that organize communications.

The impact of new technology has never been direct or deterministic. Rather, new technologies have created new resources that have sometimes enabled political leaders to change an established political balance. Thus when the cost of travel and of publishing a newspaper declined rapidly after 1820, Martin Van Buren and other ambitious new leaders found it possible to concert their forces. Through frequent personal meetings and through new party newspapers, they set up new political organizations that shouldered aside the personal factions and cabals that large landowners and city merchants had used to manage political affairs since the eighteenth century. Similarly, the proliferation of telephones and automobiles in the 1950s and 1960s, together with the introduction of jet passenger planes and computers, decisively redistributed some of the critical resources of American politics. Individual political candidates, from John F. Kennedy to John D. Anderson, and distinct interest groups, from the National Rifle Association to the Sierra Club, have found it increasingly useful to ignore the structure provided by the two-party system.

In view of the recent decline in the significance of political parties in the United States, it may be useful to recall the overwhelming importance that the most respected experts attributed to them for so many years. "The whole machinery, both of national and state governments, is worked by the political parties," asserted James Bryce in *The American Commonwealth* (1888), the single most influential study of the actual workings of the nation's politics and government ever published. "The spirit and force of party," Bryce added, "has in America been as essential to the machinery of government as steam is to a locomotive."[1]

Until the late 1960s, most political scientists continued to agree with Bryce. "The political parties created modern democracy," insisted E. E. Schattschneider, "and modern democracy is unthinkable save in terms of the parties."[2] In 1950 the Committee on Political Parties of the American Political Science Association, chaired by Schattschneider, took it for granted that "popular government in a nation of more than 150 million people requires political parties which provide the electorate with a proper range of choice between alternatives of action."[3] In his Jefferson Memorial Lectures of 1966, historian Richard Hofstadter summed up the view of party significance shared by nearly all up-to-date political scientists and historians. "Our social pluralism made itself effective within each of the two major parties," Hofstadter said. "Each major party has become a compound, a hodgepodge, of various and conflicting interests; and the imperatives of party struggle, the quest for victory and for offices, have forced the parties themselves to undertake the business of conciliation and compromise among such interests."[4]

Twenty years later the notion that political parties play a fundamental, even indispensable, role in American politics and government seemed out of date. *The Party's Over*, declared journalist David Broder; A *Decline of American Political Parties* characterized the years between 1952 and 1980, argued political scientist Martin P. Wattenberg.[5] It was time, according to Walter Dean Burnham, to write of "The Disappearance of the American Voter."[6] Nelson Polsby, one of the most acute and prolific students of contemporary American politics, concluded by the early 1980s that Hofstadter's idea of the party system no longer described reality. "The idea of a political party as a coalition of interests and groups bound together by many sorts of ties, including the hope of electing a President, is fast becoming an anachronism," Polsby wrote. "Party is increasingly a label for masses of individual voters who pick among various candidates in primary elections as they would among any alternatives offered by the mass media."[7]

The rise and decline of the two-party system pattern in American politics dramatically altered the basic structures through which political life is organized. As Schattschneider observed, such a basic change in the political structure is of the greatest importance, because to a very large extent, "what happens in politics *depends on the way in which people are divided* into factions, parties, groups, classes. . . ." In the United States, Schattschneider argued, political parties are the most significant political organizations, and they have solved "their greatest organizational problem very simply by maintaining the two-party system."[8] Or to be more precise, as V. O. Key, Richard P. McCormick, Walter Dean Burnham, and other political scientists and historians have demonstrated during the past twenty years, from 1796 at least until the 1960s successive two-party systems continuously provided the basic order for political life in the United States.

Altogether, these scholars have identified five or six distinct "party systems" in the United States, each system separated from its predecessor by one or more "critical elections." Within the period characterized by a party system, the voters have aligned themselves in a fairly stable way with two political parties, one of which has normally been stronger than the other. The first party system grew out of the conflict between the Federalists and the Democratic Republicans over the elections of 1796 and 1800; the second reflected patterns established in the conflicts between Jacksonian Democrats and Whigs in 1824, 1828, and 1832; and the third saw the rise of the battle between Republicans and Democrats that began with the Compromise of 1854 and led to the Civil War. It has been more difficult to draw boundaries between the periods dominated by the subsequent party systems, but in general a fourth was characterized by a close balance between the two parties after Reconstruction; the Republicans dominated during a fifth, which is usually dated from 1896; and the Democrats dominated a sixth, which may have begun as early as 1928 and became solidified after the onset of the Great Depression and Franklin D. Roosevelt's elections in 1932 and 1936.[9] It seems likely that this last New Deal party system has come to an end, but it is not clear whether another party system, comparable to the others, has replaced it.

New technologies provided important resources to the leaders who created, and who are now threatening to dismantle, the two-party system that structured political conflict between the 1830s and the 1970s.[10] At the outset of this very long span of time, Americans developed the first political parties that were capable of mobilizing the mass electorate of an entire nation. The resulting second party system established a basic pattern found in succeeding party systems for 140 years. Since about 1968, party organizations have decayed, many voters have ceased to identify strongly with either party, and many citizens—nearly half, in some recent presidential elections— have ceased even to vote. The New Deal party system has decayed, but no new system has arisen to replace it. Very possibly, these two episodes define the beginning and the end of the two-party period in American history. Political parties did not mediate between a mass public and the government before the late 1820s; several scholars are already suggesting that political parties no longer play a key mediating role today. Changes in transportation and communications technology help explain both how parties gained their ascendancy one hundred and fifty years ago, and why they have lost it today.

The creation of the second party system was one of the great achievements of the political leaders of the 1820s and 1830s. As Richard P. McCormick noted, the parties of this period "left an impressive inheritance to succeeding political generations." The central portion of this inheritance was the pattern of competition between two political parties, organized on a national basis and focused on the contest to secure majorities of the popular vote in enough states to win the presidency. The inheritance also entailed a "marvelously intricate and elaborate . . . party apparatus," emphasizing the delegate convention, the raucous campaign techniques that made American political meetings into democratic folk festivals, and "the highly professional party manager, with his army of workers."[11] The second party systems also left the nation with an intensively mobilized electorate, accustomed for the first time to turn out to vote in massive proportions.

McCormick argues persuasively that many factors, of which technological change was by no means the most important, brought about the construction of the second party system. Above all, he argues, a "hidden revolution" altered the constitutional and legal environment within which political contests took place. There were "many sets of rules" in 1800; by the early 1930s "the rules had become *relatively* uniform from state to state."[12] As others have pointed out, the rules governing *party* activity also changed everywhere almost at the same time, between 1828 and 1832. Before they could choose delegates for the convention that would name their presidential candidate for 1832, Democrats in virtually every state were forced to revise their selection procedures.[13]

The most important change in the rules of politics, McCormick observed, was "in the method of choosing presidential electors."[14] By 1832 every state except South Carolina chose its electors through a contest for a plurality of the popular vote in the state as a whole. Under the diverse and idiosyncratic methods of selection that had previously prevailed, local and state political elites had only to bargain with one another over the votes that chose a new president; often, their bargaining could take place within the state legislature. Now elites were forced to appeal to the voters as well as to one another.

At the same time, new suffrage rules had greatly enlarged the electorate. By the early 1830s restrictions on the suffrage that dated from the seventeenth century had been removed for all adult men (with the notable exceptions of slaves and black citizens) everywhere except in Rhode Island, Virginia, and North Carolina. Increasingly, printed and often secret ballots also replaced *viva voce* voting, allowing the more numerous voters to be more independent as well.[15] Voters now began to turn out in great numbers. Connecticut closely paralleled the national trend: whereas only 7.2 percent of the potential electorate in this state actually cast votes in the 1820 election for president, the proportion rose to 27 percent in 1828, 46 percent in 1832, and 76 percent in 1840.[16]

In state after state, astute political leaders turned the new rules to advantage by defining partisan appeals and setting up party organizations to persuade voters to support their candidates. Alert leaders also learned from their peers, capitalizing on effective party techniques introduced in neighboring states. Good organizational ideas that appeared first in New York, New Jersey, and Maryland were quickly adapted to conditions in New England, then to the circumstances of the West and the South.[17]

The new party leaders of the 1820s found that new transportation and communications technologies gave them the resources they needed to take full advantage of the new legal rules and organizational ideas. Contrary to the impression left by Alexis de Tocqueville, these technologies did not much help the political parties to mobilize a mass electorate. Instead, small but continuous improvements that made travel cheaper and more rapid, and that greatly reduced the cost of publishing limited circulation newspapers, proved very useful to the creators of the parties themselves. As early as the mid-1820s, political leaders like Martin Van Buren were using the new travel and publishing technologies to pull their organizations together, to work out differences and concert their efforts, and to impose discipline. The patterns they defined proved to be remarkably enduring.

New means of transportation were particularly important because they enabled political leaders, those who were relatively rich as well as those who were poor, to meet with one another face to face as often as political events required. Even before the establishment of a full-scale railroad system, continuous small refinements reduced transportation costs by about 50 percent and doubled the number of trips per capita between 1816 and 1840. In 1816 it cost about $7.00 to travel from New York City to Albany; within ten years the price had fallen to about $1.00. In 1790 it had taken four days to travel between these two cities; by 1840 it took less than ten hours.[18] If the cost of transportation, in both money and time, had not fallen so sharply, Van Buren and his fellow professional politicians would have found it much more difficult to put their new-model political party together. And it was through the carefully coordinated maneuvers of their party that they were able to supplant the great merchants and landowners who had dominated New York's politics since the days of Peter Stuyvesant.

While improved means of transportation have rarely been associated with the rise of the second party system, observers from Alexis de Tocqueville to the present have attributed an important role to the press. On examination, however, it turns out to be difficult to say exactly how the newspapers helped promote the new-model parties. Although most accounts suggest that the press mobilized the new mass electorate, it is much more likely that smaller party papers gave party leaders the resources they needed to set up and maintain their new state and national organizations.

The great age of mass-production newspapers was not to come until the introduction of the Hoe "lightning press" in 1847 and then the web-perfecting, stereotyping press of 1875. But flat-bed hand presses were continually improved by the introduction of stronger components and more sophisticated levers after 1800. Such gradual innovations made it possible for the printer to produce 200 sheets an hour by 1810. German and English inventors then introduced the steam-powered cylinder press, and by 1830 the New York firm of Robert Hoe and Son was turning out Napier double-cylinder, self-inking presses capable of yielding 2,000 "perfected" sheets (printed on both sides) an hour.[19] Lithography, which made it possible to produce cartoons in considerable numbers, also became available to political leaders in the 1830s.[20]

The impact of this technological change was increased by a concomitant economic effect: as new printing presses were placed into service by the most ambitious and well-financed papers in the largest cities, the number of used hand presses in the market swelled. So, too, did the number of journeyman printers who saw that large-capacity presses would require fewer master printers. Thus the 1830s saw not only the introduction of the first cheap mass-circulation dailies, the *Boston Transcript* (1830), *The Sun* (New York City, 1833), and the *New York Herald* (1835), but also an extraordinary proliferation of limited-circulation weeklies.[21] These small-town, village, and special-interest papers made good use of the older machines and the skilled printers whose services were not needed by the fledgling mass-circulation papers of the very largest cities.

Altogether, the total number of newspapers increased steadily but slowly between 1790 and 1820, then began a rapid expansion. According to Allan R. Pred, who has made the most careful recent examination of the sources, there were about 92 weeklies, biweeklies, and dailies in 1790, 235 in 1800, 371 in 1810, 512 in 1820. The number then jumped to 861 in 1828 and to 1,404 in 1840. Fewer than 10 percent of these papers were dailies based in cities; most of them were small-town weeklies. When he visited the United States in 1831, de Tocqueville concluded that in the entire nation there was "scarcely a hamlet which has not its own newspaper."[22]

The limited-circulation newspapers of this period were closely—and increasingly—tied to politics. In 1800, according to one estimate, as many as 80 percent of the daily papers were devoted primarily to the news of commerce. By 1810 only half of all dailies were commercial.[23] The intensive use of subsidies from wealthy supporters of the political parties, together with government patronage in the form of sinecures, advertising and printing contracts, and free use of the U.S. mails, changed the balance.[24] By 1850 the first comprehensive census of the American press asked not only how frequently a paper appeared, but whether it was "political, neutral, or independent"; 95 percent of all newspapers declared themselves to be "political."[25] "Every shade of political persuasion has its organ," observed a well-informed Democratic journal.[26]

De Tocqueville advanced a clever and persuasive argument to the effect that the early mass-circulation dailies played a critical part in American democracy. In aristocracies, he observed, the "principal citizens" could "discern one another from afar; and if they wish to unite their forces, they move towards each other, drawing a multitude of men after them." In democracies such as the United States, by contrast, only "numerous" associations "have any power." Yet many potential members of any large association necessarily lack the wealth and leisure that enable aristocrats to meet face to face. The press, he argued, supplied the needed means of indirect contact; newspapers brought people together into civil and political associations, "and the newspaper is still necessary to keep them united. . . . Hardly any democratic association," de Tocqueville concluded, "can do without newspapers."[27]

Historians of journalism have been tempted to conclude that newspapers did indeed play a direct role in the mobilization of the electorate for the second party system. As Bernard A. Weisberger observed, "new groups of voters had to be organized . . . the party paper became an element in the management of political life, and the official printer who conducted it found his way into executive councils."[28] Political scientists have found such conclusions congenial; in the view of V. O. Key, to take an especially influential example, "the partisan press put a degree of order into the confusing world of politics" and provided "the loyal reader" with "cues of considerable clarity."[29]

There are several reasons to doubt that newspapers, particularly the mass-circulation papers of the biggest cities, played quite so direct a role in the mobilization of the American electorate. Newspapers were not yet items of truly mass distribution and consumption in the 1830s. Despite the rapid increase in the number of individual papers, very few appeared more than once or twice a week. The largest circulations approached 10,000 only in New York and, by the end of the decade, in Philadelphia, Boston, and Baltimore. According to Pred's careful estimate, the nation's total output amounted to only 5.2 newspaper copies per capita *per year* in 1820, 6 in 1835, and only 8.6 as late as 1840.[30]

Lithographed broadsides and political cartoons, often cited as particularly effective means for reaching a mass audience, were even less widely available. Produced in cumbersome fashion on old-fashioned vertical presses, lithographs were made directly from plates that had to be drawn by the artist himself. Production was thus limited to less than 200 an hour, or at most 4,800 during a twenty-four-hour day.[31] By far the most famous and most widely distributed campaign broadside of the 1828 election was the "coffin handbill," a blistering account of "SOME OF THE BLOODY DEEDS OF GENERAL JACKSON" distributed by supporters of John Quincy Adams. The largest run of this handbill amounted to only 10,000 copies, enough for the party activists, perhaps, but far short of the number needed to reach the nation's more than one million voters.[32]

Nor did the very large big-city dailies enter directly into the partisan fray. The New York *Sun* "avoided the kind of political discussion which filled the party papers." James Gorden Bennett of the *Herald* "was not cut out for party journalism"; the Boston *Transcript* and *Daily Times* imposed a "taboo on political controversy." According to Frank Luther Mott, the most thorough of all historians of the American press, every editor of an inexpensive paper agreed that his "first duty" was to give his "readers the news, and not to support a party or a mercantile class."[33] Relying on large circulations for sales and advertising revenues, the successful "penny" newspapers of the 1830s could be independent of both the merchants' subscriptions and the politicians' subsidies. No longer, Bernard Weisberger concludes, could a political party "buy a paper for a few thousand dollars and install a 'loyal' editor at its helm."[34]

The much more limited circulation papers of the party press did play a direct (and more easily documented) role in the establishment of the second party system. The first American definition and defense of a political party appeared, appropriately enough, in 1820 in the Albany *Argus,* the organ of Martin Van Buren's Albany Regency. As Michael Wallace has demonstrated, during the Revolution and through the duration of the first party system, almost all Americans rejected political parties as "associations of factious men bent on self-aggrandizement." It was through the pages of the *Argus* that Van Buren and his associates first developed the argument for the legitimacy of political parties. Parties, the *Argus* declared, ought to be enduring institutions, "bound to the fortunes of no aspiring chief," controlled "by the fairly expressed will of the majority," and managed by those willing to conform "to the principles of their party." By 1824 the *Argus* could quote Republicans from throughout the Empire State in defense of its new view of party. "Voluntary associations for . . . the nomination of officers founded on the representative principle" were essential instruments of democracy, these political leaders now believed, because they "enabled republicans, the friends of liberty, to harmonize in their views and give efficacy to their exertions."[35]

The essential point, as the *Argus* put it, was that party organizations enabled "brethren of the same principle" to meet, allowed the minority to have its say, affirm its loyalty, and "yield to the majority—and the result is announced as the will of the whole." Those who refused to accept the decision of the majority acted contrary to the democratic spirit appropriate to the new republic. And, as Wallace pointed out, "editors of party papers were particularly subject to party discipline." Isaac Leake, editor of the *Argus*, saw himself as "a child of the Republican Party" who would, as a matter of course, seek "the concurrence of the party" in all matters of editorial policy."[36] "Without a paper [soundly and discreetly] edited at Albany," Van Buren wrote one of his associates, "we may hang our harps on the willows."[37] Like other key members of the party organizations, editors were rewarded for their services; journalists received ten percent or more of the nominations Jackson sent to the Senate during his first six months in office.[38]

Editors were necessarily subordinated because their papers served as the means of communication, not simply between the party and the voters, but between top party leaders and their lieutenants and minor functionaries. Party papers defined and defended official positions for all party members. Party papers also attacked the opposition, providing arguments and rhetoric for those who worked the barbecues and the barber shops. The long, earnest essays of the party papers were clearly intended for people who were intensively involved in politics; they contrasted sharply with the brief, personal, anecdotal feature-story journalism of the large-circulation penny press. It was through their newspapers that party leaders denounced those who broke ranks, "bolted," or rejected the authority and the discipline of the organization itself. Surely it was denunciations of this sort, and not only assaults on competing parties, that gave the papers of the period the quality of "scurrility and vulgar attack" that Frank L. Mott denounced as the "dark ages of partisan journalism."[39]

Despite the conclusion that V. O. Key and many others have been tempted to derive from de Tocqueville, the early years of the Industrial Revolution did not produce communications technologies capable of allowing political parties to mobilize a mass electorate. Cheaper, quicker transportation and inexpensive limited-circulation party newspapers, not mass-circulation dailies, were the politically significant new technologies of the 1820s and 1830s. Making creative use of these eminently useful, if limited, innovations, the political leaders of the time created patterns of party organization, party discipline, and party competition that endured for nearly one hundred and fifty years.

In the years since 1960, many of the elements of the American two-party system have come apart. Voter participation in presidential elections has steadily declined, the political parties have lost much of their coherence as organizations, and party leaders have much less influence over nominations. Leading scholars lament the "decline of intermediation" in presidential politics. They argue—and in 1984 the news media agreed—that weaker parties are less able to defend a broad public interest against the demands of special interest groups.[40] Alarmed social scientists assert that the result is an alienated electorate, a weakened central government, and even a general "crisis in political legitimacy."[41]

A new set of technological innovations has helped weaken the party organizations by multiplying the channels through which individual candidates and organized special interest groups can communicate directly with the voters. Television has of course played a critical role in recent years, and scholars have devoted a good deal of attention to the effects on voters of the content of televised news and political advertising. Equally important, however, is the impact of a variety of recent technological innovations on the patterns of communication and transportation in the United States. Altogether, these innovations have made it possible for many political actors to operate as if the party organizations did not exist.

Scholars have assigned credit—or blame—for the decline of the American two-party system to factors as numerous and diverse as those alleged to be responsible for its original appearance. The clash between American values and American realities; the general disintegration of Western society; the gradual passing of the generations that experienced the shock of the Great Depression; the increasingly diverse and contentious demands of interest groups within the Democratic party: all these explanations have been brought forward, and more.[42] In the most fully developed explanation, Byron Shafer emphasizes the "quiet revolution" in the "institutional arrangements" of the nation's political parties, just as Richard P. McCormick argued that a "hidden revolution" was essential to the appearance of the second party system.[43] In the recent period, as in the 1830s, new communications technologies have facilitated, if they did not force, these institutional changes.

Several facts are clear. The proportion of American citizens who actually turn out and vote in presidential elections has declined steadily since 1960, when it reached a postwar high of 63 percent. Despite the significant rise in participation by black voters in the South following the passage—and the substantial enforcement—of the Civil Rights and Voting Rights Acts of 1965 and 1970—the *national* participation rate hovered just above 53 percent in 1980 and again in 1984. This decline in political participation is largely an American phenomenon: in Canada and the democracies of Western Europe the turnout in national elections remained in the 75 percent to 90 percent range during the same period.[44]

During this same period, voters have also grown less and less loyal to the two major parties. Even fewer Americans vote for congressional, state, and local candidates than for president; those who do vote for these lower officers have increasingly chosen to "split the ticket," to vote for a president from one party and a congressman or state representative from the other. Between 1920 and 1944 the voters of only 10 percent to 15 percent of all congressional districts cast a majority for the presidential candidate of one party while returning a representative from the other; between 1960 and 1980 the proportion ranged from 27 percent to 44 percent.[45] Opinion surveys between 1952 and 1964 consistently found that about 75 percent of the members of the electorate identified themselves as either Democrats or Republicans; Philip Converse, a leader in election survey research, wrote at the time of the "serene stability in the expression of party loyalties." By 1972, however, only 64 percent identified clearly with either party, and less than 40 percent identified strongly.[46]

Most of the increase in the proportion of the voters who identify with neither party consists, as Martin P. Wattenberg has shown, of people who do not consider themselves "Independent," but who are entirely detached from the existing political parties. Even those who do identify fairly strongly with one party or the other have become less and less partisan. Survey research reveals, Wattenberg concludes, that the members of the electorate "no longer have much to say when asked what they like and dislike about the two parties."[47]

It is also clear that the political parties have lost much of their strength and coherence as organizations, and that their leaders' influence over presidential nominations has diminished sharply since 1960. Before 1960, the leaders of the party organizations selected the presidential nominees; Harry S. Truman could quite rightly dismiss the primaries, in which would-be nominees appealed directly to the voters, as "eyewash."[48] In the 1940s political scientists took it for granted that the parties defined themselves through their presidential nominations. "Unless the party makes authoritative and effective nominations, it cannot stay in business," declared E. E. Schattschneider.[49] By the mid-1970s, however, party organizations in the sense that Truman and Schattschneider knew them were no longer making nominations. Instead, candidates, the news media, and the participants in a lengthening series of primaries and caucuses have come to dominate the nominating process.

Nelson Polsby draws a striking parallel between the mounting of a contemporary campaign for a presidential nomination and "the production of a Broadway show":

A company is newly created. It sells tickets, books theaters, writes a script (frequently known as 'the speech'), and advertises the star. Individual contributions are solicited through the mail. As these build up, candidates become eligible for federal matching funds provided by law to assist candidates successful in their initial fund-raising efforts.[50]

"Party organizations simply are not actors in presidential politics," observes Austin Ranney, a political scientist who himself played a significant (and not entirely intended) role in the creation of the new nominating process. Instead, party organizations have become "little more than custodians of the party-label prize which goes to the winning candidate organization."[51]

Byron Shafer has argued that a series of institutional changes destroyed the parties' effectiveness and led to the alienation of the voters. Chief among these institutional changes is a series of fateful reforms in the nomination process made within the Democratic party in the aftermath of the disastrous 1968 Democratic National Convention. Before the reforms, most delegates to the parties' national conventions were selected through party caucuses and through primaries in which the names of would-be delegates appeared on the ballot. Under these arrangements, established party figures and representatives of politically active community organizations dominated the conventions. The post-1968 reforms replaced these traditional delegate selection procedures with the candidate primary and the participatory convention. As a result, most convention delegates owe loyalty to a presidential candidate rather than to a local party or community organization. The reforms also required that each state delegation include certain groups (blacks, women, and youth) in numbers proportional to their presence in the state's population at large. This requirement also reduced the likelihood that the delegates would represent and hold themselves accountable to ongoing local party and community organizations.

A later set of financial reforms further undercut the continuing state and local political organizations. These reforms required candidates for president to set up their own strongly centralized national organizations, carefully controlled by accountants and attorneys. They also required candidates to appeal directly for small donations from large numbers of individuals in order to qualify for very large grants of federal campaign funds. As a result, candidates for the presidential nominations are virtually forced to operate independently from the party organizations. Indeed, in 1984 Gary Hart sharply criticized Walter Mondale for receiving the support of the Democratic organizations in many states. During a campaign, moreover, federal law strictly limits the amount of money a candidate may spend. As a result, candidates for president have "cut the grass-roots items—pamphlets, buttons, bumper stickers," limited their contacts with local organizations, and increased their use of television.[52] Special interest political action committees are not limited in the amount they spend in support of a candidate, however, so long as the candidate does not control their expenditures. In sum, the campaign finance reforms had the (largely unintended) effect of increasing the influence of political action committees even as they crippled the political parties.

All of these institutional changes were intended to remedy the abuse of power, particularly by racist Democratic organizations in the South. They supplemented a series of reforms dating from the first years of the twentieth century—the Australian ballot provided by public authorities rather than by party organizations; the official rather than party registration of voters; the party primary governed by public law rather than by party rule—that had already weakened the parties and reduced turnout to some extent.[53] But it was the post-1968 reforms, Shafer concludes, that produced "the disengagement or the actual dismantling of intermediary organizations—the very organizations which were needed to link the public" with government and politics. The reforms deprived many ordinary voters of the ability to influence presidential nominations through local organizations integral to their lives—labor unions, religious organizations, civic clubs, and political parties. When the reformed nomination procedures have offered candidates of limited experience and appeal, like George McGovern, Jimmy Carter, and Gerald Ford, many voters inevitably feel isolated from government. Indeed, they "really *are* more insulated from political life than they were before."[54]

Technological innovations have also enabled candidates and interest groups to weaken the party organizations. Television, automobiles, jet planes, telephones, computers, and opinion polls have all multiplied the channels through which individual candidates and organized special interest groups can communicate directly with the voters. Television has of course received the most attention in this regard, both from journalists and from the several scholars who have studied the effects of the content of televised news and political advertising on the voters. Other recent technological innovations have, however, had an equally significant impact.

Nearly all careful students of the content of American television agree that it rarely favors one party over another. Instead, television news tends either to criticize political parties in general, or to suggest that they are unimportant.[55] Because television news seeks a large audience by emphasizing the dramatic actions of candidates and other individuals, and by presenting news of the widest possible interest, it neglects parties and other organizations that it deems to be of interest only to a portion of the viewers. Under the "fairness doctrine," moreover, federal regulators require television news to treat the parties equally—or not at all. In response to these varied forces, and to their own sense of mission, leaders of the television news organizations have developed a vaguely antiparty (and anti-special interest) stance as the public's watchdog. Indeed this stance strongly resembles the antipartisan position of the early publishers of the penny press.[56] Meanwhile no new medium of recent years has filled the role played by the party papers which articulated the defense of party in the 1820s and 1830s.

Television has also tended to undermine the political parties because, far more than radio or the mass-circulation daily newspapers, it has enabled candidates to appeal over the heads of party managers to the voters. Estes Kefauver, the first candidate for a presidential nomination who owed his prominence to television, adopted just such a strategy. "Where once candidates for public office had to rely on mustering organizational strength to communicate with voters," Martin Wattenberg has written, now it is "increasingly possible for them to establish direct contact through the media."[57]

Other new technologies have, however, undermined the party system in more decisive ways. The most important of these are the automobile, telephone, jet airplane, computer and word processor, and public opinion survey. Although televised hearings did win Estes Kefauver a sudden and remarkable popularity in 1952, helping him carry a string of primary elections, he did not build on his advantage by setting up an effective personal organization, and he failed to win the Democratic nomination. It is the telephone, the airplane, and the computer that allow candidates to construct their own personal organizations and to take the fullest possible advantage of their new ability to reach the voters' living rooms. John F. Kennedy's well-equipped campaign plane was even more notable than his effective use of television—and in 1960 he won the nomination that had eluded Kefauver.

The automobile and the telephone had become items of mass consumption in the United States as early as the 1920s, but they had new consequences for politics after they had been adopted by more than 80 percent of all households in the early 1960s. Domestic air transportation also became an item of mass consumption only in the 1960s; computers were not widely available to political leaders until the 1970s. Since 1960 new mass-communication technologies, not only in television but in print itself, combined with market forces to bring extensive change in metropolitan journalism.[58] Many newspapers have been forced out of business, and those that survive have either become "common carriers" of a very wide variety of information, taken on an increasingly national role, or joined the specialized, limited-audience publications that have proliferated in every metropolitan region.[59] Altogether, these technological developments have greatly increased the ability of individual Americans to escape what Nelson Polsby has aptly called "the tyranny of geographical propinquity," and to find and associate with like-minded people on their own, without the aid of the neighborhood political club.[60]

Even more important, these new technologies make it far easier for political leaders to create the personal organizations and political action committees that have dominated presidential campaigns since 1960. It is the up-to-date telephone bank, the jet plane, and above all the computerized list of the names, addresses, and telephone numbers of potential workers and contributors that enable the large political action committees to function. Without telephones, jet travel, and word processors, would-be candidates would find it nearly impossible to assemble effective personal organizations during the year or two that precede an election campaign. Indeed, it is only with the aid of computers capable of generating tens or even hundreds of thousands of appeals for small donations that candidates for the presidential nominations are able to comply with contemporary campaign finance laws. And it is their personal organizations that enable candidates to take advantage of television and become independent of the established parties.[61]

The telephone and the computer also make possible one other new technology that has helped political leaders and political action committees to undermine the party system: the technology of opinion polling. During its long period of dominance, the national political party, built on a structure of state, county, and precinct-level party organizations, provided the best information about the voters' opinions. But the parties lost this advantage when social scientists developed systematic opinion surveys in the 1940s and 1950s. The rise of the pollster was made final and complete when the near-universal adoption of the telephone and the rapid development of computerized data processing facilities in the 1960s made it possible to conduct surveys with considerable reliability at a manageable cost. By the early 1960s candidates were turning to social scientists and professional pollsters for the information on voter preferences they had traditionally obtained from party leaders. Ten years later, Jimmy Carter relied more on his pollsters than on party leaders as he defined his campaign—and then his presidency.[62]

New technologies of communication and transportation—television, telephone, automobile, jet aircraft, computerized mailing list, opinion poll—have reinforced the institutional changes that have weakened American political parties since 1960. Earlier technological innovations—the party newspaper, scheduled stagecoach, and railroad—similarly reinforced the new organizations that created the American two-party system in the 1820s and 1830s. Lest the argument presented here seem closer to technological determinism than is intended, it may be well to conclude with the point that new technologies do nothing more than create new resources. Political leaders and ordinary citizens then use these resources in the pursuit of their own objectives.

For the past twenty years, new technologies have strengthened the hands of those who worked against the two-party system based on long-established local and state political organizations. In the mid-1980s, however, there are signs that leaders of the national (if not the state or local) parties may be finding ways to turn contemporary technology to their own advantage. First the Republicans and then the Democrats have made significant efforts to maintain computerized lists of contributors, advertise the *party* through the mass media, carry out regular opinion surveys for party members, and provide a wide variety of modern, professional services to candidates throughout the nation.[63] It is not yet clear whether the parties will strengthen themselves sufficiently to create a new two-party system like the half-dozen that succeeded one another between 1828 and 1968. Whether they succeed will depend not so much on the nature of modern technology as on the uses men and women learn to make of it.

Notes

1. James Bryce, *The American Commonwealth*, 2d ed. (London: Macmillan, 1891), 1:5, 2:3.
2. E. E. Schattschneider, *Party Government* (New York: Farrar and Rinehart, 1942), p. 1, quoted in Hofstadter, *The Idea of a Party System: The Rise of Legitimate Opposition in the United States, 1780–1840* (Berkeley: University of California Press, 1970), p. 7.

3. "Toward a More Responsible Two-Party System: A Report of the Committee on Political Parties, American Political Science Association," *American Political Science Review* (September 1950, supplement), 44:15. Italics in the original. Quoted in Austin Ranney, *Curing the Mischiefs of Faction: Party Reform in America* (Berkeley: University of California Press, 1975), p. 6.

4. Richard Hofstadter, *The Idea of a Party System*, pp. 71–72.

5. David S. Broder, *The Party's Over: The Failure of Politics in America* (New York: Harper and Row, 1971); Martin P. Wattenberg, *The Decline of American Political Parties, 1952–1980* (Cambridge: Harvard University press, 1984).

6. Walter Dean Burnham, "The Appearance and Disappearance of the American Voter," in Burnham, *The Current Crisis in American Politics* (New York: Oxford University Press, 1982), pp. 121–165.

7. Nelson W. Polsby, *Consequences of Party Reform* (New York: Oxford University Press, 1983), p. 132.

8. E. E. Schattschneider, *The Semisovereign People* (New York: Holt, Rinehart, and Winston, 1960), pp. 60, 57.

9. Leading contributions to the literature on party systems and critical elections in the United States start with V. O. Key, Jr., "A Theory of Critical Elections," *Journal of Politics* (February 1955), 17:3–18, and continue through the influential collection of essays in William Nisbet Chambers and Walter Dean Burnham, eds., *The American Party Systems* (New York: Oxford University Press, 1967) and Burnham's *Critical Elections and the Mainsprings of American Politics* (New York: Norton, 1970) and *The Current Crisis in American Politics*, to sophisticated reconsiderations of these notions by James L. Sundquist, *Dynamics of the Party System: Alignment and Realignment of Political Parties in the United States*, rev. ed. (Washington, D.C.: Brookings Institution, 1983), and Jerome M. Clubb, William H. Flanigan, and Nancy H. Zingale, *Partisan Realignment: Voters, Parties, and Government in American History* (Beverly Hills: Sage Publications, 1980).

10. Richard L. Rubin has suggested as much in a broad survey of the interaction among *Press, Party, and Presidency* (New York: Norton, 1981).

11. Richard P. McCormick, *The Second Party System: Party Formation in the Jacksonian Era* (Chapel Hill: University of North Carolina Press, 1966), pp. 353–354.

12. *Ibid.*, p. 343.

13. Byron E. Shafer, *Quiet Revolution: The Struggle for the Democratic Party and the Shaping of Post-Reform Politics* (New York: Russell Sage Foundation, 1983), p. 6.

14. McCormick, *Second Party System*, p. 343.

15. Chilton Williamson, *American Suffrage from Property to Democracy, 1760–1860* (Princeton: Princeton University Press, 1960). In New York, to take the example of one of the most populous states, the restriction of the vote to freeholders was removed in 1821.

16. Burnham, "The Appearance and Disappearance of the American Voter," p. 129; McCormick, *Second Party System*, pp. 350–351.

17. McCormick, *Second Party System*, pp. 333–342. Chilton Williamson similarly found that "western [constitutional] conventions drew liberally upon the institutions and practices of the seaboard." *American Suffrage*, p. 217.

18. Allan R. Pred, *Urban Growth and the Circulation of Information: The United States System of Cities, 1790–1840* (Cambridge: Harvard University Press, 1973), pp. 145–146, 181.

19. Bernard A. Weisberger, *The American Newspaperman* (Chicago: University of Chicago Press, 1961), pp. 52–53, 73–74.

20. Frank Luther Mott, *American Journalism, A History of Newspapers in the United States Through 260 Years: 1690 to 1950*, rev. ed. (New York: Macmillan, 1950), p. 400; Stephen Hess and Milton Kaplan, *The Ungentlemanly Art: A History of American Political Cartoons* (New York: Macmillan, 1975), p. 50.

21. Weisberger, *American Newspaperman*, pp. 93–98.

22. Pred, *Urban Growth and the Circulation of Information*, p. 21. Weisberger, *American Newspaperman*, p. 65.

23. Alfred McClung Lee, *The Daily Newspaper in America: The Evolution of a Social Instrument* (New York: Macmillan, 1937), p. 59, cited in Rubin, *Press, Party, and Presidency*, p. 8.

24. For an excellent survey of political subsidies to the press, see Rubin, *Press, Party, and Presidency*, chs. 2 and 3.

25. Mott, *American Journalism*, p. 216.

26. *Democratic Review* (April, 1852), 30:359, 361, quoted in Mott, *American Journalism*, p. 253.

27. Alexis de Tocqueville, *Democracy in America*, Phillips Bradley, ed. (New York: Knopf, 1945), 2:119–120.

28. Weisberger, *American Newspaperman*, p. 78; according to Robert A. Rutland, "newspapers catapulted Jackson into the White House," *The Newsmongers: Journalism in the Life of the Nation, 1690–1972* (New York: Dial Press, 1973), p. 112.

29. V. O. Key, *Public Opinion and American Democracy* (New York, 1961), p. 393, quoted in Rutland, *The Newsmongers*, p. 84. Rubin asserts that "by sharply politicizing and polarizing political elites and rank and file, the partisan press deepened political cleavages and provided a key stimulant for mass mobilization" during the 1820s and 1830s. Rubin, *Press, Party, and Presidency*, p. 18.

30. Mott, *American Journalism*, pp. 220–241; Pred, *Urban Growth and the Circulation of Information*, p. 21.

31. *The New Encyclopedia Britannica*, 15th ed. (Chicago: Encyclopedia Britannica, 1984), 14:1056.

32. Rubin, *Press, Party, and Presidency*, p. 49.

33. Weisberger, *American Newspaperman*, pp. 95, 98; Mott, *American Journalism*, pp. 238, 242–243. These generalizations about the political orientation of the penny press of the 1830s are based primarily on Frank Luther Mott's indefatigable reading; no one seems to have applied to these papers the content-analysis techniques employed so fruitfully by Richard L. Merritt in *Symbols of American Community, 1735–1775* (New Haven: Yale University Press, 1966).

34. Weisberger, *American Newspaperman*, p. 108.

35. Michael Wallace, "Changing Concepts of Party in the United States: New York, 1815–1828," *American Historical Review* (December 1968), 74:458–468.

36. Wallace, "Changing Concepts of Party," p. 464.

37. Mott, *American Journalism*, p. 254.

38. Rubin, *Press, Party, and Presidency*, p. 38.

39. Mott, *American Journalism*, p. 168; Weisberger, *American Newspaperman*, pp. 78–84. For minor party figures, Weisberger notes, the party paper "was not only a propaganda sheet but a kind of continuing "communique" from headquarters; *American Newspaperman*, p. 81.

40. Shafer, "Reform and Alienation: The Decline of Intermediation in the Politics of Presidential Selection," *Journal of Law & Politics*, (Fall 1983), 1:93–132, and *Quiet Revolution, passim*; Polsby, *Consequences of Party Reform*, ch. 10.

41. Morris Janowtiz, *The Last Half-Century: Societal Change and Politics in America* (Chicago: University of Chicago Press, 1978); Samuel P. Huntington, *American Politics:*

The Promise of Disharmony (Cambridge: Harvard University Press, 1981); Burnham, *The Current Crisis in American Politics.*

42. Burnham, *The Current Crisis in American Politics;* Huntington, *American Politics: The Promise of Disharmony;* Paul Kleppner, *Who Voted? The Dynamics of Electoral Turnout, 1870–1980* (New York: Praeger, 1982); Norman H. Nie, Sidney Verba, and John R. Petrocik, *The Changing American Voter,* enl. ed. (Cambridge: Harvard University Press, 1979); Sundquist, *Dynamics of the Party System;* J. Morgan Kousser, "Voters, Absent and Present," *Social Science History* (1985), 9:215–227.

43. Shafer, *Quiet Revolution,* p. 4; Polsby, *Consequences of Party Reform;* Wattenberg, *Decline of American Political Parties;* Ranney, *Curing the Mischiefs of Faction.*

44. Burnham, "The Appearance and Disappearance of the American Voter," in Burnham, *The Current Crisis in American Politics,* pp. 121–165; U.S. Bureau of the Census, *Statistical Abstract of the United States, 1981* (Washington, D.C.: Bureau of the Census, 1981), p. 496, table 824.

45. Wattenberg, *The Decline of American Political Parties,* p. 19. Wattenberg identifies similar trends in voting for senatorial and local candidates. Although there was some increase in ticket splitting between 1944 and 1960, the clearest break with the old pattern came in 1960; p. 21.

46. Wattenberg, *The Decline of American Political Parties,* p. 23.

47. *Ibid.,* p. 69.

48. Polsby, *Consequences of Party Reform,* p. 9.

49. Schattschneider, *Party Government,* p. 64, quoted in Wattenberg, *The Decline of American Political Parties,* p. 74.

50. Polsby, *Consequences of Party Reform,* p. 72. The fullest account of "the diminution, the constriction, at times the elimination, of the regular party in the politics of presidential selection" is Byron Shafer, *Quiet Revolution.* Also relevant is Jeane J. Kirkpatrick, *Dismantling the Parties: Reflections on Party Reform and Party Decomposition* (Washington, D.C.: American Enterprise Institute, 1978).

51. Ranney, "The Political Parties: Reform and Decline," in Anthony King, ed., *The New American Political System* (Washington, D.C.: American Enterprise Institute, 1978), p. 215; for Ranney's role in the reforms that changed the role of the parties see his *Curing the Mischiefs of Faction.*

52. The quoted statement was made by James A. Baker, III, campaign manager for George Bush in 1980, in Shafer, "Reform and Alienation," p. 113.

53. For discussions of these turn-of-the-century reforms in voting procedures, see J. Morgan Kousser, *The Shaping of Southern Politics: Suffrage Restriction and the Establishment of the One-Party South* (New Haven: Yale University Press, 1974); Peter H. Argersinger, "A Place on the Ballot: Fusion Politics and Antifusion Laws," *American Historical Review* (April 1980), 85:287–306; Herbert J. Bass, "The Politics of Ballot Reform in New York State, 1888–1890," *New York History* (July 1961), pp. 253–72; Richard L. McCormick, *From Realignment to Reform: Political Change in New York State, 1893–1910* (Ithaca: Cornell University Press, 1981); and David C. Hammack, *Power and Society: Greater New York at the Turn of the Century* (New York: Russell Sage Foundation, 1982), pp. 54, 100, 129, 321.

54. Shafer, "Reform and Alienation," pp. 116, 130, *et passim,* and *Quiet Revolution;* also relevant is Polsby, *Consequences of Party Reform,* pp. 132 ff.

55. For a particularly careful and persuasive analysis of the political content of television news, see Michael J. Robinson and Margaret A. Sheehan, *Over the Wire and on TV: CBS and UPI in Campaign '80* (New York: Russell Sage Foundation, 1983). Martin P. Wattenberg's *Decline of Political Parties,* ch. 6, also contains a very good discussion. Other important studies are those of Doris A. Graber, *Mass Media and American*

Politics, 2d ed. (Washington, D.C.: Congressional Quarterly, 1984); Thomas Patterson and Robert McClure, *The Unseeing Eye: The Myth of Television Power in National Elections* (New York: Putnam, 1976); and Patterson, *The Mass Media Election: How Americans Choose Their President* (New York: Praeger, 1980). Content analysis of election news began in the 1940s with the classic studies of newspapers by Paul Lazarsfeld, Bernard Berelson, and Hazel Gaudet, *The People's Choice,* 3d ed. (New York: Columbia University Press, 1968), and Berelson, Lazarsfeld, and William McPhee, *Voting* (Chicago: University of Chicago Press, 1954).

56. The best discussion of the stance of the leaders of television news is Robinson and Sheehan, *Over the Wire and on TV.* Herbert J. Gans studied the content of television news and of *Time* and *Newsweek,* and came to the conclusion that the news presented in all these instruments shares, he says, a "common advocacy of honest, meritocratic, and anti-bureaucratic government" as well as an "antipathy to political machines and demagogues, particularly of populist bent." Gans, *Deciding What's News* (New York: Pantheon, 1979), p. 69. As Gans points out, these values "are very much like the values of the Progressive movement of the early twentieth century." Another useful discussion is Polsby, *Consequences of Party Reform,* pp. 142–146.

57. Wattenberg, *The Decline of American Political Parties,* p. 90.

58. The following table demonstrates the critical increase in the diffusion of new communications and transportation technology between 1950 and 1960:

Percent of U.S. Households Owning Selected Items, 1940–1980

	1940	1950	1960	1970	1980
Automobiles	40	59	77	82	84
Telephones	37	62	79	91	96
Television Sets	—	9	87	95	98

Source: U.S. Bureau of the Census, *Historical Statistics of the United States, Colonial Times to 1970* (Washington, D.C.; GPO, 1975), pp. 717, 783; *Statistical Abstract, 1981,* pp. 559, 628.

During this period, daily newspaper circulation per capita declined from .35 in 1950 to .28 in 1980, while the total number of domestic airline revenue passenger miles increased from 8 billion in 1950 to 254 billion in 1980. *Statistical Abstract, 1981,* pp. 559, 642.

59. Anthony Smith, *Goodbye Gutenberg: The Newspaper Revolution of the 1980s* (New York: Oxford University Press, 1980), offers a sweeping interpretation of the impact of recent technological and market forces on American newspapers.

60. Polsby, *Consequences of Party Reform,* p. 138.

61. For a general description of the campaign finance reform laws, see Shafer, "Reform and Alienation," pp. 107–108; for an extended discussion, see Michael J. Malbin, ed., *Parties, Interest Groups, and Campaign Finance Laws* (Washington, D.C.: American Enterprise Institute, 1980). Malbin's own contribution to that volume, "Of Mountains and Molehills: PACs, Campaigns, and Public Policy," is an excellent introduction to its subject. Also useful are Theodore J. Eismeier and Phillip H. Pollock, III, "Political Action Committees: Varieties of Organization and Strategy," and Margaret Ann Latus, "Assessing Ideological PACs: From Outrage to Understanding," in Malbin, ed., *Money and Politics in the United States: Financing Elections in the 1980s* (Washington, D.C.: American Enterprise Institute, 1984); and Larry Sabato, "Parties, PACs, and Independent Groups," in Thomas E. Mann and Norman J. Ornstein, eds., *The American Elections of 1982* (Washington, D.C.: American Enterprise Institute, 1983).

62. A brief overview of the history and use of public opinion surveys in American politics is contained in Philip M. Hauser, *Social Statistics in Use* (New York: Russell Sage Foundation, 1975), chs. 14 and 15.

63. David Adamany, ''Political Parties in the 1980s,'' in Malbin, *Money and Politics*, pp. 95–115.

6. The Impact of Technological Change on Urban Form

Kenneth T. Jackson
Columbia University

The shape of cities, indeed their very existence and growth, is in large measure a function of technological development. Before the invention of even simple agricultural tools and methods, primitive man was nomadic, moving regularly from place to place, collecting berries and fruits, and stalking small animals and fish for sustenance. As long as there was no surplus to barter for more desirable goods, permanent settlements were impossible. As Lewis Mumford tells us, the first cities were places of the dead, to which wandering peoples would return periodically to visit the graves of their parents or children.[1]

With the passage of several millennia, farming was introduced, small agricultural surpluses appeared, and for the first time towns began to dot the planet. Uncertainty surrounds the founding of the first cities, but historians of the ancient world report that Ur and Babylon, as well as several other Near Eastern cities, had populations in the tens of thousands by 2500 B.C., and that as many as a million people lived within the gates of Rome during the lifetime of Jesus Christ.

In order to evaluate the impact of technology upon urban form we can do no better than to return to the classification scheme of epochs devised by the great Scottish planner Sir Patrick Geddes and modified by Lewis Mumford. According to this model, the history of towns can be divided into three successive, but overlapping and interpenetrating, phases: the eotechnic, the paleotechnic, and the neotechnic. Each produced a different type of urban settlement and both internal structure and outer form responded to technological innovation.[2]

The eotechnic period lasted essentially from the great age of Rome until about 1750. It was characterized by the handicraft industry, the use of materials made of wood and glass, and the exploitation of wind and water as nonanimate energy sources. Urbanization in this epoch occurred at a very slow rate, and indeed for much of the period cities actually declined in population and influence. Rome, for example, fell drastically from about one million to as few as 40,000 inhabitants. Mechanical innovations were infrequent, although both the clock and the printing press date from these years.

The paleotechnic epoch, which began in the middle of the eighteenth century and continued through the nineteenth century, witnessed a quickening in pace of technological change and urban growth. The prime energy source in this period was coal, the most characteristic invention was the steam engine, and the dominant materials were iron and steel. Urban form during this 150-year era underwent more drastic changes than had occurred in all previous years combined. There were two important categories of technological innovation which brought about this fundamental reordering of urban form. In the first place, we can point to changes in transportation and communication technology. In this regard, the development of public transit systems in cities and the improvement in telecommunications via the telegraph and telephone were paramount. In the second place, there were changes in industrial and building technology of a revolutionary nature. The development of a cheap and inexpensive method of making steel, coupled with the successful demonstration of the metal cage theory of skyscraper construction, made possible the vertical city that was to be so characteristic of the twentieth century.

The neotechnic epoch is that with which we are most familiar. Energy now comes primarily from oil and natural gas, and the prime mover of people has become the internal combustion engine. Similarly, the shift from steam to electric power had a crucial impact upon industrial location. During the paleotechnic period, for example, when steam engines were the chief power source for factories (and as late as 1914 they still supplied 70 percent of installed primary power in manufacturing) power was distributed from a single engine by means of inumerable shafts, pulleys, and belts. Factories were best built several stories high, and the best locations for such activities were sites near the central business district.

As the neotechnic period took hold, however, electric motors took over. In this new world, each machine could have its own motor drive, and a single-story building would be more efficient in terms of materials handling, especially with the development of forklift trucks and large trailer vehicles. Thus, the electric motor, when coupled with the moving assembly line, caused industry to seek space on the urban periphery (where land was cheaper) for its long, low, one-story structures. The automobile and more importantly the truck provided the necessary flow of labor and materials to the new manufacturing locations.[3]

Because technological innovations were more frequent and more significant after 1815, it should not be surprising that the basic form of cities changed more between 1815 and 1985 than in all the forty-five hundred or so previous years of urban settlement on the planet. This can be demonstrated by reviewing the five spatial characteristics shared by every major city in the world in 1815. When wind, muscle, and water were the prime movers of Western civilization, the easiest, cheapest, and most common method of getting about was by foot. It is appropriate, therefore, to refer to such preindustrial agglomerations as "walking cities."[4]

The first important characteristic of the walking city was congestion. When Queen Victoria was born in 1819, London had about 800,000 residents and was the largest city on earth. Yet an individual could easily walk the three miles from Paddington, Kensington, Hammersmith, and Fulham, then on the very edge of the city, to the center in only two hours. In Liverpool, Birmingham, Manchester, and Glasgow, the area of new building was not even two miles from the city hall. On the European continent, where medieval fortifications typically posed barriers to outward expansion, as in Vienna, Berlin, and Verdun, the compact nature of life was equally pronounced. Gross densities normally exceeded 75,000 per square mile and were rarely less than 35,000 per square mile, which is about the level of crowding in New York City in the 1980s. Although North American cities were newer and smaller than their European counterparts early in the nineteenth century, they exhibited the same degree of intense, inner-city congestion.

The second important characteristic of the walking city was the clear distinction between city and country. In part, this was a legacy from earlier centuries, when the walls of a community were inviolable, indeed almost sacred. Even in the New World, where walls were less common, there was no blurring of urban-rural boundaries, and there were no signs announcing the entrance of a traveler into a community. Before the age of technological change, a sharp-edged dot on the map was an accurate symbol for a city. There was an obvious visual distinction between the closely built-up residential precincts of a city and whatever rural sections surrounded it, and there were no fast food restaurants and motels stretching far along the radial highways.

The third important characteristic of the walking city was its mixture of functions. Except for waterfront warehousing and red-light districts there were no neighborhoods exclusively given over to commercial, office, or residential functions. Factories were almost nonexistent, and production took place in the small shops of artisans.

The fourth important characteristic of the walking city was the short journey to work of its inhabitants. In 1815, even in the largest cities, only about one person in fifty traveled as much as one mile to his place of employment. Work and living spaces were often completely integrated, with members of the family, as well as apprentices, literally living above or behind the place of employment.

The final important characteristic of the walking city was the tendency of the most fashionable and respectable addresses to be located close to the center of town. In Europe, this affinity for the city's core represented the continuation of a tradition that dated back thousands of years. To be a resident of a big town was to enjoy the best of life, to have a place in man's true home. Although American cities were not rigidly segregated by class before 1815, and the poor often lived in alleys hard by the more opulent dwellings of the wealthy, there were clear indications that the suburbs were in every way inferior to the core of the city. The word itself had strong pejorative connotations. Ralph Waldo Emerson referred to the "suburbs and outskirts of things," while Nathaniel Parker Willis lamented that, in comparison to England, America had "sunk from the stranger to the suburban or provincial."

The Erosion of the Walking City

Between 1815 and 1875, large cities, especially in the United States and Great Britain and to a lesser extent in Europe, underwent a dramatic spatial change. The power of steam and new machinery transformed nineteenth-century society. Enormous growth to metropolitan size was accompanied by functional differentiation, and neighborhoods, individuals, and activities were affected in nonrandom ways. Cities were turned inside out as a new pattern of peripheral affluence and center despair began to emerge. The shift was not sudden, but it was no less profound for its gradual character. Indeed, the phenomenon was one of the most important in the history of society, for it represented the most fundamental realignment of urban structure in the forty-five-hundred-year past of cities.

In addition to the redistribution of the highest socioeconomic groups outward, four other patterns were also developing by 1875. First, peripheral areas were growing more rapidly than core cities. Second, the density curve began to level out. Third, the innermost sections of large American cities were experiencing an absolute loss in population by 1860. Fourth, middle-class citizens were commuting increasing distances to work.

New Forms of Transportation Technology

The half century between 1810 and 1860 witnessed the introduction of the steam ferry, omnibus, commuter railroad, and horsecar. These innovations gave additional impetus to an urban exodus that would remake the spatial patterns of large cities, and inaugurated an era of greater separation between classes and races. The result was hailed as the inevitable outcome of the desirable segregation of commercial from residential areas and of the disadvantaged from the more comfortable. Frederick Law Olmsted wrote that the city, no less than the private home, had to be divided into various segments which could perform specialized functions.

The Time of the Trolley

The generation after the Civil War was notable for the wave of invention which transformed the ways in which middle-class people lived and worked. Among the more notable developments were the air brake (Westinghouse, 1868), the electric light (Edison, 1879), the telephone (Bell, 1876), the small camera (Eastman, 1888), the fountain pen (Waterman, 1894), the adding machine (Burroughs, 1885), the linotype (Mergenthaler, 1885), the pneumatic tire (Dunlop, 1888), and the zipper (Judson, 1891). Some insight into the nature of the momentous changes involved is suggested by contrasting the ages of steam and electronics: heat, sweat, and grime gave way to the cool glitter of the metropolis at night, to the glistening, mathematically perfect shapes of mass-produced alloys, to the button-pushing leverage of new sources of energy. No invention, however, had a greater impact on the European and American city between 1885 and 1920 than the visible and noisy streetcar and the tracks that snaked down the broad avenues into undeveloped land.[5]

The cable car was actually the first successful application of mechanical power to the problems of intraurban transport. Developed first in New York City in 1869, it had a number of advantages over the only available alternative—the horsecar. The cable car was cleaner (no dirt or cinders and no stable stench), quieter (most of the gear was underground), and more powerful (it could easily carry heavy loads up the steepest grades). As an added benefit, it involved no cruelty to man's faithful friend, the horse.

Over the long term, however, the disadvantages of the cable car were more weighty than its advantages. The most serious problem was its enormous capital cost. Another major difficulty was inefficient operation—more than 95 percent of the power was expended to move the cable alone. A third major problem was the cable itself. With annoying frequency, conductors were unable to disengage their grips.

The electric streetcar, also known as the trolley, was developed in the 1880's by many inventors, most of them working alone. The most successful of the early trolley ventures and the one that would spawn a revolution in urban transport was that of Frank Julian Sprague. He founded the Sprague Electric Railway and Motor Company in 1884, and entered into an agreement in 1887 with the Richmond Union Passenger Railway to devise a system that would serve Virginia's largest city in its entirety. Although the Richmond undertaking cost Sprague more money than he made on it, the well-publicized attempt to move many cars simultaneously by means of overhead wires demonstrated the feasibility of transit electrification on a broad scale. Thereafter, Richmond became a temporary mecca for railway investors and operators. By the turn of the century, half the streetcar systems in the United States were equipped by Sprague, and 90 percent were using his patents.

Pollution-free electric traction possessed many advantages. Faster than either the cable car or the horse-drawn tram, it raised the potential speed of city travel to 20 miles per hour (the average was 10–15 miles per hour), and was capable of additional acceleration in low-density or undeveloped areas. Similarly, it achieved substantial economies over alternative forms of transit. It required neither the extensive underground paraphernalia of the cable car nor the heavy investment in animals, feed, and stables of the horsecar. Because the trolleys themselves tended to be larger than the horse trams, the cost per passenger mile was reduced by at least half, and the average price of a fare dropped from a dime to a nickel.

The American people especially embraced the trolley with extraordinary rapidity and enthusiasm. In 1890, when the federal government first canvassed the nation's rail systems, it enumerated 5,700 miles of horsecar track, 500 miles of cable cars, and 1,260 miles for the trolley. By 1893, only six years after Frank Sprague's successful Richmond experiment, more than 250 electric railways had been incorporated in the United States, and more than 60 percent of the nation's 12,000 miles of track had been electrified. By the end of 1903, America's 30,000 miles of track was 98 percent electrified. Meanwhile, the proportion of cable mileage had fallen from 6 percent to 1 percent and that of horsecar mileage from 69 percent to 1 percent. It was, as a distinguished transportation historian has written, "one of the most rapidly accepted innovations in the history of technology." By comparison, the automobile, which was invented at about the same time, was a late bloomer.

The rapidity of the American adoption of the trolley was especially striking in comparison with Great Britain and Europe. In 1890, for example, the number of passengers carried on American street railways (including cable and elevated systems) was more than two billion per year, or more than twice that of the rest of the world combined. In cities of more than 100,000 inhabitants, the average number of rides per person each year was 172, a figure that included children and other persons who traveled scarcely at all. Berlin, which had the best system in Europe, would have ranked no higher than twenty-second in the United States. At the turn of the century, when the horsecar had virtually disappeared from American streets, it remained the dominant form of urban transport in Britain. In Tokyo, the electric streetcar did not make its first appearance until 1903, and in 1911, its system was less than one-tenth as large as that of New York City.

Streetcar Technology and the Spatial Distribution of Economic Activity

In the nineteenth-century metropolis, industrial location was largely determined by steamships and railroads. Only where they met could factories assemble the masses of coal—their driving power—and the basic raw materials necessary to fuel industrial enterprise. And only at the railroad-navigable waterway juncture could factories ship products to distant markets. The trolley did not affect this equation, except to make it easier for workers to reach the plant from more distant residences. This simply created more favorable conditions for factories, a point noted by Edward Ewing Pratt in his 1911 study of *Industrial Causes of Concentration of Population in New York City.*[6]

As more steam railroad lines were built late in the nineteenth century, however, more intersections of freight-hauling tracks were created. At these nodal points, new factory locations became possible, and more regional industrial activity moved away from the core city. Olivier Zunz has carefully detailed this process for Detroit, showing how the manufacturing enterprises of the Motor City tended toward the crossing of railroads in the years between 1880 and 1920. A few older concerns continued to reflect the industrial design of the past and remained downtown, but industries that required a great deal of space and those dealing with warehousing activities moved away from the core, where there was room to expand.[7]

The central business districts of large cities thrived during the time of the trolley. There were many centralizing forces unrelated to the electrification of public transport. The steel-frame skyscraper, developed in the last two decades of the nineteenth century, was the perfect physical embodiment of the heavily centralized city. The telephone and the elevator made life in tall buildings bearable and possible, as did the electric light bulb. But the extraordinary prosperity and vitality of most urban cores between 1890 and 1950 cannot be understood without reference to the streetcar systems. Unlike the railroads, the streetcars penetrated to the very heart of the city. The tracks radiated out from the center like spokes on a wheel, tying residential areas far distant to the heart of the metropolis. Because the routes almost always led downtown, with only an occasional cross-town or lateral line, the practical effect was to force almost anyone using public transit to rely on the central business district.[8]

The New Age of Automobility

It was not clear early in the twentieth century what shape the automotive future might take. The costs associated with driving fell between 1900 and 1970. In conjunction with better roads and the abundant fuel that became available following the 1906 Spindletop discoveries in Texas, the motor vehicle lowered the marginal cost of transportation. This meant that once a household had purchased a motor vehicle, short trips were cheap, and children and spouses could be transported without the additional fare that would have been necessary on a streetcar. Automotive families had neither to wait nor to walk. New possibilities in shopping, living, and working were opened. In 1925, Columbia University sociologists Robert and Helen Lynd completed the field work for their now classic study of "Middletown." In all six areas of social life in Muncie, Indiana, the private car played either a contributing or a dominant role.

The automobile made it infinitely easier to commute in directions perpendicular to the trolley tracks. But of even greater significance in changing the way city people lived and worked was the truck. Even in its primitive form before World War I, the truck could do four times the work of a horse-drawn wagon which took up the same street space, and as engines became more powerful the truck became a marvel of efficiency. Prior to 1916, when there was only one truck for every ten thousand Americans, factories clustered around the rail junctions of large cities. As Joel Tarr has pointed out, it was essentially easier and more economical to move people in and out of the core by public transit than it was to move freight by horses and wagons to and from scattered businesses. Thus, workers fanned out in the metropolis while factories crowded near the rail junctions.

Industry, which had not historically been associated with cities in the age of wind and sail, began moving from the urban cores even at the height of the age of steam power. The high price and scarcity of land in central areas, coupled with municipal regulations and taxes, were important encouragements to dispersal. In 1859, for example, the Boudinot Mill in Paterson, New Jersey was transplanted from the center of the city to the open land of the periphery. And in 1873, the Singer Sewing Machine Company pulled out of Manhattan for more space in bucolic Elizabeth. (Elizabeth was not so bucolic in 1982, when Singer closed its big plant after one-hundred-nine years of continuous operation, allegedly because of foreign competition.)[9]

With the twentieth century came the electrical revolution. The typical power unit was no longer a steam engine, but a thousand horsepower turbogenerator. Most importantly, electric power transmission and the introduction of small electric motors to replace large steam machines altered the technology of factory manufacture by making it more economical to build single-story rather than multistory plants.

Trucks greatly stimulated a tendency that was already well under way. They were not generally available before 1910, but their impact was rapid. Richard Schaeffer and Elliot Sclar have calculated that manufacturing employment in Boston's inner ring grew much faster than those either closer in or farther out between 1909 and 1919. Between 1915 and 1930, when the number of American trucks jumped from 158,000 to 3.5 million and the proportion of trucks to private automobiles doubled, industrial deconcentration began to alter the basic spatial pattern of metropolitan areas. In conjunction with better highways and new methods of materials handling that emphasized one-story manufacture, the truck created a new efficiency for outlying industries that was not matched by similar economies in inner city operations. Between 1920 and 1930, the proportion of factory employment located in central cities declined in every city of more than 100,000 residents in the United States.[10]

Conclusion

The densely concentrated cities of the nineteenth century, with their industries, stores, and offices crowded together toward the middle, were a short-lived phenomenon brought on by the fact that inter-urban transportation was better than intra-urban transportation. The automobile so vastly changed the equation that it had a greater social and spatial impact on cities than any technological innovation since the development of the wheel. As early as 1938, William F. Ogburn wrote that "the invention of the automobile has had more influence on society than the combined exploits of Napoleon, Genghis Khan, and Julius Caesar," and in 1975, James J. Flink concluded that Henry Ford's major contributions—the moving assembly line, five dollar day, and Model T—had affected America more in the twentieth century than the Progressive Era and the New Deal combined. The liberation of our culture from the limitations of horse-drawn transport has yet to receive analytical treatment, however. Walter Prescott Webb showed the consequences of barbed wire, the revolver, and the windmill on the Great Plains; William F. Ogburn has analyzed the impact of the radio and the airplane, and Lynn White has imaginatively written of the importance of the stirrup. But no one has yet gone beyond Flink's provocative *The Car Culture* and attempted to resolve the persistent paradox of the American love affair with the car and the less happy assessment of what happens to the environment when a society takes to the road.

No other invention has altered urban form more than the internal combustion engine. The automobile allowed its owner to leave and return when he wanted, and along routes of his own choosing. Public transport, which had only recently broken the historic and close connection between work and residence, no longer seemed so attractive or wonderful. Some observers of this shift have argued that the car is creating a new and better urban environment, and that the change in spatial scale, based upon swift transportation, is forming a new kind of organic entity which will render obsolete the older urban forms.

Lewis Mumford, the most productive and intelligent urban historian of the twentieth century, has persuasively disagreed with the disciples of modernity. Writing from his small town retreat in Amenia, New York, he has suggested instead that technological change is destroying the very meaning of the city. His prize-winning book, *The City in History*, was a celebration of the medieval community and an excoriation of "the formless urban exudation" that he saw American cities becoming. He noted that the automobile metropolis was not a final stage in city development, but an anti-city which "annihilates the city whenever it collides with it."

Notes

1. Lewis Mumford has thought and written as much about the influence of technology upon urban form as any person. Among his major publications in this area are: *Technics and Civilization* (New York: Harcourt, Brace and World, 1934); *The Highway and the City* (New York: Harcourt, Brace and World, 1963); and *The Myth of the Machine: The Pentagon of Power* (New York: Harcourt Brace Jovanovich, 1970).

2. I am particularly indebted to Joel Tarr of Carnegie-Mellon University for sharing his insights with me on this topic. Among his many publications in this field, I have found his *Transportation Innovation and Changing Spatial Patterns: Pittsburgh, 1850–1910* (Pittsburgh: Transportation Research Institute of Carnegie-Mellon University, 1972) especially useful.

3. A thoughtful recent treatment of changing attitudes toward technology through the perspective of American visionaries is Howard P. Segal, *Technological Utopianism in American Culture* (Chicago: University of Chicago Press, 1985).

4. My own attitudes about technology and the city are summed up in Kenneth T. Jackson, *Crabgrass Frontier: The Suburbanization of the United States* (New York: Oxford University Press, 1985), especially chs. 2, 5, 6, 9, 13, 14, 15, and 16.

5. The classic work on urban transportation remains Sam Bass Warner, Jr., *Streetcar Suburbs: The Process of Growth in Boston, 1870–1900* (Cambridge: Harvard University Press, 1962). Other distinguished books on this subject include John P. McKay, *Tramways and Trolleys: The Rise of Urban Mass Transport in Europe* (Princeton: Princeton University Press, 1976); Edward S. Mason, *The Street Railway in Massachusetts: The Rise and Decline of an Industry* (Cambridge: Harvard University Press, 1932). Carl W. Condit, *The Railroad and the City: A Technological and Urbanistic History of Cincinnati* (Columbus: Ohio State University Press, 1977); and Clay McShane, *Technology and Reform: Street Railways and the Growth of Milwaukee, 1887–1900* (Madison: State Historical Society of Wisconsin, 1974).

6. Edward Ewing Pratt, *Industrial Causes of Congestion of Population in New York City* (New York: Columbia University Press, 1911).

7. Olivier Zunz, *The Changing Face of Inequality: Urbanization, Industrial Development, and Immigrants in Detroit, 1880–1920* (Chicago: University of Chicago Press, 1982).

8. On the suburbanizing influence of the streetcar systems, see Jackson, *Crabgrass Frontier*, ch. 6; Robert M. Fogelson, *The Fragmented Metropolis: Los Angeles, 1850–1930* (Cambridge: Harvard University Press, 1968); and Roderick S. French, "Chevy Chase Village in the Context of the National Suburban Movement, 1870–1900," *Records of the Columbia Historical Society* (1973–1974), 49:300–329.

9. The best work on industrial deconcentration is Leon Moses and Harold F. Williamson, "The Location of Economic Activities in Cities," *American Economic Review*, (May 1967), 57:214–215. See also James B. Kenyon, *Industrial Location and Metropolitan Growth: The Paterson-Passaic District* (Chicago: University of Chicago Department of Geography Research Study No. 67, 1960); and Victor R. Fuchs, *Changes in the Location of Manufacturing in the United States Since 1929* (New Haven: Yale University Press, 1962), pp. 90–95.

10. The best overview of this topic is K. H. Schaeffer and Elliott Sclar, *Access for All: Transportation and Urban Growth* (Baltimore: Johns Hopkins University Press, 1975).

7. Technological Change and American Worker Movements, 1870–1970

Melvyn Dubofsky
State University of New York at Binghamton

Fernand Braudel has written that "technology is the queen: it is she who changes the world."[1] Few economic or modern historians would challenge that assertion. Indeed two of the most comprehensive and significant histories of economic development and growth in the modern era—David Landes' *The Unbound Prometheus*, (1969) and Alfred D. Chandler, Jr.'s *The Visible Hand*, (1977)—assign primary influence to technological innovations as the source of economic growth. Both Landes and Chandler see the past in much the same way. At some point in the late eighteenth century in Landes' history of economic growth and in the mid-nineteenth century in Chandler's history of the development of corporate enterprise, human existence moved onto a new course. In Landes' words, which Chandler would undoubtedly second, "the industrial revolution marked a major turning point in man's history. . . . It was the Industrial Revolution that initiated a cumulative, self-sustaining advance in technology whose repercussions would be felt in all aspects of economic life."[2]

As economies grew and developed and change begat change, the lives of working people inexorably altered. Industrialization and technological change created a new breed of worker, one habituated to the discipline of the time clock and the routines of the machine rather than the more irregular rhythms of nature and social tradition. If first-generation industrial workers had to learn a new way of life, their heirs did not have it easier. For one of the constants of economic development in the nineteenth and twentieth centuries was the cyclical regularity of technological innovation, which in changing how goods were produced transformed the way people labored. Not only did succeeding generations of workers tend to labor in different ways, fabricating new products with innovative machines; they toiled under changing systems of supervision for shifting forms of intrinsic and material rewards.

That technological change during the past two centuries has had an enormous impact on working people is without challenge. That trade unions have been simultaneously shaped by and themselves sought to control technology is also scarcely subject to serious doubt. Today, more clearly than ever, we can perceive aspects of that process. Two immediate examples may suffice as illustrations. In the late summer of 1983 employees of the American Telephone and Telegraph Company walked off their jobs when contract negotiations between their unions and the company collapsed. Although nearly one hundred percent of the production workers (operators, installers, linespeople, and repairers) struck, most users of the company's services remained unaffected. Modern communications technology enabled a smaller number of managerial and supervisory employees to provide satisfactorily all the services ordinarily performed by the great mass of strikers. About the same time a similar story repeated itself in New York City. There the local utility workers struck but they, too, failed to disrupt electrical and gas service to the city's consumers. Once again computerized communications and control systems enabled the utility company to operate effectively despite its employees' solidarity as strikers. On the one hand, then, contemporary, computerized technology rendered organized workers' ultimate weapon, the strike, relatively harmless. But on the other hand, the firms affected by the strikes, AT&T and Consolidated Edison, did not use their new technology to smash the unions as would undoubtedly have been the case at any other time between the 1870s and 1930s. Clearly, something decisive had changed which was related in yet little understood ways to the manner in which technology affected the distribution of power between capital and labor, employers and workers. Perhaps I can suggest some tentative hypotheses concerning the relationship between trade unions and technological change.

Today it can be said that we have a substantial body of literature concerning the impact of technology on work, if far less on the relationship between technology and trade unions. Ever since Harry Braverman published *Labor and Monopoly Capital* in 1974 a veritable subfield of the social sciences dedicated to the study of what is labeled "the labor process" has boomed. By now all must be familiar with Braverman's contention that the history of technological innovation under capitalism has been the unilinear story of labor's deskilling and the expropriation of workers' crafts and skills by managers and scientists in the service of capital. A whole school of scholars has built elaborations on Braverman's theory of the progressive degradation of labor under capitalism, from Stephen Marglin's analysis of English employers' attempts to deskill labor in the early industrialization of the seventeenth century to Katherine Stone's description of the tactics used by American steelmasters to eliminate all skills and autonomy on the job possessed by their employees.[3] All of these students of the labor process, unlike Landes and Chandler, see the primary impetus for technological change in capitalists' urge to control labor, and not in their desire to increase productivity through the application of science to industry.

Other scholars less prone to see technological innovation as a single-minded attempt by employers to deskill their workers and hence gain control over production nevertheless describe a similar process. Whether in David Brody's study of steelworkers in the nonunion era or Daniel Nelson's description of managerial reforms in the late nineteenth to early twentieth centuries, the result appears the same: innovation leads to the loss of skills which in turn causes workers to lose all or part of their autonomy and power on the job.[4] Indeed almost all of the literature on the history of work, in particular crafts or industries, describes a steady transformation of traditional patterns of work in which established skills are persistently diluted or erased.

Because most of the literature focuses on how old skills were diluted and not on how new ones emerged, much of what we know about the impact of technology on unions concerns traditional craft unions of skilled workers. We have case studies of the impact of technology on specific craft unions and their responses as well as more general models exploring the parameters of the craft unions' reactions to technological change. But we know less about the impact of technological change on the shape of the overall labor movement and how the labor movement as a whole has behaved under changing technologies.

At this point I prefer to venture an hypothesis to explain trade union behavior and how it relates to different historical periods. The strength of craft unions was based initially on their control over entry into the trades and hence on their ability to establish monopolies in the labor market. As long as employers could not produce profitably without the skills possessed by craft unionists, such workers could secure their jobs, statuses, and incomes through what Giovanni Arrighi defines as marketplace bargaining power (MBP). As technological change diluted existing skills, craft unionists lost both their strategic place in the shop or factory and their power in the labor market. In Arrighi's words:

The process is completed in machinofacture, which turns upside down the relationship between the workman and the means of production, transforming the former into an appendage/instrument of the latter. The expansion of capital is thus freed from its previous dependence on the personal strength and personal skill with which the detail workmen in manufacture, and the manual laborers in handicraft, wielded their implements. The MBP of workers, that is, as sellers of labor-power, is thus progressively undermined by the very process of capitalist accumulation.[5]

Yet, as workers lose their bargaining power in the market (MBP), they ineluctably regain it at the point of production (WBP). The ever growing division of labor in the factory, the increasing scale and complexity of factories and their machinery, and the concomitant concentration of workers in ever larger productive units make capital (employers) more vulnerable to work stoppages and passive forms of resistance at the shop-floor level. Moreover, the greater the organic value of the capital in an establishment the greater the damage created by an interruption or slowdown in production even by a small number of workers. Again, in Arrighi's words: "The downward tendency of labor's MPB, emphasized by Marxist theory, is thus always matched by an upward tendency of its WBP.[6]

Arrighi's hypothesis, which I find convincing in the abstract, presents problems when set to the test of history. The major difficulty is that the history of capitalism is so uneven that its development pattern or trajectory does indeed seem to follow what many Marxists refer to as "combined and uneven development." Technological change occurs at varying rates of speed in different sectors of the economy. Some craft workers see their skills eliminated by technology; others simultaneously find that technological change intensifies the demand for their labor. Some firms use the most innovative production methods; other firms in the same industry resist change and even remain profitable, for a time at least, under the old regime. And even the most modern, technologically advanced economy exhibits large pockets of traditional production. Thus it is impossible to state that from the 1870s, say, to the present all workers experienced a decline in MBP and a rise in WBP. Or that all craft workers had MBP and all machine operators had WBP. But by examining the history of American workers and their trade unions since the mid-nineteenth century, we can see under precisely what conditions or circumstances the hypothesis fits.

In seeking to periodize the history of technology's impact on American unions, we cannot do better than use the eras suggested in David Gordon, Richard Edwards, and Michael Reich's recent economic history of American labor, *Segmented Work, Divided Workers,* (1982). Their first period, the early 1800s through 1870s, what they label "initial proletarianization," saw little technological innovation or machine production outside the textile industry. Employers in this period transformed the labor process in various ways but seldom by technology. The second period, the 1870s through 1920s, what Gordon et al. call the era of "homogenization," saw technology thoroughly transform the manner in which work was done. The third period, from the 1930s through 1960s, which Gordon et al. label as "segmentation," resembled the first more than the second era. Employers continued to transform work but technology played a smaller role. In the third era, unlike the first, however, unions proved central to the reorganization of work and the discipline of labor. The final period, the 1960s to the present, lacks a rubric but is clearly a time, like era two, in which technology is transforming totally, if not revolutionizing, work.

What remains constant throughout the four periods and what I will be examining in more detail below is the one inescapable reality of American labor history, the never-ending struggle between workers and bosses for power. David Brody has put this point well. "The struggle of workers to retain a degree of job satisfaction, of managers to subordinate them to a rationalized system of production," he writes, "is a continuing story, and not one ending at any given stage of industrialism."[7]

For most of the nineteenth century advanced technology scarcely impinged on the world of the worker and trade unions. Skilled workers, the vast majority of all union members, either themselves owned the tools of production or controlled the actual process of production using tools and machines provided by the boss. Skill was acquired neither through formal schooling nor management-initiated training programs. Instead it was passed on through families—father to son or uncle to nephew—and union-controlled apprenticeship programs. The skilled workers who acquired the knowledge to puddle and mold iron, set type, cut garments, machine metal, blow glass, or brew beer, to name just a few of the multifarious skilled crafts in existence, were absolutely indispensable to production. Employers had no alternative source for the knowledge and skill possessed by craftsmen. David Montgomery describes the work routine of skilled unionized iron workers at a Columbus, Ohio mill in the 1870s:

The three twelve-man rolling teams, which constituted the union, negotiated a single tonnage rate with the company for each specific rolling job the company undertook. The workers then decided collectively, among themselves, what portion of that rate should go to each of them . . . how work should be allocated among them; how many rounds on the rolls should be undertaken each day; what special arrangements should be made for the fiercely hot labors of the hookers during the summer; and how members should be hired and progress through the various ranks of the gang. To put it another way, all the boss did was to buy the equipment and raw materials and sell the finished product.[8]

Despite some of the hyperbole in Montgomery's words, they contain a large measure of truth. Prior to the machine age, coal miners, for example, worked with minimal supervision and at their own pace. They decided where and how to undercut a vein, how large an explosive charge to set, and how rapidly to load the coal. As befit an autonomous skilled worker, the miner provided his own tools (even paid for sharpening his drills and the blasting powder he used), quit when he chose, and used his own judgment in working his room in the coal face. In the words of a third-generation miner, John Brophy, "that was one of the great satisfactions that a miner had—that he was his own boss within his workplace." He was also the living embodiment of an older tradition that would be passed on to his children.[9]

Other vignettes illustrate the pride and place of the nineteenth-century skilled craftsmen. When Robert and Helen Lynd in their classic study of Muncie, Indiana during the 1920s chose to suggest the impact of the modern factory on the city's workers, they compared the workers of the prosperity decade to their predecessors of the 1890s. Muncie's skilled glassblowers and building tradesmen of the 1890s, according to the Lynds, were among the town's most respected citizens, loyal union members, autodidacts, and community activists. They were truly full and equal citizens in a people's republic.[10] In the larger industrial city of Chicago skilled iron molders proved their indispensability to the production process in the McCormick Harvester works when during a walkout they initiated in 1885 the company's determination to carry on production proved fruitless.[11]

Their indispensability to production determined the structure and behavior of the unions that skilled workers built. With few exceptions, the only unions that survived economic cycles in the nineteenth century consisted of highly skilled workers, those Benson Soffer has referred to as "autonomous workmen." Their power as individuals and as union members derived from their relative scarcity in the marketplace. As long as they monopolized the skills they possessed, and employers lacked an equally productive alternative, such workers wielded real power.[12] Some indeed felt powerful enough to do without unions and collective action, as the inability of most craft unions to organize a majority of workers in a trade proved. But those for whom collective action proved efficacious used trade unions to buttress their power in the marketplace. Most of the local craft unions in the nineteenth century, which subsequently evolved into the dominant national and international trade unions, based their constitutions, rituals, and practices on securing MBP. They limited membership, adopted stringent apprenticeship regulations, restricted the number of helpers a journeyman might employ, set daily production quotas (or stints), required all members to pledge never to work alongside a nonunionist, and often sought, and successfully at that, to make the union headquarters a hiring hall for employers. To the extent that they succeeded in achieving their goals, such unions became as indispensable to skilled workers as the latter were to employers.

At first, the threat to the MBP of such workers and unions did not come from innovations in the actual production process. Until the 1890s most products continued to be made in traditional ways and most of the skilled workers maintained their vital role. But the market in which they sold their labor and in which the goods they manufactured circulated changed. The dual transport-communications revolution of the mid-nineteenth century created a national labor and products market. In response, as Lloyd Ulman describes so well in *The Rise of the National Union,* (1955), local unions combined into national and international federations. Trades, such as building and carting, in which there was no national product competition, developed national offices to coordinate the movement of tramping artisans (those nineteenth-century "Knights of the Road" who traveled from place to place seeking better jobs or the improvement of their skills as journeymen). As workers became more mobile, it was essential that craft unions develop policies to even the flow of labor to disparate markets and prevent local gluts from arising. The unions did so by issuing traveling cards, coordinating information on local labor market conditions, and warning tramping artisans away from glutted localities. Those unions whose members manufactured goods increasingly competitive in a national marketplace had an equally strong motivation to transfer institutional authority from the local to national level. These unions sought to even the costs of production across space by establishing uniform wage, hour, and production standards, denying employers in one region or locality an advantage over their competitors elsewhere. Their ability to do so, of course, depended on their real MBP. As it turned out in practice in the late nineteenth and early twentieth centuries, the craft unions concentrated in local product markets had much more effective MBP than those in more nationally competitive product markets. Thus unions of printers, carpenters, and teamsters, among others, grew and flourished over time, while the unions of iron molders, puddlers, and glassblowers, among others, dwindled into impotency.

All this is not to say that the actual organization of work scarcely changed in the nineteenth century. Such a statement would be far from accurate. The imperatives of more stringent competition in an ever enlarging national marketplace impelled employers to seek cheaper methods of production. In the absence of substantial technological innovations, the simple division of labor became the most commonly used approach. American economic growth proved the acuity of Adam Smith's observation that the extent of the market governs the division of labor. As canals, railroads, and telegraph lines widened the American market, employers hired increasing numbers of green hands, women, and children, all of whom could be assigned extremely specialized production tasks which could be learned and mastered in a short time. Such cheap laborers spent their toiling hours performing a few simple repetitive operations, which left them ignorant of the place of their job in the larger production process. In this system, in Karl Marx's terse comment, "it is not the workman that employs the instruments of labour, but the instruments of labour that employ the workman."[13]

Until the 1890s, however, the division of labor and specialization were not urgent concerns for most autonomous skilled craftsmen. Even in the shoemaking and garment trades, where specialization and the task system had been carried to extremes by the end of the 1870s, the most highly skilled workers, the cutters, retained their craft and its indispensability. As a consequence, they still possessed MBP and used it to keep their limited membership craft unions alive and well. But the last two decades of the nineteenth century were to change all that; they would usher in a great technological transformation which would leave few forms of work, laborers, or unions untouched.

Between the 1890s and the 1920s employers totally transformed the world of work as it had existed heretofore. Not all traditional skills were eliminated nor did all craft unions lose their power. But the main drift moved in precisely those directions. In the economy of the late nineteenth century, a time of falling prices, recurrent business slumps, and intensifying competition among firms, employers had little choice but to reduce their costs of production. This compulsion had an immediate impact on both workers and unions. In many trades and industries the traditional ways of skilled workers and union practices posed an obstacle to the intensification of labor and reductions in the cost of production. As Andrew Carnegie noted concerning the policies of the Amalgamated Association of Iron, Steel, and Tin Workers, they placed a "tax" on production at his company's Homestead steelworks.

Employers responded to this situation in a variety of ways, all of which diluted skills and threatened union power. As Daniel Nelson has shown in his history of managerial reform between 1880 and 1920, employers slowly but steadily altered the actual factory environment and the flow of work in the plant, limited the arbitrary authority of plant foremen while increasing central office control of labor, and instituted new hiring policies and personnel practices to obtain a more docile and productive labor force. And what Nelson calls the "new factory system" successfully diluted the power of craftsmen and unions.[14] At the same time employers rapidly innovated new production methods and introduced new machinery. The advanced technology of the steel industry did away with many of the skills possessed by iron workers and the whole thrust of technological innovation in the industry sought economy of labor, domesticating or eradicating the Amalgamated Association, and severing the customary connection between productivity and wages. In the steel industry's future, the fruits of innovation would go to capital, not labor, and wages would be set in the marketplace where technology and unrestricted immigration had reduced the power of the skilled and their unions.[15] Other industries followed a similar pattern. In the glass industry between 1890 and 1905, first semiautomatic and then fully automatic machines replaced the skilled hand glassblowers. In the printing trades, linotype machines and power presses displaced hand composition and printing. Granite and stonecutters watched nervously as mechanical planers eliminated customary hand skills.[16] Sometimes employers introduced new machinery even when it was less economical than the use of skilled workers, as was the case with the McCormick Harvester Company in 1886 when it used molding machines to break a strike among its unionized molders.[17]

These practices and tendencies reached their fullest expression in the policies associated with Frederick Winslow Taylor and his many disciples and imitators. Taylorism, or scientific management, sought to organize production systematically and induce workers to perform their assignments in the "one best way." The goal of scientific management, in the words of one associate of Taylor's, was "the establishment of standards everywhere, including standard instruction cards for standard methods, motion studies, time study, time cards . . . [and] records of individual output." The essential aim of Taylorism was to place the worker "at the bottom level of a highly stratified organization . . . [where] his established routines of work, his cultural traditions . . . [were all] at the mercy of technical specialists." And as David Montgomery observes, scientific management "implied a conscious endeavor to uproot those work practices which had been the taproot of whatever strength organized labor enjoyed in the late nineteenth century."[18]

Absolute control of the production process and elimination of worker autonomy reached their peaks in the meat packing and automobile industries in the pre-World War I era. In both industries moving production lines (a disassembly line in the slaughterhouses and the famous assembly line at Ford's Highland Park plant) determined the pace of work and could be intensified or moderated solely at the discretion of management. Packinghouse workers and car assemblers spent their whole work days engaged in the same simple repetitive operations, which left them as devoid of skill as the day they entered the plant.[19]

Throughout the four decades of transformation, a continuous and simultaneous process of deskilling and reskilling of workers repeated itself. Certainly, skilled glassblowers, granite cutters, hand compositors, iron molders, coopers, and all-around machinists found their hard-acquired crafts obsolescent. At the same time, common laborers, who once merely fetched and hauled materials for the skilled production workers, found themselves located directly in production as machine operators or parts assemblers. The former common laborer, now redefined as a semiskilled operator, undoubtedly experienced a real improvement in status and perhaps even in skill. And the demand for common, casual day labor, which never entirely disappeared, could be readily satisfied by the ever flowing stream of new immigrants for whom any form of steady employment signified material betterment.[20] But new forms of skill also emerged and, as Andrew Dawson writes: "The skilled stratum proved to be a highly adaptive social group in the face of innovation." All the basic industries, including steel, automobiles, coal mining, and the railroads, needed highly skilled machine makers and maintenance people. In the maritime trades skilled machinists, boilermakers, and stationary engineers replaced general seamen, as steam substituted for sail. Even during the acme of technological innovation and scientific management, skilled workers were never, in Dawson's words, "a moribund excrescence upon the body of the labor force, but, for better or worse, a vital force within the working class."[21]

As a vital presence within the working class, skilled workers kept alive not only the traditions of craftsmanship but also the spirit of unionism. The craft unions sought, as best they could, to cope with the twin threats of technological innovation and scientific management. Generally, they tried to accommodate to technological change, not to resist it. They also attempted to adjust to the transformed market for their labor by widening their union jurisdictions, allying with competing craft unions, and diluting the eligibility requirements for union membership. In the end, however, their relative success or failure in accommodating to technological change depended more on their actual or residual MBP than on any concrete policies or practices they adopted.

Basically, as George E. Barnett and Sumner Slichter pointed out in their classic studies of labor and technological change, unions exhibited three primary ways of reacting to new production methods. They resisted change, chose to compete directly with new technology, or sought to obtain union control of machinery. Historically, unions, in fact, tried all three methods. Typically, before it became apparent that new technology would eliminate traditional skills, many craftsmen believed that their indispensability would enable them either to resist change or compete successfully with new machines by continuing to produce at a lower cost. As Slichter somewhat dyspeptically noted, "the history of the attempt of unions to adjust themselves to technological changes suggests that they have a strong tendency to do the right thing too late." By "the right thing," Slichter meant the choice to accommodate to technology and gain union control over machinery.[22]

By and large, most craft unions indeed tried to do "the right thing." It was rare for a union in the late nineteenth century ever to oppose directly management's right to use new machines. At most, unions sought to contain the speed of change and preserve jobs by reducing the hours of work, despite the fact that most skilled workers probably agreed with a fellow worker who asserted that "labor saving machinery has made some men richer, most things cheaper, and the working classes poorer."[23] After studying carefully the response of printers',

glassblowers', and stonecutters' unions to technological change between roughly 1900 and the 1920s, George Barnett concluded:

Not only is trade unionism officially committed to the view that resistance to
machinery is futile, but it is almost unanimous in holding further that resistance to the introduction of machinery delays, or makes impossible, the
adoption of measures which may mitigate the hurtful effects of the introduction of machinery.[24]

Most craft union leaders made quite clear their receptivity to technological change. George W. Perkins, the president of the Cigar Makers' International Union, an institution shaken by the introduction of
the automatic cigar-making machine, said at his union's 1923
convention.

No power on earth can stop the at least gradual introduction and use of
improved machinery and progressive methods of production. Any effort in
that direction will react against those who attempt it. Our own condition
proves that efforts at restriction were futile, and ineffective, and injurious.
Without an exception, every organization, since the beginning of the factory
system, that has attempted to restrict the use of improved methods of production has met with defeat.

At the end of the 1920s, William Green, president of the AFL, and
Matthew Woll, one of its more influential spokesmen, reiterated Perkins' position. "The American labor movement," asserted Green,
"welcomes the installation and extension of the use of machinery in
industry." To which Woll added, "It is not the function of the labor
movement to resist the machine. It is the function of the labor movement to turn the installation of machinery to the good of the
worker."[25]

How successful were the labor movement and the craft unions in
turning technological change to the advantage of the worker? Not
especially! Why? To begin with, technological change fundamentally
transformed labor's MBP. In industry after industry, new or better
machines eliminated the need for skilled workers. McCormick's mechanical molders, which in 1885 replaced skilled molders but at a
higher cost, soon also turned out a superior product at a lower cost.
In the steel industry, as Charles Schwab commented, an employer
could hire an entirely green hand and within two weeks turn him
into an efficient, productive worker. This trend repeated itself persistently. Hand glassblowers, practicing a highly skilled craft, first pro-

tected their jobs by competing directly with new machines and then by applying their skills to the control of semiautomatic machines, which were run more productively by craftsmen.[26] But then employers introduced fully automatic machines on which skilled workers produced no cost advantage.[27] When the Lynds studied Muncie, a center of glass bottle production, in the 1920s, they found unionism in the industry dead.[28]

Only in those cases in which skilled workers continued to possess MBP did their unions succeed in controlling the introduction of machinery or growing. Printers and pressmen, whose skills proved as necessary and economical on the new linotypes and power presses as they had been for the old hand processes, retained much autonomy on the job and belonged to stable, flourishing unions. Less skilled workers were simply noncompetitive in the labor market.[29] The same was true of many building trades workers, whose skills were yet to be made obsolescent, who were much in demand in the 1920s, and who competed only in local labor and product markets. At a time (the 1920s) when the labor movement in general declined (between 1921 and 1929 total union membership fell from over five million to about 3.5 million), the printing and building trades unions actually grew in size. Elsewhere, however, workers and unions saw their MBP diminish, and, as it did, they suffered. Unions never penetrated the oligopolistic mass-production industries in which technological innovation and scientific management had progressed furthest. In railroad shops and small machine shops, where new tools and managerial methods had been introduced, all-around machinists lost out to newly trained specialists who did not belong to the union. And in the coal mines, mechanical undercutting machines plus competition from more productive nonunion mines created an enormous labor surplus. The United Mine Workers of America was reduced from being the largest single union in the country, with over 500,000 members in 1920, to a paralyzed union with fewer than 100,000 dues-paying members only ten years later.[30]

Throughout this long era of technological change and transformation of the labor process, trade unionists sought to grapple with the new order of production. From the mid-1880s on, labor leaders increasingly lamented the passing of the craftsman and demanded a labor movement which would organize workers regardless of skill.

Part of the rationale for the Knights of Labor, the first labor federation in the United States to achieve mass membership (an estimated 700,000–800,000 members in 1886), lay in its effort to organize those workers lacking clearly defined skills. Declaring craft unions an anachronistic relic from the handicraft era of production, the Knights tried to function as a general union which opened membership to all regardless of skill, gender, or race. They failed. Only the allegedly antiquarian craft unions, whose members still possessed MBP, survived the business cycles of the late nineteenth century and flourished during the economic expansion from 1897 through 1903.

In 1905 the Industrial Workers of the World (IWW) repeated part of the experience of the Knights of Labor. Its founding manifesto declared that "laborers are no longer classified by differences in trade skill, but the employer assorts them according to the machines to which they are attached. These divisions, far from representing differences in skill, or interests among laborers, are imposed by the employers that workers may be pitted against one another."[31] Thus the IWW, like the Knights of Labor before it, tried to organize unskilled as well as skilled workers, to make the American labor movement as "modern" as the corporations with which they contended. But the IWW also proved less than a success. It never developed an alternative to the MBP of the craft unions, and at a time when unrestricted immigration regularly replenished the market for machine operators and common laborers, its successes proved ephemeral.

Craft unionists, too, took cognizance of their new universe of work. "Every day our trade is becoming more and more specialized," remarked James O'Connell of the International Association of Machinists, "and if we hope to . . . protect our craft it is necessary that our qualifications for membership be radically changed." By 1900 leaders of the Butcher Workman's Union realized that "today it is impossible to draw the line where the skilled man leaves off and the unskilled man begins. . . . [This] makes it necessary to organize all working in the large plants under one head."[32] The United Mine Workers of America (UMWA) had always operated on that principle, organizing all who worked in and around mine pits, including carpenters, pumpmen, engineers, and machinists. And at its 1901 convention in Scranton, the AFL formally recognized the right of the coal miners to organize workers heretofore deemed within the exclusive jurisdiction of specified craft unions. To that degree, the AFL's "Scranton declaration" sanctioned industrial or general unionism. But the AFL made other attempts to bring trade unionism structurally into a new technological era. Its leaders encouraged the formation of federated union departments—the mining trades, building trades, metal trades, and railway trades departments, among others—which would enable related craft unions to act as a unit against concentrated capital.[33] Individual craft unions also tried to make their own separate peace with the new technology. The Carpenters' Union, the largest and perhaps most successful of the building trades unions, followed the principle of "once of wood, always of wood." It allowed its members to work with all sorts of new construction materials and recruited among people who had never worked with wood and belonged to or fell within the jurisdiction of other unions.[34]

Before and during World War I, many labor leaders also began to sense or act on the shift in labor's strength from MBP to WBP. That, after all, was at the root of the IWW's assertion that the real struggle between labor and capital occurred at the point of production, and that the new capital-intensive technology made large firms especially vulnerable to conventional strikes, intermittent strikes, slowdowns, passive resistance, and even sabotage. It was also partially behind the militant strike wave of 1916–1922, which involved mostly conventional AFL unions and which, as David Montgomery argues, was fought over control issues at the point of production. He also suggests that, even in the absence of strikes, conventional unionists fought a daily battle with management over control within the workplace.[35] But in this period, as Montgomery's research also demonstrates, workers' struggles remained closely associated with MBP, their intensity rising as unemployment fell and declining as unemployment rose.[36]

As we have already seen, until the end of the 1920's, industrial or general unionism had proved itself a failure. Not only had the IWW failed, but AFL attempts to organize steelworkers, meat packers, and nonoperating railway employees all collapsed between 1919 and 1922, as did such previously successful industrial unions as the UMWA and the International Ladies' Garment Workers. The craft unionists, who had never really been eager to unionize the less skilled (many of the craft unions that made halfhearted efforts to organize the nonskilled offered them only subordinate, so-called Class B status in the union), had a ready explanation for the failure of industrial unionism. Union strength could not be built in the absence of MPB, alleged the craft unionists, and nonskilled machine operators were merely interchangeable bodies in a glutted labor market, people whom Dan Tobin, president of the Teamsters' Union, could readily dismiss as "the rubbish at labor's door." There was an element of truth in that belief. As David Brody has written of the American labor movement as it existed in the 1920s: "The bitter truth was clear: depending on their own economic strength, American workers could not defeat the massed power of open-shop industry.[37] But they could use their imperceptibly rising WBP, which craft unionists did not yet perceive, on the shop floor level to limit partially management's efforts to increase labor productivity. Stanley Mathewson's 1931 study, *Restriction of Output by Unorganized Workers*, showed precisely how workers informally practiced the stint, the slowdown, and even sabotaged production in the most technologically advanced plants. Research sponsored directly by corporations and conducted by such social scientists as Elton Mayo, F. J. Roethlisberger, and W. J. Dickson also revealed how vulnerable capital-intensive industry was to worker resistance. But not until the Great Depression of the 1930s would it become evident how the informal WBP exposed by Mathewson and others would transform itself into the formal power exercised by institutionalized trade unions.

One of the great puzzles of American labor history is how and why trade unions for the first time breached the antiunion defenses of mass-production industry at a time of deep depression and mass unemployment. It should not be necessary here to describe the details of the history of the unionization of mass-production industry or the specifics of what has come to be known as the New Deal "revolution in labor law." Suffice it to say that by the end of the 1930s, trade unions had organized the automobile, steel, and electrical goods industries, among others, and that the labor movement was three times as large as it had been in 1933. Except for Sweden, no other labor movement in the industrial world advanced as rapidly and successfully as that in the United States. The American labor success story during the Great Depression was closely associated with the concentrated character of American industry and its technological virtuosity.

Although continuous-flow production and the assembly line, characteristics of the American mass-production system, homogenized labor and subjected the mass of workers to the dictates of machine technology, it also increased the potential vulnerability of capital to direct action by workers at the point of production. If the size and scale of American corporate enterprises provided capital with enormous material resources with which to confront and defeat workers' resistance, this capital-intensive structure also intensified the damage that could be done to an entire corporation by a strike in only one of its key plants and the disruption that could be wrought in the national economy by a strike in an essential industry. As one steelworker quoted by David Montgomery observed, "bringing the workflow to a crunching halt is both easy and commonplace for those who are familiar with the intricacies of their machinery." The truth of this observation was established by the Goodyear rubber workers who sat down on the job in 1936, the Flint auto workers who did the same in January-February 1937 and won recognition and a union contract from General Motors, and also the steelworkers who by threatening to strike U.S. Steel won a contract in March 1937 without even walking off the job.[38]

These successes were all linked to the emergence of the Congress of Industrial Organizations as a direct competitor to the AFL and one that recognized the significance of capital intensity and WBP for trade unionism. But the AFL unions learned quickly from the example of the CIO. Craft unionists became more receptive to recruiting the nonskilled and used their superior resources to grow more rapidly after 1938 than their industrial union competitors. By 1940 the AFL was far larger than the CIO and its affiliates acted just as aggressively at the workplace.[39]

World War II further revealed the vulnerability of concentrated capital to the shop-floor power of its employees. As recent books by Nelson Lichtenstein and Howell John Harris have shown, corporations were deeply troubled by a lack of discipline among their workers, which they attributed to the rise of the CIO in the late 1930s and the labor scarcity caused by the war.[40] During the war itself, wildcat strikes, lax work habits, and absenteeism, especially among women workers, caused a great deal of trouble for plant managers. Because government policy during the war also favored unions to the extent that it guaranteed their security through federal administrative rulings, corporations sought a way to live with unions and yet regain shop floor discipline. By 1945, they had no choice in a world in which almost 15 million workers (nearly 35 percent of the nonagricultural labor force) belonged to trade unions.

The postwar social contract between management and labor flowed directly from capital's vulnerability to direct action at the point of production. In order to reassert its authority at the workplace, management recruited the assistance of union officials. Corporations promised unions recognition, security, and peaceful relations; they offered their employees higher wages, annual productivity increases, protection against inflation, attractive fringe benefits, and stable jobs. In return, workers promised higher productivity and unions agreed to police discipline on the shop-floor. Unions also promised not to interfere with management's prerogatives, generally defined as the right to manage by allocating capital, introducing new technology, or reorganizing work routines. And unions guaranteed not to strike during the duration of contract, which was more and more often a multiyear agreement. In a sense, then, capital paid labor well to establish management's right to do what it wanted to do. "By so agreeing," David Brody has written, "companies and unions revealed what was, at rock bottom, the common intent of their encompassing contractual relationship—the containment of spontaneous and independent shop-floor activity." And he adds, "company and union were drawn into unacknowledged collaboration against shop-floor militancy.[41]"

For a quarter of a century after World War II that unacknowledged bargain between management and unions effectively contained worker resistance at the point of production while conceding capital the prerogatives it demanded. Management introduced new technology, reorganized the labor process, and greatly increased per capita productivity, all with minimal union resistance. As long as workers received higher wages for increased productivity, job security through seniority systems, and supplementary unemployment benefits to guarantee full earnings during momentary periods of cyclical unemployment, unions proved less resistant to technological change than ever. For corporations finally seemed to have accepted what had always been the union *sine qua non* for accepting new technology: that its impact on the worker be cushioned and the worker's fate not be left to the vagaries of the marketplace. Thus technological change, which proceeded steadily in the 1950s and 1960s, caused many pessimists to worry about the impact of automation, but produced few changes in union structure, behavior, or attitudes toward new methods of production.

By the 1970s, however, it became evident that workers and trade unions were caught up in a second "great transformation" in technology and the labor process comparable to that of the period from the 1890s through 1920s. Once again, corporations found themselves faced with increasingly competitive markets and shrinking profits. This time the competition arose externally as well as internally and in some ways proved even more threatening to established corporate enterprises. And once again firms responded by seeking to increase productivity and lower labor costs by reorganizing work routines and computerizing machinery. It goes without saying that this application of computer technology to industry has reduced total employment in the traditional mass-production industries and substantially lowered membership in the major industrial unions formed during the late 1930s and 1940s. Since the end of the 1960s, as we all know, union membership has grown less rapidly than the total labor force and in years of higher than normal unemployment has actually fallen absolutely.

Not only have corporate enterprises increased labor productivity through technological innovation; they have also moved those jobs still requiring a measure of labor intensity to low-wage areas overseas. That, too, has been made possible by the new technology of almost instantaneous international transmission of data and managerial decisions. Computerization and international mobility of capital have thus combined to imperil the American labor movement as it has functioned since the 1940s.

Overall the trade union response to this second great transformation seems quite in character with past forms of behavior. Unions, by and large, have sought to accommodate the new technology, not resist it. At most, they have tried to slow the pace of change in order to soften its potential negative impact on workers. Thus the longshoremen's unions on both coasts accepted containerization in return for a combination of guaranteed jobs and annual wages. The International Typographical Union with its long history of accommodating technological change through control of work followed tradition. As computerized typesetting replaced the linotype machine and made ordinary typists as productive as skilled printers and also cheaper, the union continued to insist that "the better the operator [meaning a union person] the lower the cost of production."[42] For a time, the printers' union even sought to remain ahead of employers in technological change by operating an advanced school in technology for printers at ITU headquarters in Colorado Springs. But printing technology had become so complex and capital intensive by the late 1960s that the union could not match the investments of private enterprise and had to close its training school.[43] Indeed, today traditional printers, outside of a few speciality job shops, are a dying breed as their union has surrendered all control over technology in order to guarantee the income, if not the skills and jobs, of currently employed printers.

Even the sector of the labor force that benefited from the technological transformation of the 1890–1920 era, the highly skilled metal workers, now suffers as the electronics revolution and microprocessors bring numerically controlled machine tools to small shops as well as large firms.[44] As a U.S. Commerce Department official recently commented, "the problem is that there is nothing in between. If you are not a banker, you are in McDonalds."[45] Indeed. For today McDonalds and Burger King employ more workers than the steel industry, and jobs grow most rapidly in the service and clerical sector of the economy which has long been impervious to the penetration of unions.

Aside from unions' customary tactic of accommodating technological change, they have sought to cope with current realities through a series of mergers. For example, in 1980 the Amalgamated Meat Cutters and Butcher Workmen (who had earlier swallowed the Fur and Leather Workers' Union) merged with the Retail Clerks to form the United Food and Commercial Workers, now the largest single union in the AFL-CIO. Even earlier, the Steelworkers' Union had taken over the Mine, Mill, and Smelter Workers, and the Amalgamated Textile Workers had allied with the United Textile Workers. These and other union mergers will likely reduce the total number of affiliated AFL-CIO unions and appear to be a logical response by the labor movement to the continued centralization and concentration of capital. But neither union accommodation to technological change nor union mergers have enabled the labor movement to make much headway among young employees in widely scattered service establishments, clerks in increasingly computerized work settings, or workers in the so-called high technology firms.

The future of the American labor movement remains highly problematic. In those industries in which unions exist and capital intensity renders firms vulnerable to worker resistance at the point of production, unions are probably here to stay. On the whole, as David Brody notes, where unions and collective bargaining were well rooted, their stabilizing effects for the employer exceeded the potential benefits of seeking to uproot unionism.[46] The big question concerns the future of the service and clerical sectors. As those sectors grow more capital intensive, as seems to be happening especially in office work, will they too become more vulnerable to worker resistance at the point of production (WBP) and hence more open to unionism? I prefer to close with a question, not an answer or a prophecy.

Notes

1. Cited in Laszlo Makkai, "Ars Historica: On Braudel," *Review* (Spring 1983), 6:452.
2. David Landes, *Unbound Prometheus* (London: Cambridge University Press, 1969), p. 3.
3. Stephen A. Marglin, "What Do Bosses Do?" *Review of Radical Political Economics* (Summer 1974), 6:60–112; Katherine Stone, "The Origins of Job Structures in the Steel Industry," in David M. Gordon et al., *Labor Market Segmentation* (Lexington, Mass.: Heath, 1975).
4. David Brody, *Steelworkers in America: The Nonunion Era* (Cambridge, Mass.: Harvard University Press, 1960), chs. 2 and 3; Daniel Nelson, *Managers and Workers* (Madison: University of Wisconsin Press, 1975), chs. 3–8.
5. Giovanni Arrighi, "The Labor Movement in Twentieth-Century Western Europe," in Immanuel Wallerstein, ed., *Labor in the World Social Structure* (Beverly Hills: Sage, 1983), pp. 55–56.
6. *Ibid.*, p. 56.
7. David Brody, "The Old Labor History and the New," *Labor History* (Winter 1979), 20:117.
8. David Montgomery, *Workers' Control in America* (New York: Cambridge University Press, 1979), pp. 12–13.
9. Jerold S. Auerbach, *American Labor: The Twentieth Century* (Indianapolis: Bobbs-Merrill, 1969), pp. 43–48; John Brophy, *A Miner's Life* (Madison: University of Wisconsin Press, 1964), ch. 4.
10. Robert and Helen Lynd, *Middletown* (New York: Harcourt Brace Jovanovich, 1956 ed.), pp. 76–79.

11. Robert Ozanne, *A Century of Labor-Management Relations at McCormick and International Harvester* (Madison: University of Wisconsin Press, 1967), pp.13–19.

12. Benson Soffer, "A Theory of Trade Union Development: The Role of the 'Autonomous' Workman," *Labor History* (Spring 1960), 1:141–163.

13. Karl Marx, *Capital* (New York: International, 1967 ed.), 1:423–424.

14. See Nelson, *Managers and Workers*.

15. Brody, *Steelworkers*, ch. 3.

16. On these developments, see George Barnett, *Chapters on Machinery* (Carbondale: Southern Illinois University Press, 1969), chs. 1–4.

17. Ozanne, *A Century of Labor-Management Relations*, pp. 20–25.

18. The quotations are from D. Montgomery, *Workers' Control*, pp. 26–27, 33. For a more sober evaluation of Taylorism, see Daniel Nelson, *Frederick W. Taylor and the Rise of Scientific Management (Madison: University of Wisconsin Press, 1980).*

19. David Brody, *The Butcher Workmen: A Study of Unionization* (Cambridge, Mass.: Harvard University Press, 1964), ch. 1; Stephen Meyer, III, *The Five Dollar Day: Labor Management and Social Control at the Ford Motor Company, 1908–1921* (Albany: SUNY, 1981), chs. 2 and 3.

20. Andrea Graziosi, "Common Laborers: Unskilled Workers, 1890–1915," *Labor History* (Fall 1981), 22:512–544.

21. Andrew Dawson, "The Paradox of Dynamic Technological Change and the Labor Aristocracy in the United States, 1880–1914," *Labor History* (Summer 1979), 20:325–351, esp. 338–339.

22. The quotation is from Sumner Slichter, *Union Policies and Industrial Management* (Washington, D.C.: The Brookings Institution, 1941), p. 203. Cf. Barnett, *Chapters on Machinery*, ch. 6.

23. Irwin Yellowitz, *Industrialism and the American Labor Movement, 1850–1900* (Port Washington, N.Y.: Kennikat Press, 1977), p. 93.

24. Barnett, *Chapters on Machinery*, p. 141.

25. The statements by Perkins and Green are both quoted in Slichter, *Union Policies*, pp. 205–206.

26. Barnett, *Chapters on Machinery*, ch. 3.

27. *Ibid.*, ch. 4.

28. *Middletown*, pp. 76–80.

29. Barnett, *Chapters on Machinery*, ch. 1; Elizabeth F. Baker, *Printers and Technology* (New York: Greenwood, 1957).

30. Melvyn Dubosfsky and Warren R. Van Tine, *John L. Lewis: A Biography* (New York: Times Books, 1977), chs. 4, 7–8.

31. Melvyn Dubofsky, *We Shall Be All: A History of the IWW* (Chicago: Times Books, 1969), p. 79.

32. David Brody, *Workers in Industrial America* (New York: Oxford University Press, 1980, pp. 29–30.

33. Philip Taft, *The A.F. of L. in the Time of Gompers* (New York: Octagon Press, 1957), ch. 13.

34. Robert Christie, *Empire in Wood* (Ithaca: Cornell University Press, 1956).

35. Montgomery, *Workers' Control*, pp. 82, 91–112.

36. *Ibid.*, pp. 94–95.

37. Brody, *Workers in Industrial America*, p. 45.

38. Montgomery, *Workers' Control*, p. 156; Giovanni Arrighi and Beverly Silver, "Labor Movements and Capital Migration: The U.S. and Western Europe in World-Historical Perspective," in Charles Bergquist, ed., *Labor in the World Capitalist Economy* (Beverly Hills: Sage Publishers, 1984), pp. 183–216, esp. pp. 191–200.

39. Christopher Tomlins, "AFL Unions in the 1930s: Their Performance in Historical Perspective," *Journal of American History* (March 1979), 65:1021–1042.

40. Nelson Lichtenstein, *Labor's War at Home: The CIO in World War II* (New York: Cambridge University Press, 1982); Howell John Harris, *The Right to Manage* (Madison: University of Wisconsin Press, 1982).

41. Brody, *Workers In Industrial America*, pp. 204–207.

42. Elizabeth F. Baker, *Technology and Woman's Work* (New York: Columbia University Press, 1964), p. 175.

43. Conversations with Secretary Treasurer Thomas Kopeck, International Typographical Union (ITU), July 1981.

44. Robert Asher, "Connecticut Workers and Technological Change, 1950–1980," *Connecticut History* (March 1983), 24:47–60.

45. *Ibid.*, p. 59.

46. Brody, *Workers in Industrial America*, p. 250.

8. Technological Change and American Farm Movements

Morton Rothstein
University of California, Davis

Since its inception as a nation, the United States has been a land virtually without peasants and with little of the Old World peasant attitudes and traditions. To be sure, several of the colonies established in the seventeenth and early eighteenth centuries were initially marked by efforts to replicate European feudal institutions and relationships. The residue of such efforts could be seen in the early nineteenth century in such places as the Eastern shore of Maryland's Chesapeake Bay and in the Hudson River valley of New York, where many families lived on the land as tenants of large estate owners and in a poverty little different from that of the lowest ranks of European peasantry.[1] But these examples were exceptions. For various reasons most of the 300,000 or more American farmers counted in the 1790 census owned that land in fee simple, and most of them bore relatively light tax burdens. The farmer as owner occupier of at least enough land from which he made a comfortable, independent living for his family, and could leave enough to keep his children in the same status, had become the national ideal, the model citizen so eloquently praised by Thomas Jefferson.

This emerging consensus, influenced by current eighteenth-century Enlightenment ideas about the fundamental importance of farmers to the nation's well-being was manifest in many ways, but perhaps none more important than the two basic laws passed under the Articles of

Confederation: the Land Ordinance of 1785 and the Northwest Ordinance of 1787. Together they have served as an extraordinarily enlightened "colonial policy" for virtually all of the nation's lands west of the Appalachian Mountains, the area once claimed by several colonies and ceded in 1781 to the newly formed central government. The two ordinances established procedures for the orderly surveying and sale of these federal lands, known since as the public domain, and for both the governance of the public domain as territories and the admission of those territories into the Union on the same basis and with the same standing as the original thirteen states. In effect, these laws set a pattern that applied to all the other lands that the federal government acquired by purchase or by conquest until the nation's boundaries extended to the Pacific Ocean and beyond.[2] By removing virtually all political barriers to the spread of farm settlements, this institutional framework became a key element in accounting for the accelerating growth in the number of farms that was one of the hallmarks of the nation's agricultural history throughout the nineteenth century. Such easy access to land ownership pushed the number of farms to about two million at the time of the Civil War, and to roughly six million by World War I, primarily through policies that steadily lowered the economic barriers to ownership and made the transformation of much of the continental land mass into productive, commercial farms the main concern of settlers.

As they pushed into the continent's interior during the generation after the Revolution, settlers had to concentrate first on clearing the heavily forested land and surviving at little more than subsistence levels in areas remote from older settlements and cheaper transportation to markets. But the westward movement of pioneers into what was thought to be an empty frontier wilderness (though occupied for centuries by native Americans)—the stuff of much American lore and legend—was also a consummate act of faith in future technological change, a belief that innovations in transportation and communication would soon give farmers the access to markets that would vindicate the decisions that millions of them made to spread across the American landscape. In little more than a century they transformed the land in accordance with that faith.

Not only were the barriers to entry for farm ownership low, but land could be generally acquired in units large enough to provide relatively high levels of living for a family. Futhermore, incipient farmers could also count upon access to public lands for their children and heirs. There was less need to concern oneself about dividing the farm among the next generation, and, therefore, virtually no constraint on family size. Indeed, American population growth during the colonial period, when virtually every colony had liberalized its land policies in order to attract migrants, was at a rate so high that it set an English country person named Thomas Malthus worrying about the future pressure of people on land resources.[3]

Malthus' concerns stemmed from an assumption that there would be little improvement in yields from either better farming practices or technological innovations. In some ways, it was an understandable assumption at the time. Much of European and American farming had shown little gain in the productivity of either the land or the laborer on that land since antiquity, except at a painfully slow, incremental pace, with many setbacks. In Western Europe, the gradual improvements in livestock breeding, the adoption of better tools and implements, and the introduction of new crops and selected seeds began to gain momentum at roughly the time the colonies were first founded, in what historians would call the Agricultural Revolution.[4] As those changes began to transform farming practices in England and parts of the German principalities, immigrants from those places brought the new knowledge with them, especially those who settled in Pennsylvania during the generation or so before the outbreak of the American Revolution. They made the hinterland of Philadelphia a virtual showplace of advanced farm practices in the colonies. But they were the exception to the rule.[5] Until well into the nineteenth century most people who lived on the land and constituted the great majority of the nation's workers used techniques little different from those of farmers in Biblical times except for the more prodigal waste of soil and forest resources. As George Washington had explained, in America the concern was to maximize the productivity of labor, since that was the scarce resource, in contrast to Europe, where the relative scarcity of arable land and cheapness of labor focused attention on improving yields per acre.[6]

Thus there was little impact from technology directly on the methods of American farmers before the 1840s. The major changes derived from the influence of gradually cheapening transportation, which made commercial agricultural production more feasible by bringing markets in the principal industrializing areas of Europe within reach, and the mechanization of some processing stages, such as cotton ginning or flour milling. The automation of flour milling by Oliver Evans improved its quality and helped sustain it as a moderately significant export item during the first half of the nineteenth century. Eli Whitney's introduction of a greatly improved cotton gin made the growing of upland varieties a profitable undertaking after the 1790s for southern slaveholders and modest yeomen, who seized the market opportunities for that crop.[7] Nowhere in the world was there a larger or stronger response to the rapidly increasing Western European demand for this raw material. By 1860, the United States accounted for seven-eighths of the cotton shipped by overseas suppliers to European factories, a demonstration in itself of the prevailing commercial orientation of American farming.

From its beginnings, therefore, American farming was marked by two conflicting ideals. One identified farmers who owned the land they worked as endowed with the highly regarded virtues of self-reliance and independence. The second regarded success in commercial farming as a means of accumulating the patrimony that would be the major reward for the hardships endured in farm making, even as it forced the producer into greater dependency on those who supplied his inputs and bought his produce. Such tensions underlay most of the sporadic, highly localized, and often violent protest movements that took place during the late seventeenth and much of the eighteenth centuries. The first of note, Bacon's Rebellion during the 1670s in Virginia, seems to have gathered support as much because of the felt disappointments of the second generation of tobacco growers in their slow progress toward prosperity as from the ostensible resentment against constraints imposed by a rigid British governor. The more recently arrived settlers chafed against efforts to stop them from retaliating against raids by native Americans which allegedly threatened their security of landholding, a complaint that would surface a century later in the Paxton Riots of Pennsylvania.[8]

Bacon's Rebellion collapsed with the death of the leader in the midst of short-term victory, and his supporters were severely punished. None of the other colonial outbreaks did much better. Mostly they fall into the same category of seeking short-term relief from real or perceived threats to their survival or ownership of land. The thrust of such incidents as the plant-cutting riots of Virginia in 1682, or the rebellions in New York or Maryland, named after Leisler and Coode respectively, were much like the maneuvering of various factions in other colonies for political advantage during the turmoil in the mother country that accompanied the "Glorious Revolution" of 1689. They were more significant for adding to the power of colonial legislatures than for reflecting agrarian discontent.[9]

The next group of settler protests came after 1763, when the end of the protracted wars between the United Kingdom and France brought peace to the back country districts of the Carolinas. Tensions in both colonies surfaced between tidewater authorities and frontier farmer-planters, with the latter group loosely organized into informal and extralegal Regulators, as they called themselves. In North Carolina, few settlers had managed to attain more than a bare living and all were hampered by the lack of seaport or navigable waterways within easy reach. Their immediate goal, however, was to forestall a sudden effort to collect long overdue taxes, since it would inevitably mean foreclosures and loss of farms for many of them. The climax to their resistance came in 1771, in a short confrontation on the banks of the Alamance River that completely routed the protesters. By contrast, the South Carolina Regulators more closely resembled a vigilante group at first, organized primarily to establish law and order in a part of the state inhabited by lawless elements, or at least social outcasts. Within a generation, after the Revolutionary War took its toll on their prosperity, these same promoters of law and order resorted themselves to violating the law in hopes of preventing foreclosures. For them, one of the gains of independence was a state legislature that alleviated some of their problems.[10]

Similar efforts to postpone foreclosure proceedings for failure to pay taxes on farm land triggered one of the best-known social movements in American history, the so-called Shays' Rebellion in western Massachusetts in 1786. During that outbreak, several bands of farm owners, only one of them led by the Revolutionary War veteran Daniel Shays, forcibly prevented the court at Northampton from issuing foreclosure orders. Within a few months the bands were broken up and several leaders arrested and convicted. As a protest against tax increases that had been designed to restore that commercially oriented state's mercantile credit standing, it has profound significance in the state's history. But it also provided the leaders of the movement for a constitutional convention with ammunition for their argument that government under the Articles of Confederation was so weak that it encouraged such allegedly anarchistic behavior.[11]

The same impulse to assert the power of the central government played a large role in suppressing two other agrarian uprisings that erupted briefly in the period following the adoption of the Constitution. One protest, known as the "Whiskey Rebellion," took place in a then remote area of western Pennsylvania where several community leaders resisted a new federal excise tax on alcoholic beverages on the grounds that it was an unduly oppressive burden for growers located so far from market that they could not profitably ship their corn in any other form. The objection may not have had much basis in fact, but Secretary of the Treasury Alexander Hamilton saw in the ensuing confrontation an opportunity to assert the authority of the new federal government. He urged President Washington to send troops swiftly and they collected the tax with a minimum show of force. The episode took on a political symbolism that had little to do with agrarian unrest.[12] Five years later, in 1799, a more familiar form of farm protest took place in northeastern Pennsylvania, when a group of farmers led by John Fries set free some of their imprisoned fellow tillers of the soil who had objected too vigorously to new state taxes that threatened them with foreclosures and had interfered with local assessors. Fries was himself convicted and sentenced to death, but pardoned by President Adams. It was Shays' Rebellion over again, but replayed on a smaller scale.[13]

Such violent reactions, even in characteristically scattered, episodic forms, virtually disappeared during the first half of the nineteenth century. For one thing, ordinary farmers were gaining more importance as voters during the spread of Jeffersonian and Jacksonian democratic ideals and practices that transformed the American political system. Farmers began to obtain leverage in the political arena that matched their numbers in the larger society. On another level, the election of Jefferson to the presidency marked the beginning of liberalization in land policy and the setting of examples in Congress that were soon translated at state and local levels into laws and court decisions that gave farmers more and more protection for the equity they had created by their labor in improving frontier homesteads, as well as for the title to the land itself.[14]

Instead, a second major strand of organized activity among farmers emerged which emphasized reform, uplift, and "improvement." This movement carried over from the Enlightenment a growing, increasingly widespread faith in the capacity of science and education to solve practical farm problems, as well as an emphasis on self-reliance that occupied a central place in the credo of most Americans. Several state legislatures subsidized a variety of learned societies (though on a smaller scale) of a kind that European governments had fostered during the first half of the eighteenth century, such as the Royal Agricultural Society. These state societies in America were at first little more than gentleman's clubs, organized and run by leading townspeople with some interest in farming but little direct experience. Whether they were in New York, Massachusetts, South Carolina, Pennsylvania, or Virginia's Albemarle County, they mainly held meetings, listened to lectures, and printed learned papers, awarding the best authors with prizes of a showy but impractical kind. Within a generation after the Revolution, similar organizations were spawned at the local level, on a county or township basis, and also received help from state governments. They met increasingly at annual fairs that they sponsored, in which the best animals and crops were exhibited, and shared whatever information they had about the most recent innovations and experiments with implements and seeds.[15]

This localized quest for improvement led to a loose, highly diffuse network of farmer clubs whose importance is difficult to exaggerate. They were crucial to the dissemination of ideas and information to farmers who were rapidly becoming the most literate, on the whole, in the world. The uniquely American drive for practical and demonstrable results from innovations reinforced the receptivity of many farmers. But the need to demonstrate results was shown in Pittsfield, Massachusetts in 1807 when the well-known promoter of transport improvements, Elkanah Watson, encountered resistance among his farm neighbors to the idea that they could improve the quality of wool, and the income from its sale, if they changed to a different breed of sheep. When they refused to visit him to inspect some new Merinos he had imported, he brought the animals to the town square to prove to his risk-averse, or perhaps simply stubborn, fellow farmers the superiority of the wool compared with what they had been producing. This early form of demonstration work would take other forms later in the century, but it involved teaching farmers about improvements by direct evidence. Watson tried a different experiment along those lines a few years later when he moved to a run-down farm he had purchased outside of Albany, New York and turned it into a model of what could be accomplished in restoring soil productivity by the application of advanced techniques in crop rotation and animal husbandry.[16] In so doing, he was again directly demonstrating the efficacy of the "reform" messages being pressed in the agricultural weeklies and monthlies springing up in all parts of the nation. For the rest of the century these farm journals championed diversified production and the adoption of European formulas for success in improving yields per acre.[17]

The original purpose in founding agricultural societies at all levels had been tied to spreading the lessons of the European Agricultural Revolution, but their activities were redirected as farmer clubs spread across the newly settled areas of the trans-Appalachian West and consisted of members with diverse experiences and ethnic backgrounds who were jointly grappling with new realities in terms of soil and climate. There was a powerful incentive in most cases for them to share their experiences, both failures and successes, and thereby support each other in confronting a common environment. On the other hand, there was little or no advantage to be gained from withholding such information from neighbors. These virtually submerged "voluntary associations," of the kind that had so impressed de Tocqueville, could be found at the township and county levels in all sections of the nation. While some affiliated themselves with statewide organizations and drew modest support from governmental bodies, others remained fiercely independent, refusing to involve themselves in any way with the wave of virtually national farm movement activity that marked the last third of the nineteenth century.[18] They represented the kind of grass-roots efforts at self-help that also involved farmers in many communities of the Old Northwest in contributing land, labor, and funds to help bring railroads and other improvements to their farmsteads.[19]

The work of these new institutions became particularly significant during the 1840s, when the first major advances in agricultural technology were introduced. They helped to spread the word, for example, about the relative merits of the several reaping machines introduced by Obed Hussey, Cyrus McCormick, and others, and about the steel plows turned out by John Deere. These items were first shown and demonstrated in "contests" at county and state fairs, with prizes awarded to the best performers. Making better plows had become an imperative matter for settlers moving onto the prairies of the Midwest, where the tough sod, imbedded with extensive root systems of tall grasses, made the task of preparing the ground for planting almost impossible, unless one could afford to hire the custom plowers who worked in teams in northern Illinois, southern Wisconsin, and much of Iowa in the 1840s and 1850s.[20]

Still, it was the age-old harvesting bottleneck that formed the chief impediment for the individual farmer's expansion of small grain production. Maize, or Indian corn, could stand until it was convenient to bring it into the barn and shell it; the paramount pioneers' crop, it gave large yields relative to seeds, and resisted diseases and pests better than any of the small grains. But rye, barley, and especially wheat could find markets; for the newer settlements in the Great Lakes states and the upper Mississippi Valley, wheat quickly became the dominant cash crop, even though the acreage a farmer could sow was essentially limited to the labor available in his family or for hire. The innovation of the reaper effectively removed such limitations. Whether or not casual harvest labor was on tap, even at the higher wages prevailing in the cities for such workers, farmers were increasingly free to plant as much as their acreages permitted. The new horse-drawn machines removed labor constraints on the productive capacity of a farmstead and could be introduced with little need to reorganize crop patterns, since most landholdings were more than large enough to absorb the full capacity of the new technology.[21] An additional benefit from the reapers' speed lay in their reduction of harvest-time risks; a heavy hail or rain storm soon after it ripened could easily ruin much of the crop, whereas getting the grain cut and stored more than ten times faster than with hand labor reduced the chances of such a calamity.[22]

The effects of the incentive provided by these machines, and the improved plows and planters, could be seen clearly over the 1850s and 1860s, as the devices became steadily more reliable for working on the prairie soils, which were both richer in potential yields and more quickly brought under cultivation. At the same time, replacement parts and other services were more readily available, and improvements in transport and marketing services reduced the costs of reaching the farmers' customers at home and abroad. With the convergence of these elements, per capita production of wheat rose dramatically from roughly six to almost ten bushels at a time when per capita consumption remained steady at about five and a half bushels. Clearly, one of the fruits of what Wayne Rasmussen has identified as the "First American Agricultural Revolution," the diffusion of horse-drawn machinery from about 1840 to 1880, was the powerful encouragement it gave to the rapid extension of wheat output, by increasing the yield per man hour rather than per acre. Indeed, it amounted to an overexpansion that could only be handled over the rest of the century by fortuitous increases in exports.[23]

Consequently, western farmers found themselves increasingly dependent not only on the suppliers of a growing array of machines and implements, but also upon the providers of a chain of transport and warehousing services. These intermediaries were themselves grappling with a changing business climate in which the requirements of such novel adaptations of old technological principles as the mechanized grain elevators forced the adoption of uniform grading standards and negotiable warehouse receipts, by-products of the startling new role of steam and electricity, a veritable communications revolution that centered on the impact of railroads, steamships, the combination of telegraph and transoceanic cables. Fostering stronger competition in both national and international markets, the new business environment produced survivors who proved more capable of adapting their practices and organizing in self-defense than did the farmers whose crops they handled. For example, the emergence of trunk-line railroads such as the Pennsylvania, New York Central, Baltimore, and Ohio railroads, which all had direct connections between Chicago or St. Louis and the eastern seaports by the early 1870s, and the development of line elevator firms that helped create futures trading on such vital grain exchanges as the Chicago Board of Trade and also introduced shipping procedures which bypassed many of the old intermediaries, were all part of the necessary adjustments to a rapidly integrating national market.[24]

The spread of these transitions left many farmers feeling more vulnerable in dealing with larger, more impersonal market institutions, and resentful about their relative helplessness. There were evidences of such resentment as early as the 1850s in southern Michigan, where some farmers carried on a kind of guerrilla war against a railroad that had beaten them in courts on the question of compensation for losses of livestock that had wandered onto tracks or for fires, allegedly caused by sparks from locomotives, that destroyed fields of crops.[25] In Massachusetts and New York, farm representatives eagerly supported the earliest efforts by state governments to regulate freight rates, which growers claimed were forcing them into unfair competition with cheaper western crops. At the same time, farmers in western states were making every effort, including contributing their labor and mortgaging their farms, to provide the financial support needed to attract the railroads that would make commercial farming feasible.[26]

Such tensions remained largely submerged during the Civil War, although at least one historian has seen in the Copperhead movement of the wartime Midwest a drive to preserve the old political coalition of agrarians reacting against special treatment for railroads and other businesses. By the early 1870s, diverse antimonopoly forces aimed mostly at railroads were participating in the political struggles of several midwestern states with enough strength to make a critical difference, and were joining forces with the first national farm organization of consequence, the Grange. Founded in Washington, D.C. by a handful of government clerks in the aftermath of the Civil War on the general model of the Masonic order, the Patrons of Husbandry, to use its official name, was primarily conceived as a nonpartisan order with the basic goal of improving farm life by reducing the social and cultural isolation that afflicted American rural families. The lonely farmhouse had kept many of them in ignorance and isolation. The relative indifference of farm community leaders to this rather innocuously idealistic enterprise kept it in virtual abeyance for a time after its beginnings in 1867. Yet it soon became the vehicle for the first truly widespread agrarian movement in the nation.[27]

Within five years, the Granger movement began enlisting literally thousands of members, representing the aspirations and concerns of the more prosperous, middle-class farmers who sought direct, practical solutions to their complaints about new market institutions. Even before a single pomona (the county-level unit of the order) had been established in Illinois, a majority of that state's legislators had pushed through the first effective commission regulating railroads and warehouses, granting it authority to limit the rates those businesses charged for their services. The law passed also as much if not more because of backing from Chicago commission merchants who were losing their place in the new market arrangements wrought by railroads and large-scale warehousemen. But since a few representatives who supported it were avowed members of the Patrons of Husbandry, it was quickly labeled a "Granger law."[28]

Although the order's leaders insisted that it was nonpartisan, such direct political action at the state level attracted members by the thousands from the farmer clubs and antimonopoly groups across much of rural America, with more than 800,000 belonging to the Grange at the high point of its strength in 1875. In this way, it served as a vehicle for a more broadly based movement for economic reform. Moreover, a vindication of the effort to use the power of state governments for regulating businesses "clothed in the public interest" came in the Supreme Court decision in *Munn v. Illinois.* When the Court retreated from that interpretation a decade later, public sentiment across the nation and among many occupations was strong enough to influence Congress to pass the Interstate Commerce Act, shifting regulation of the businesses embodying the new technology to the federal government.[29] But the shift came only after a period of experimentation in several Midwestern states, where the Grange membership was most concentrated, with "Granger laws" similar to those of Illinois.[30]

But railroad regulation was not the only area of activity for the Grangers. Their leaders did not lose sight of the original educational and social purposes of the order, which to this day keep many a meeting hall in small towns of rural America alive and flourishing. In addition, many units experimented with the founding of cooperatives for greater market power in buying supplies and selling their produce. In California, where Grangers had leaders from among the most prominent farmers in the state, they circumvented a monopoly in ship chartering and in the importing of grain sacks, both vital local issues, with some success. In DeKalb, Illinois, an enterprising young merchant named Montgomery Ward laid the basis for an extensive and enduring mail-order house by recognizing the power of the local Grange and giving its members special discounts. Often they tried to run factories that made machinery and implements or wagons and other equipment and that were on the verge of failure when the farm group bought them. For whatever reason, they almost invariably sank into bankruptcy in short order. Few of the cooperative elevators and livestock shipping agencies lasted much longer. The more enduring work along these lines was in founding mutual fire and life insurance companies, a few of the business exchanges, and several agencies for pooling orders to buy in bulk.[31]

The cause of these failures in cooperative activity lay at least partly in a lack of experience in such efforts and in the widespread assumption that little skill or knowledge was needed to perform intermediary functions. Part of the problem also was the reluctance of cooperative organizers to impose requirements of loyalty and discipline upon its members. When a delegation of leaders from the British Wholesale Cooperative Society visited the United States in 1874, hoping to join forces with the Grangers in eliminating all middlemen between American farmers and consumers in the United Kingdom, they were appalled to learn that virtually none of the American cooperative ventures adhered to the "Rochdale" principles that had been instrumental in the success of the movement in Britain.[32]

With such a spotty record of achievement in economic affairs, the Grange went into a decline almost as meteoric as its rise. Membership dropped most sharply in the Midwest, but the decline was only temporary in other parts of the country. Efforts to revive it after 1880 were rewarded with steady growth in the Far West and in the Northeastern quadrant of the nation, from Maine to Ohio, where Grange strength has lasted to the present. Except in the Northwest, however, it had become a rather tame movement, appealing through its social programs to the values that its largely family-oriented, middle-class constituents saw as more important than protest or demands for changes.[33]

There were other farm groups willing to take up the cry for reform during the last two decades of the nineteenth century. The locus of radical efforts shifted to the South and to the High Plains, areas where concentration on the staple crops of cotton and wheat respectively set the context for spreading discontent. The leadership in the Alliance movement that emerged on the state level in Texas and Louisiana during the early 1880s and gradually swept across most of the South by 1890 still came from the relatively well-to-do farmers, augmented by rural preachers, doctors, and newspaper editors. But they spoke for a rank and file drawn by and large from lower income groups, farmers who were trapped in the production of crops whose prices were set in world markets and were unable to find alternatives. The leaders spoke in an increasingly strident hyperbole, which was the fashion of the day in political discourse, but also appealed to a latent class consciousness that drew distinctions between producers of goods and those who provided capital or services. This strain of radicalism could be seen from the movement's early insistence on excluding merchants, lawyers, and bankers from membership. They were regarded by the Alliance as representing an increasingly suspect and complicated credit and market system that seemed to pervert rather than promote the agrarian quest for independent security.[34]

Most significant, the Southern Alliance, the larger and more vociferous of the two wings of the movement, spoke for a region barely touched by technological change in the production process. Plows were somewhat better than at mid-century, but they were still generally pulled by a single mule, and the tasks of hoeing, picking, and ginning cotton were performed in a manner little different from the time when Cotton Kingdom was first settled. The major changes were in the shifts of population, black and white, from the older cotton states to the newly opened portions of the region—the marginally better lands of central Texas and southeastern Oklahoma for small operators, or the large, new plantations carved out of recently reclaimed alluvial soils such as in the Yazoo delta of northwestern Mississippi.[35]

It was in their efforts to address the broader problems of dealing with the integrating market system and the changes wrought by technology off the farm that southern leaders of the mounting but still diffuse farmers' movement found common ground with northern staple producers. But irreparable divisions prevented the Northern Alliance leaders from fully joining those from the South. The divisions were partly based on residues of sectional antagonisms carried over from the Civil War. There were also real conflicts in their economic interests which forced the leaders of the two Alliances to appreciate the fact that the existence of divergent forms of specialization was making American agriculture a cluster of highly differentiated industries. A major stumbling block in the effort to make a single national Alliance was in the disagreement over whether or not to call for the prohibition of oleomargarine as a cheap substitute for butter, a demand that was being pressed then by dairy farmers in the North but was anathema to cotton farmers, who hoped they had finally found a potential market for cottonseed oil.[36]

If such a dispute seemed narrow, the Southern Alliance's major newspaper, the *National Economist,* articulated several broad goals by which they hoped to appeal to other reform groups, such as the nationalization of railroads and the telegraph system, the abolition of futures markets, the creation of postal savings banks, the direct election of senators, and the revamping of electoral procedures. Only in their proposal for a "subtreasury plan," which would require the federal government to provide a sizeable advance payment on each farmer's output of certain designated crops, was there a recognition that the alleviation of the basic problem of low prices would require unprecedented measures. This suggestion was dropped from the program as a radical impediment to fusion with the Northern Alliance. Far more successful in both organizations was the revival of cooperatives, often in the form of buying and selling agencies serving an entire state and run with an efficiency that showed that the lessons of the Grange experience had been learned.[37]

The major effort to fuse the two Alliances came in 1890; soon after its failure, in May 1891, the Populist party was formed and a new, climactic phase attained by the agrarian political movement, which had been erratically gathering a determined following. The Populists folded many elements of the farm-led challenges to orthodoxy into a broader, diffuse reform party that also included elements of the Greenback party of the 1870s and the Silverites (both seeking remedies in antideflation mechanisms), the Prohibitionists, the champions of woman's suffrage, remnants of the Knights of Labor (which had gone into eclipse after the 1886 Haymarket tragedy), and such influential critics of the dominant industrial order as Henry Demarest Lloyd. In 1892, the Populists ran a presidential candidate who got a million votes and won some impressive congressional and gubernatorial contests, but clearly had a relatively slender and highly sectional base. Four years later, they were probably beginning to lose strength, and were coopted at the national level by a Democratic party that repudiated its own sitting president and nominated instead a virtually unknown young Nebraskan, William Jennings Bryan, who as a congressman had shown considerable sympathy for many elements of the Populist program. He suffered an overwhelming defeat, which ended what many supporters and some historians deemed the last effort of the agrarians to reclaim the control of the national government and consigned farm spokemen ever since to narrow, pressure-group activities. Less credible is the interpretation that makes the movement, with its tentative alliance between whites and blacks in the South and between farmers and workers in the North, the last gasp of true democracy, and its demise a turning point that lost Americans their last chance to reclaim many of the old republican virtues now submerged in an increasingly urbanized America.[38]

While stormy political activity during the agrarian crusade submerged the older, long-dormant tradition of sporadic, violent protests during the second half of the nineteenth century, the impulses behind the self-help tradition, which stressed improved productivity through the encouragement of science and technology, continued working steadily. In the 1850s the United States Agricultural Society, composed largely of members from the eastern states who sought to apply scientific endeavors to the service of farmers, began agitating anew for congressional action to fulfill John Quincy Adams' old dream of a federally endowed university. Their effort had received added impetus from the beginnings of agricultural scientific research in special institutional settings at Harvard, Yale, and other private universities by those seeking better, more practical knowledge about the biological and chemical processes in farming that Justus Liebig's work on soil chemistry had promised. The commitment to this kind of effort in publicly supported universities was also growing under the influence of such leaders as Jonathan Baldwin Turner.[39]

The belief in federal support for improving the lot of commercial farmers had already produced the rather strenuous efforts in gathering and disseminating information that included additional data in the national census of 1850 and 1860 and the supplementary annual volumes in the Patent Office reports of the 1840s and 1850s. The removal of southern opposition to such aid during the Civil War opened the way for the passage of several laws that established a permanent new relationship between the federal government and farmers. In 1862, the same year that brought the Homestead Act, Congress provided subsidies for transcontinental railroads that would open the West to commercial markets, created a Department of Agriculture (the first special interest bureaucracy within the federal government, though it would not gain cabinet status until late in the century), and perhaps most significant, the Morrill College Land Grant Act. Representatives from Western states generally opposed the Morrill Act, since it gave each state in the Union 30,000 acres from the public domain for each of the state's congressmen with the stipulation that income from the land be used to support a university where the agricultural and mechanical arts could be taught. Since most of the population was still in the East, and most of the public lands in the West, they considered the formula grossly unfair.[40]

Nevertheless, the act created a system of public universities dedicated in large part to a mission of offering practical help through science and technology for farmers. It has been called one of America's greatest and most widely imitated social inventions. It was also an act of faith with few immediate results. Scientific teaching and research would have little apparent effect on farming until late in the century. The first demonstration of its utility came from the laboratories of the United States Department of Agriculture, which uncovered in 1890 the cause of the dreaded "Texas fever" afflicting western cattle (and cattlemen). It was a lowly tick that acted as vector for the disease; putting the cattle through a dip that would kill the insects effected the cure. A second practical solution to farm problems also came in 1890 from the University of Wisconsin, where a scientist named Babcock took a little time out from what he considered more serious research to develop a test measuring the butterfat content of milk, a test simple enough for a child to administer. It opened the way to employing objective standards for judging the quality of milk and a revolution in the marketing of that commodity.[41]

Such advances, important enough in their way, seemed meager during the first generation of investment in research at land grant universities. There were more benefits to farmers and ranchers opening the Great Plains after the Civil War from the technology that brought them barbed wire, windmills, and cheap side arms, to help them contend with fencing problems, water scarcity, and the new fauna of the semi-arid region beyond the Missouri River, than from findings in the laboratories. The political activists were consequently often inclined to be skeptical, if not scathingly critical, of the apparent failure of those institutions to teach useful courses or to engage in research that addressed the farmers' immediate problems.

To some extent, there was a sense that farmers were victimized rather than helped by scientific progress. Many a fake nostrum, impractical machine, and bag of nonsprouting seeds was sold to ingenuous farmers, to mention only a few items in their litany of complaints.[42] Many dairy farmers suddenly felt besieged in the 1890s when the germ theory of disease led urban reformers to call for the tuberculin testing of all cows whose milk entered their markets, though the test was soon shown to be unreliable.[43]

The faith in progress through science was undiminished, however, within the informal network that emerged in virtually every state, binding together the leading (which usually meant most prosperous) farmers, who were usually active in the state agricultural societies and the growing numbers of producers' associations, with the elected representatives at the state and federal levels and the administrators of the land grant universities. From this interlocking support group came the impetus for the Hatch Act of 1887, which set up agricultural experiment stations with the sole mission of serving the farm communities of their states with special research and testing. In some states these laboratories were incorporated into the body of the land grant university; in others they were made and kept separate. Less than twenty years later, after it became obvious that the small staff of these stations had much of their time taken up by routine service functions while real, severe problems lacked attention, the network pushed through the Adams Act, which increased the appropriations for the stations, but required that all of the additional support be devoted solely to research. The justification for this decentralized strategy was that it would best help solve each state's unique farm problems.[44]

While these new institutions were still gathering strength at the beginning of the twentieth century, reaching out to their constituency through such novel efforts as Farmers' Institutes, where professors and deans from the agricultural colleges visited farm communities around their states in the winter months, lecturing for farm youngsters uninterested in the regular academic curriculum of these colleges, farmers in some parts of the nation remained bitter and resentful in the aftermath of the Populist defeat.[45] Many southern cotton farmers, who saw little improvement in prices during the so-called "golden age" of agriculture that lasted from 1900 to 1914, attempted to revive the Alliance system of exchanges and other cooperative ventures in an organization known by the short title of Farmers' Union, the nation's second general farm group. It added one additional weapon to the small arsenal of antimonopoly devices used earlier, a general withholding action designed to constrict supply in order to force prices upward. A widely touted effort along that line attracted considerable attention in 1907, but a better cotton crop the next year undermined much of the belief in the campaign's promise, and farmers in the South abandoned the Union as quickly as they had joined it in this poverty-ridden region. This loss of membership was at least partially offset by gains among farmers in the grain-growing districts of the High Plains, from northern Texas and western Oklahoma to eastern Colorado and parts of Montana, which has remained its chief geographic base until the present.[46]

It was a measure of the desperation of cotton farmers that the opening years of the century also brought to parts of the lower Mississippi Valley a wave of "whitecapping" or racist violence and intimidation in a brutal rural counterpoint to the contemporaneous high tide of lynching incidents against blacks in America. More directly connected to sharp market changes were the night-riding incidents of the "Black Patch War" in western Kentucky, where growers of dark tobacco used violence and intimidation to protest against price changes associated with the rise of cigarette consumption and the increased market power of large-scale tobacco manufacturing firms connected with that product. In both sets of incidents there was a return to the kind of sporadic protest that had marked earlier efforts to deal with threats to farmer survival.[47]

More articulate and more directly descended from the Alliance experiments was the rise of the Equity movement, an effort by J. A. Everitt to formulate a broad goal for farmers of attaining some fair share of the nation's growing wealth by exerting some leverage in the market. The movement had its greatest appeal in the grain-growing regions of the upper Mississippi Valley, but quickly disintegrated into at least three separate groups which had little more than localized influence, except for a few successful statewide grain elevators operated on a cooperative basis. A more surprising residue of radical efforts from the Populist era was the victory of rural-based socialism in North Dakota in 1916. The belief in private property for farmers remained undiminished there, even as the leaders of the Nonpartisan League

(NPL) called for state ownership of grain elevators, banks, flour mills, and insurance companies. In a hard-fought campaign, which on the national level brought the reelection of Woodrow Wilson as president, the farmers of North Dakota captured control of both the legislature and the governorship, and began instituting their program. The movement was undercut, however, by America's entry into World War I, when the NPL made themselves easy targets of repression by counseling against cooperation with conscription and the war effort, partly because of religious, as well as ideological, beliefs and partly because of the German background of many farmers in that state.[48]

The turmoil associated with farmer movements in the late nineteenth and early twentieth centuries came after the impact of gains in productivity from the technology of animal-powered machines had largely run its course. Few farmers benefited from the gradual spread of electricity, telephones, paved roads, or the better schools—including high schools—for their children, all of which began to change the lives of more and more urban Americans. The social isolation of most farmers remained, widening the gap between the shifting attitudes and values of an urbanizing America and the farmers who fed it, though it never was as great as in many other societies. A distinct, uneasy awareness of this disparity lay behind many of the efforts to close the gap between the amenities available to farmers and those enjoyed by town and city people, such as in the work of the Country Life Movement, various church groups, and educational organizations. But the results were rather modest before 1917.[49] Better transportation facilities and services for obtaining inputs and marketing outputs and making it easier to get to town (or to get a doctor or mail) was still the most sought-after technological change.

It was the internal combustion engine, especially Henry Ford's "Tin Lizzie," that began breaking down that isolation. The automobile was a major factor in organizing the NPL in North Dakota in 1916–17. At the same time, it also provided an effective means for bringing directly to farmers a growing number of young men, newly trained at the land grant universities and eager to demonstrate new, and presumably better, methods and deliver information that would improve the farmers' livelihood. Farm leaders and educators were convinced that the occasional involvement of the universities in farmer institutes and short courses did not give farmers the regular, practical, and immediate help they needed. This conviction grew with the achievement of Seaman Knapp, a transplanted Iowan who organized teams to help the semiliterate sharecroppers of the Louisiana and Texas backcountry in their struggle against the boll weevil during the opening years of the century. By literally showing marginal farmers how to cultivate their cotton plants in ways that would disrupt the weevils' life cycle, these nascent extension workers proved their value. The idea spread quickly to the North and was given strong support by such leaders as Kenyon Butterfield. The culmination of this movement was the passage of the Smith-Lever Act in 1914, which provided federal funding to supplement state, county, and private funding for the work of these "county agents." This agricultural extension effort was quickly and demonstrably a success, though inevitably the "clients" who were most receptive to the latest discoveries were already the most effective producers and the easiest to teach. Nevertheless, this adjunct to the diffusion of scientific and technical knowledge was a second great social invention that shaped our highly diverse agricultural institutions.[50]

It was also virtually inevitable that as the network of county agents began to spread—rapidly, across the northeastern quadrant of the nation, and somewhat more slowly in the Southeast and West—the private supporters among the more prosperous farmers and rural businessmen would organize themselves into more formal interest groups, pushing for additional legislative aid at both the state and federal level. In parts of the Midwest such as Iowa and Illinois, they were also self-consciously serving as a counterweight to the radical influence of movements such as the NPL. The Farm Bureau movement soon reached national scope; by 1920 the American Farm Bureau Federation (AFBF) had become the most active general farm organization in the United States, with a lobbying office in Washington, D.C.[51]

In the aftermath of World War I, which had brought a relative prosperity such as farmers had not seen in two generations, there came a sharp reaction, a farm crisis marked by the collapse of prices during the year following June 1920. The American Farm Bureau Federation's lobbyist, Grey Silver, was instrumental in organizing a group of progressive congressmen on a nonpartisan basis into a "farm bloc," which pushed through a series of laws meeting long-standing demands of rural constituents. Among these were the regulation of stockyards, packing plants, and futures markets, and extension of credit and enlargement of land bank activities, secondary highway construction, and the Capper-Volstead Act of 1922, the "Magna Carta" of the cooperative movement, so called because it authorized state governments to exempt producers' cooperatives from prosecution under antitrust laws.[52] The act came at the height of an effort to apply the techniques of close-knit specialty producer cooperatives, primarily in California, to the more widespread, disorganized livestock and staple growers, who confronted depressed world prices that would prevail throughout the 1920s and 1930s. The charismatic leader of the effort to organize staple producers into cooperatives that could administer prices through monopolistic power was Aaron Sapiro, a young lawyer who as a protege of David Lubin and Harris Weinstock of Sacramento had helped specialty producers obtain such market power during the previous decade. It was one of the first efforts to confront realistically the need to curtail output, but not enough of the basic commodity producers—whether specialists in livestock, grain, or tobacco—could be brought into the single, large-scale cooperative required to make such market power possible. The scheme soon collapsed amid considerable recrimination.[53]

For the rest of the 1920s, the Farm Bureau, as the major effective voice of farm interests, backed an export-dumping scheme advocated by George N. Peek. They were successful enough to get Congress twice to pass the McNary-Haugen Bill to implement that scheme, only to have it vetoed by President Coolidge. Persuaded that the "farm problem," as the persistence of low prices and inadequate income was called, could be best handled by cooperative action, incoming President Hoover called a special session of Congress in the summer of 1929. He pushed through an Agricultural Marketing Act that in effect provided for federal loans and administrative help to implement the logic of the Sapiro plan. The timing was dreadful, however, and a further collapse of prices after 1929 undermined the experiment, leaving to the New Deal the task of rescuing commercial farmers through production controls by restricting acreage, with allotment payments as compensation for foregone output.[54]

Meanwhile, the new crisis of 1929–1933 generated considerable discontent in bedrock conservative Iowa and among its neighboring states, again involving both short-lived withholding actions such as had been tried in the 1920–21 debacle and violent resistance to foreclosures. Similar encounters took place in milk withholding actions (and forced dumping) on roads leading to market in Wisconsin and upstate New York. An emergency farm mortgage refinancing act enacted during the famous "Hundred Days" under Franklin Roosevelt was as critical as the Agricultural Adjustment Act (AAA) in allaying the desperation of farmers afraid of losing their equity and willing to flirt with the most radical solutions to prevent it.[55]

The injection of liquidity into the farm economy slowly began to make possible a resurgence of investment in long-delayed technical improvements. Foremost among the machines was the stable tractor with power takeoff, making feasible the use of a wide range of attached implements, such as cotton pickers, that dramatically increased output per man hour. Hybrid seeds and other products of genetic research, along with better fertilizers, began to make significant improvements in yields per acre as well. None of these changes took place fast enough during the 1930s to have a noticeable effect.[56] But the subsidization of cooperatives to provide farmers with cheap electricity through the Rural Electrification Administration did bring a rapid change. In 1930, less than 10 percent of American farms had access to "juice"; by 1940, almost 90 percent did, with revolutionary effects on the engineering of farms and their machines, as well as the lot of the homemaker, who was able at last to use the same appliances as her city counterpart.[57]

At first, the New Deal gave the Farm Bureau a chance to increase its influence. Asserting that "membership is power," its president, Edward O'Neal, launched a vigorous drive to sign up new members. He could claim, with some justice, that Farm Bureau pressure had been instrumental in drafting the AAA and other helpful laws. The drive was also helped considerably by the willing cooperation of county agents, who dispensed allotment payments. Increasingly, however, the Farm Bureau leadership became troubled by various other rural experiments, such as the Subsistence Homestead Act and Bankhead-Jones Tenancy Act. Farm Bureau support had turned a demonstration against the Supreme Court decision declaring the AAA unconstitutional into one of the largest marches on Washington ever seen. But two years later the second AAA of 1938 went through

Congress without the support of the AFBF. Instead, a revitalized Farmers' Union, based in Denver, Colorado and calling for prices that would cover "the cost of production," was gaining influence in Washington lobbies and the U.S. Department of Agriculture. Less effective were the protests mounted by the Southern Tenant Farmers' Union and other groups representing those farm dwellers who were being displaced instead of helped by New Deal policies.[58] Indeed, both tenants and farm laborers were far more vulnerable to displacement by technological change in production over the last century than farm owners, who at least had access to credit to help them make adjustments.

It was World War II that began the true transformation of farming in the United States, just as it ended the Depression at large. The sudden shortage of labor pulled many of the submerged lower half of income receivers in American farming, particularly those underemployed on the land, into factory and other urban jobs, while providing those who stayed with parity prices for the first time since 1920. During the war, farmers received special exemptions and extra rations of tires and gasoline, and in turn pressed every available machine into service to produce 25 percent more food and fiber with 25 percent fewer workers. Their congressional representatives, however, insisted on a floor of fixed price supports at 90 percent of parity in return for accepting a ceiling of 110 percent in conformity with anti-inflation measures. The postwar period brought squabbles over support prices for perishable crops (soon dropped), and over the "Brannan Plan," effectively resulting in a stalemate over policy, and the spectacle in the mid- and late 1950s of Secretary of Agriculture Benson—a conservative leader of his state's Farm Bureau and the National Council of Cooperatives—struggling mightily to return subsidies to the level set in the basic second AAA, which he had once despised.[59]

This squabble took place at the same time as a virtual explosion of productivity in farming, accompanied by a massive outmigration of people from farming (the latter in part a transfer of welfare problems to cities). The productivity increase, which was roughly three times greater than the analogous increase in manufacturing, came from the final displacement of draft animals by tractors, the improvement of the entire range of mechanized equipment, the application of new, powerful herbicides and insecticides, and advances in seed and livestock breeding. But it also made farming to a much greater degree capital intensive rather than labor intensive, and required farmers to go deep into debt to keep and add to their land and buy equipment.[60]

By the late 1950s a new group of farmers in the Midwest, mostly hog and dairy farmers in their thirties and forties from northern Missouri, Iowa, Wisconsin, and Minnesota who were disillusioned with the perceived ineffectiveness of the AFBF, the Grange, the Farmers' Union, and the National Council of Cooperatives (the four major "spokesman" organizations), had founded the National Farmers Organization. They stressed the need to emulate labor unions, which then seemed quite successful in dealing with large-scale enterprises, and to "bargain collectively" with the purchasers of their farm products. Only that way, they believed, could they secure prices fair enough to release them from the lifetime of indebtedness they saw ahead. The peak of their militancy, and their effectiveness, came in the 1960s. They stumped futilely in 1962 on behalf of the Kennedy farm program proposals but then led a series of "withholding actions" that forced several midwestern creameries and meat-packing plants to sign contracts with them. Since then, they have been almost indistinguishable from the older organizations.[61]

By the 1970s farmers had truly become one of the last minorities in America, members of a highly diverse outdoor high-technology industry—or more properly, a cluster of industries divided against themselves.[62] Many of their members have seen in the Russian wheat deal of the early 1970s, the energy crisis, and the succeeding "stagflation" a plot to undermine the family farm. As the burden of debts at new, higher interest rates strained their resources, the nation was treated to the spectacle in 1979 of a newly formed American Agriculture Movement mounting a "drive" on Washington that involved farmers moving their huge, rumbling equipment up Pennsylvania Avenue in a virtual parade of technology that left most observers awestruck by the productive capacity of farmers, rather than by their plight as debtors.[63] Meanwhile, the Reagan administration was finding that in spite of an ideological commitment to removing the federal government from direct involvement in the farm economy, it was trying to save commercial farmers by unprecedented outlays for a Payments-in-Kind (PIK) program, and by sponsoring short-term moratoria on farm foreclosures.[64]

Since then, the deflation and reduction in exports because of the strong dollar has had similar adverse effects, and during the 1983–84 winter the same movement led groups of protesting farmers in demonstrations on Wall Street and the commodity exchanges of Chicago. Meanwhile, the real stress and pain of farmers threatened with the loss of their land, marked once more with small, sporadic outbursts of violence, shows up regularly on the television news. They are now but a small fraction of the two percent of the national population drawing a living, or at least part of one, from the land, but are no closer to articulating their cause in a coherent fashion than they were a century ago.[65] Agriculture may represent the nation's largest employer when broadly defined, but the farmers' movement offers little new hope to that small segment of the industry that still lives on the land.

Notes

1. Gregory A. Stiverson, *Poverty in a Land of Plenty: Tenancy in Eighteenth-Century Maryland* (Baltimore: Johns Hopkins University Press, 1977); Sung Bok Kim, *Landlord and Tenant in Colonial New York: Manorial Society, 1664–1775* (Chapel Hill: University of North Carolina Press, 1978). These revisionist works deal with two of the most notable states in which efforts to maintain manorial arrangements bred continuing tensions. A debate is currently raging over the extent to which colonial settlers established a kind of "moral economy" akin to those perceived in Third World rural societies, and resisted involvement in the cash nexus of markets, a position championed by James Henretta, "Families and Farms: *Mentalité* in Preindustrial America," *William and Mary Quarterly*, 3d series (1978), 35:3–32, and supported by Michael Merrill, "Cash Is Good to Eat: Self-Sufficiency and Exchange in the Rural Economy of the United States," *Radical History Review* (Winter 1977) 4(1):42–71, and Bettye H. Pruitt, "Agriculture and Society in the Towns of Massachusetts, 1771: A Statistical Analysis," Ph.D. dissertation, Boston University, 1981. The chief criticisms come from James T. Lemon, "Early Americans and their social environment," *Journal of Historical Geography* (1980), 6(2):115–131; Carole Shammas, "How Self-Sufficient Was Early America?" *Journal of Interdisciplinary History* (Autumn 1982) 13(2):247–272, and such works as David L. Coon, "The Development of Market Agriculture in South Carolina, 1670–1785," Ph.D. dissertation, University of Illinois, 1972. For comparisons with the Canadian and South African frontiers, see William Norton, "Frontier Agriculture: Subsistence or Commercial," *Annals of the Association of American Geographers*, (September 1977), 67(3):463–468.

2. The classic evaluation of these two ordinances as major achievements by government under the Articles of Confederation remains Merrill Jensen, *The New Nation: A History of the United States During the Confederation, 1781–1789* (New York: Knopf, 1950), pp. 234–244, 350–359. The standard survey of federal land laws since the

passage of the ordinances is Paul W. Gates, *History of Public Land Law Development* (Washington, D.C.: Public Land Law Review Commission, 1968). A thoughtful collection of articles on how those laws worked as they changed over time is Vernon Carstensen, ed., *The Public Lands: Studies in the History of the Public Domain* (Madison: University of Wisconsin Press, 1963). For a wide-ranging discussion that stresses the gradual commercialization of farming in most of the United States during the "frontier-rural period" from 1720 to 1870, see Walter Nugent, *Structures of American Social History* (Bloomington: Indiana University Press, 1981), pp. 74–86.

3. Jim Potter, "The Growth of Population in America, 1700–1860," in David V. Glass and D. E. Eversley, *Population in History: Essays in Historical Demography* (Chicago: Aldine, 1965), pp. 631–688.

4. J. D. Chambers and G. E. Mingay, *The Agricultural Revolution, 1750–1880* (London: Batsford, 1966) is the standard work on the British phase of these changes. For a broad discussion of the cultural context of these changes in Western Europe and North America, and the critical role of land ownership, along with a capitalistic mind-set by those owners, in the diffusion of more productive methods and organization, see William N. Parker, "The Magic of Property," *Agricultural History* 54:4 (October 1980), 54(4):477–489.

5. James T. Lemon, *The Best Poor Man's Country: A Geographical Study of Early Southeastern Pennsylvania* (Baltimore: Johns Hopkins University Press, 1972); the relatively static nature of eighteenth-century agriculture in the British North American colonies and in the United States into the nineteenth century forms the basis for Clarence H. Danhof, *Change in Agriculture: The Northern United States, 1820–1870* (Cambridge: Harvard University Press, 1969).

6. Washington's letters to Arthur Young, the leading publicist and advocate of the "Agricultural Revolution," included a letter from Jefferson explaining the same phenomenon, cited in Lewis C. Gray, *History of Agriculture in the Southern United States to 1860*, 2 vols. (reprinted Gloucester, Mass.: Peter Smith, 1958), 1:449.

7. John Storck and Walter D. Teague, *Flour for Man's Bread: A History of Milling* (Minneapolis: University of Minnesota Press, 1952), pp. 158–174. For a full discussion of Evans, see Greville and Dorothy Bache, *Oliver Evans: A Chronicle of American Engineering* (Philadelphia: Historical Society of Pennsylvania, 1935). On Whitney, see Constance McL. Green, *Eli Whitney and the Birth of American Technology* (Boston: Little, Brown, 1956) and Nathan Rosenberg, *Technology and American Economic Growth* (New York: Harper and Row, 1972), pp. 26–27. For an excellent overview of the antebellum cotton market, see Stuart Bruchey, comp. and ed., *Cotton and the Growth of the American Economy: 1790–1860* (New York: Harcourt, Brace and World, 1967).

8. For an accessible overview see Joseph P. Cullen, "Bacon's Rebellion," *American History Illustrated* (December 1968), pp. 22–27. A judicious selection of relevant documents, with helpful headnotes, is Robert Middlekauf, ed., *Bacon's Rebellion*, Berkeley Series in American History, Charles Sellers, ed. (Chicago: Rand, McNally, 1964). For a probing inquiry into the causes of the incident, see Warren W. Billings, "The Causes of Bacon's Rebellion: Some Suggestions," *Virginia Magazine of History and Biography*, (October 1970), 78(1):409–435. There is an interesting effort to link the incident to declining tobacco prices and shrinking opportunities, along with an accelerated use of black slaves, in Edmund Morgan, *American Slavery, American Freedom: The Ordeal of Colonial Virginia* (New York: Norton, 1975), pp. 250–275, but it has come under sharp attack. A different approach, linking it to disappointed hopes of "middling settlers," is taken in Darrett B. Rutman and Anita H. Rutman, *A Place in Time: Middlesex County, Virginia, 1650–1750* (New York:

Norton, 1984). A recent effort to return to political rather than economic explanations, and to interpret Bacon again as a "torchbearer of the Revolution" is in
Stephen S. Webb, *1676: The End of American Independence* (New York: Knopf, 1984).
On the Paxton Boys and their protest against insufficient "protection" from Indians,
see Wilbur R. Jacobs, ed., *The Paxton Riots and the Frontier Theory,* Berkeley Series
in American History, Charles Sellers, ed. (Chicago: Rand McNally, 1967).

9. David S. Lovejoy, *The Glorious Revolution in America* (New York: Harper and Row,
1972). For a classic account of such movements, and an effort to lump all farmers'
attempts to preserve and improve their condition into a single "movement," see
Carl C. Taylor, *The Farmers' Movement: 1620–1920* (New York: American Book
Company, 1953).

10. Robert M. Brown, *The South Carolina Regulators* (Cambridge: Harvard University
Press, 1963), the standard account, must be supplemented with Rachel N. Klein,
"Ordering the Backcountry: The South Carolina Regulation," *William and Mary
Quarterly* (October 1981), 38(4):661–680), and her Ph.D. dissertation, "The Rise
of the Planters in the South Carolina Backcountry, 1767–1808," Yale University,
1979, which compares that group with the more "democratic" North Carolina
Regulators. For a broader treatment of these outbreaks in the context of violent
episodes across the history of the United States, see Robert M. Brown, *Strain of
Violence: Historical Studies of American Violence and Vigilantism* (New York: Oxford
University Press, 1975), pp. 30–33, 69–83. For a recent effort to provide an eco-
nomic interpretation of the North Carolina movement, see A. Roger Ekirch, *"Poor
Carolina": Politics and Society in Colonial North Carolina, 1729–1776* (Chapel Hill:
University of North Carolina Press, 1981) and the perceptive review of it by Richard
L. McCormick in *William and Mary Quarterly* (October 1983), 40(4):598–615.

11. It is curious that this incident has not yet received the balanced study it deserves.
For a recent discussion, see Richard D. Brown, "Shays' Rebellion and its Aftermath:
A View from Springfield, Massachusetts, 1787," *William and Mary Quarterly* (Oc-
tober 1983), 40(4):598–615. A useful discussion of the background for the protest
is in Van Beck Hall, *Politics Without Parties: Massachusetts, 1780–1791* (Pittsburgh:
University of Pittsburgh Press, 1972), pp. 190–226. Important new work is under-
way, as shown in a session on the social context of Shays' Rebellion at the American
Historical Association Meetings, December 1984, Chicago, with papers by John L.
Brooke and Gregory H. Nobles.

12. A good discussion of the literature is contained in David O. Whitten, "An Economic
Inquiry into the Whiskey Rebellion of 1794," *Agricultural History* (July 1975),
49(3):491–504 and in the work on a virtually neglected parallel protest, Mary K.
Bonsteel Tachau, "The Whiskey Rebellion in Kentucky: A Forgotten Episode of
Civil Disobedience," *Journal of the Early Republic* (Fall 1982), 2:239–259. This last
essay is reproduced, along with several others and some newly edited documents,
in Stephen R. Boyd, ed., *The Whiskey Rebellion: Past and Present Perspectives* (Contributions in American History, Number 109; Westport, Conn.: Greenwood Press,
1985).

13. Taylor, *The Farmers' Movement,* pp. 53–56.

14. Paul W. Gates, "Tenants of the Log Cabin," *Mississippi Valley Historical Review* (June
1962), 49:3–31. On the general early thrust for "improvement," see Curtis P.
Nettels, *The Emergence of a National Economy, 1775–1815* (New York: Holt, Rinehart
and Winston, 1962), pp. 243–262.

15. Wayne C. Neely, *The Agricultural Fair* (New York: Columbia University Press, 1935),
pp. 27–109; Danhof, *Change in Agriculture,* pp. 49–72; Roy V. Scott, *The Reluctant
Farmer: The Rise of Agricultural Extension to 1914* (Urbana: University of Illinois Press,

1970), pp. 3–36; David E. Lindstrom, *American Farmers' and Rural Organizations* (Champaign, Ill.: Garrard Press, 1948), pp. 59–74.

16. Donald Marti, "Agrarian Thought and Agricultural Progress: The Endeavor for Agricultural Improvement in New England and New York, 1815–1840," Ph.D. dissertation, University of Wisconsin, 1966.

17. The standard work on farm newspapers and magazines as disseminators of information is Albert L. Demaree, *The American Agricultural Press, 1819–1860* (New York: Columbia University Press, 1941).

18. Two examples of such clubs are found in Cat Spring Agricultural Society, *The Cat Spring Story* (San Antonio, Texas: Lone Star Printing Company, 1956) and the records of the Rosendale, Wisconsin Agricultural Society, State Historical Society of Wisconsin, Madison.

19. On the broad aspects of social development in that region, see William N. Parker, "From Northwest to Midwest: Social Bases of a Regional History," in David C. Klingaman and Richard K. Vedder, eds., *Essays in Nineteenth-Century Economic History: The Old Northwest* (Athens: Ohio University Press, 1975), pp. 3–34. For a detailed discussion of early support for railroad construction by individual farmers and farm communities in Wisconsin, see Frederick Merk, *Economic History of Wisconsin During the Civil War Decade* (Madison: State Historical Society of Wisconsin, 1916) pp. 238–288. For a more recent survey of all sources of support for railroads, including donations of labor and funds by farmers, see Edward T. Morgan, "Sources of Capital for Railroads in the Old Northwest," Ph.D. dissertation, University of Wisconsin, 1964.

20. For the general context of farming activities and the associated institutions during the antebellum period, see Paul W. Gates, *The Farmer's Age: Agriculture, 1815–1860* (New York: Holt, Rinehart and Winston, 1960). The innovation of the steel-tipped plow, and the implement business that grew out of it, is treated in Wayne G. Broehl, Jr., *John Deere's Company: A History of Deere and Company and its Times* (New York: Doubleday, 1984). On an early rival, see Douglas L. Meikle, "James Oliver and the Oliver Chilled Plow Works," Ph.D. dissertation, Indiana University, 1958. On the use of hired farm labor in custom plowing, threshing, etc., see David E. Schob, *Hired Hands and Plowboys: Farm Labor in the Midwest, 1815–60* (Urbana: University of Illinois Press, 1975).

21. The best brief discussion of the reaper is in William N. Parker, "Agriculture," in Lance E. Davis, et al., eds., *American Economic Growth: An Economist's History of the United States* (New York: Harper and Row, 1972). For a sophisticated effort to explain its diffusion, see Paul A. David, *Technical Choice, Innovation, and Economic Growth* (Cambridge: Cambridge University Press, 1975), pp. 195–232. See also Paul P. Christensen, "Land Abundance and Cheap Horsepower in the Mechanization of the Antebellum United States Economy," *Explorations in Economic History* (October 1981), 18:309–329.

22. Alan L. Olmstead, "The Mechanization of Reaping and Mowing in American Agriculture, 1833–1870," *The Journal of Economic History* (June 1975), 35:327–352 and "The Diffusion of the Reaper: One More Time," *ibid.* (June 1979), 39:475–476.

23. Wayne D. Rasmussen, "The Impact of Technological Change on American Agriculture, 1862–1962," *Journal of Economic History* (December 1962), 22:578–591; Danhof, *Change in Agriculture*, pp. 228–249.

24. Lee Benson, *Merchants, Farmers and Railroads: Railroad Regulation and New York Politics, 1850–1887* (Cambridge: Harvard University Press, 1955). On the fragmented nature of early nineteenth-century markets in the nation, see Allan R. Pred, *Urban*

Growth and the Circulation of Information: The United States System of Cities, 1790–1840 (Cambridge: Harvard University Press, 1973). On marketing innovations in grain exchanges, see Jeffrey C. Williams, "The Origins of Futures Markets," *Agricultural History* (January 1982), 56(1):306–316; Richard O. Zerbe, "The Origin and Effect of Grain Trade Regulations in the Late Nineteenth Century," *ibid.*, pp. 172–193; and Thomas S. Ulen, "The Regulation of Grain Warehousing and Its Economic Effects: The Competitive Position of Chicago in the 1870s and 1880s," *ibid.*, pp. 194–210.

25. Charles Hirschfeld, *The Great Railroad Conspiracy: The Social History of a Railroad War* (East Lansing: Michigan State University Press, 1953).

26. Frederick Merk, "Eastern Antecedents of the Grangers," *Agricultural History* (January 1949), 23(1):1–8; Merk, *Economic History of Wisconsin*. This phenomenon was repeated later, when the late nineteenth-century protest movement swept up farmers in eastern Nebraska at the same time that those in the western parts of the state were seeking to attract railroads and other services for their enterprises; see Stanley B. Parsons, *The Populist Context: Rural Versus Urban Power on a Great Plains Frontier* (Westport, Conn.: Greenwood Press, 1973).

27. Frank L. Klement, *The Copperheads of the Middle West* (Chicago: University of Chicago Press, 1960); Solon J. Buck, *The Granger Movement: A Study of Agricultural Organization and Its Political, Economic and Social Manifestations, 1870–1880* (Cambridge, Mass.: Harvard University Press, 1913); D. Sven Nordin, *Rich Harvest: A History of the Grange, 1867–1900* (Jackson: University Press of Mississippi, 1974).

28. Harold D. Woodman, "Chicago Businessmen and the 'Granger' Laws," *Agricultural History* (January 1962), 36(1):79–90; Roy V. Scott, *The Agrarian Movement in Illinois, 1880–1896*, Illinois Studies in the Social Sciences, vol. 52 (Urbana; University of Illinois Press, 1962).

29. For a convenient collection of excerpts from original sources associated with the Grangers, and trenchant comments on the post-Civil War farmers' movements in general, see Vernon Carstensen, ed., *Farmer Discontent, 1865–1900* (New York: Wiley, 1974); for the legal background of this case, see Harry N. Scheiber, "The Road to *Munn:* Eminent Domain and the Concept of Public Purpose in the State Courts," *Perspectives in American History* (1971), 5:329–402.

30. George H. Miller, *Railroads and the Granger Laws* (Madison: University of Wisconsin Press, 1971).

31. Ezra S. Carr, *The Patrons of Husbandry on the Pacific Coast* (San Francisco: Bancroft, 1875); George Cerny, "Cooperation in the Midwest in the Granger Era, 1869–1975," *Agricultural History* (October 1963), 38(4):187–205; Joseph G. Knapp, *The Rise of American Cooperative Enterprise: 1620–1920* (Danville, Ill.: Interstate Printers and Publishers, 1969), pp. 46–57.

32. Philip N. Backstrom, "The Mississippi Valley Trading Company: A Venture in International Cooperation, 1875–1877," *Agricultural History* (July 1972), 46(3):425–437.

33. George B. Ridgeway, "Populism in Washington," *Pacific Northwest Quarterly* (October 1948), 39(4):284–311; Thomas W. Riddle, "Populism in the Palouse: Old Ideals and New Realities," *Pacific Northwest Quarterly* (July 1974), 65(3), 98–109; Robert L. Tontz, "Memberships of General Farmers' Organizations, United States, 1874–1960," *Agricultural History* (July 1964), 38(3):143–156. For the later history of a business-oriented offshoot of the Grange that was mostly confined to New England and New York, see Thomas E. Milliman and Frances E. Sage, *The GLF Story, 1920–1964: A History of the Cooperative Grange League Federation Exchange* (Ithaca, N.Y.: Wilcox Press, 1967).

34. Robert C. McMath, Jr., *Populist Vanguard: A History of the Southern Farmers' Alliance* (Chapel Hill: University of North Carolina Press, 1975); Michael Schwartz, *Radical Protest and Social Structure: The Southern Farmers' Alliance and Cotton Tenancy, 1880– 1890* (New York: Academic Press, 1976); Floyd J. Miller, "Black Protest and White Leadership: A Note on the Colored Farmers' Alliance," *Phylon* (Summer 1972), 33(2):169–178; Theodore Saloutos, *Farmer Movements in the South, 1865–1933* (Berkeley: University of California Press, 1960). For state-level studies, see Nick Adzick, "Agrarian Discontent in Missouri, 1865–1880: The Political and Economic Manifestations of Agrarian Unrest," Ph.D. dissertation, St. Louis University, 1977; Ronald Briel, "Preface to Populism: A Social Analysis of Minor Parties in Nebraska Politics, 1876–1890," Ph.D. dissertation, University of Nebraska-Lincoln, 1981; Donna A. Barnes, *Farmers in Rebellion: The Rise and Fall of the Southern Farmers' Alliance and People's Party in Texas* (Austin: University of Texas Press, 1984). On the special role of lecturers and the difference between the rhetoric of the Alliance and the later Populists, see Lois Scoggins Self, "American Chatauqua: The Lecture System of the Southern Farmers' Alliance Movement," Ph.D. dissertation, University of Wisconsin, 1981.

35. Pete Daniel, *Breaking the Land: The Transformation of Cotton, Tobacco, and Rice Cultures Since 1880* (Urbana: University of Illinois Press, 1985); Robert L. Brandfon, *Cotton Kingdom of the New South: A History of the Yazoo Mississippi Delta from Reconstruction to the Twentieth Century* (Cambridge; Harvard University Press, 1967); Steven Hahn, *The Roots of Southern Populism: Yeoman Farmers and the Transformation of the Georgia Upcountry, 1850–1890* (New York: Oxford University Press, 1983).

36. H. Clarence Nixon, "The Cleavage Within the Farmers' Alliance Movement," *Mississippi Valley Historical Review* (June 1928), 15:22–33; Lawrence Goodwyn, *The Populist Moment: A Short History of the Agrarian Revolt in America* (New York: Oxford University Press, 1978), an abridged, paperback version of his *Democratic Promise: The Populist Moment in America* (New York: Oxford University Press, 1979) has numerous references to the sectionalist divisions within the movement. It is a major, but flawed, work, extending the sympathetic interpretations of such classic, but now somewhat outmoded accounts as John D. Hicks, *The Populist Revolt: A History of the Farmers' Alliance and the People's Party* (Minneapolis: University of Minnesota Press, 1931) to claim much larger importance for this agrarian "crusade" as a turning point that did not turn, a last chance to preserve older democratic forms and values in the United States. For two friendly but not uncritical discussions of this theme, see Robert C. McMath, Jr., "The Movement Culture of Populism Reconsidered: Cultural Origins of the Farmers' Alliance of Texas, 1879–1886," in Henry C. Dethloff and Irvin M. May, Jr., eds., *Southwestern Agriculture: Pre-Columbian to Modern* (Texas A&M University Press, 1982), pp. 197–225, and Bruce Palmer, "The Southern Populists and the American Dream," *ibid.,* pp. 226–239. For a thoughtful discussion of recent works on the Populists from a more radical point of view, see James Green, "Populism, Socialism, and the Promise of Democracy," *Radical History Review* (Fall 1980) 24:7–40; and Goodwyn's response to critics in his "The Cooperative Commonwealth and Other Abstractions: In Search of a Democratic Premise," *Marxist Perspectives* (Summer 1980), pp. 8–42.

37. Schwartz, *Radical Protest,* pp. 203–245; McMath, *Populist Vanguard,* pp. 90–109, 125–6, 148; Knapp, *Rise of Cooperative Enterprise,* pp. 57–68; Stanley B. Parsons et al., "The Role of Cooperatives in the Development of the Movement Culture of Populism," *Journal of American History* (March 1983), 69(4):866–887.

38. Charles M. Destler, *Henry Demarest Lloyd and the Empire of Reform* (Philadelphia: University of Pennsylvania Press, 1963); Paul W. Glad, *McKinley, Bryan, and the People* (Philadelphia: Lippincott, 1964); and Robert F. Durden, *The Climax of Populism* (Lexington: University of Kentucky Press, 1965) deal with the political movement on a national basis. There is a growing literature on the identity, at least by income or commodity groupings, of Populists among farmers, and their motivations—rational or irrational. See Walter T. K. Nugent, "Some Parameters of Populism," *Agricultural History* (October 1966), 40(4):255–270; James Turner, "Understanding the Populists," *Journal of American History* (September 1980), 67(2):354–373; Dwight B. Billings, Jr., *Planters and the Making of a "New South": Class, Politics, and Development in North Carolina, 1865–1900* (Chapel Hill: University of North Carolina Press, 1979); John Dibbern, "Who Were the Populists? A Study of Grass Roots Alliance Men in Dakota," *Agricultural History* (October 1982), 56(4):677–691; Peter H. Argersinger, "Ideology and Behavior: Legislative Politics and Western Populism," *Agricultural History* (January 1984), 58(1):43–58; George B. Tindall, *The Persistent Tradition in the New South* (Baton Rouge: Louisiana State University Press, 1975), pp. 24–47. For sociological explanations, see Arthur Stinchcombe, "Agricultural Enterprise and Rural Class Relations," *American Journal of Sociology* (1961–1962), 67:165–176 and Barnes, *Farmers in Rebellion*, pp. 9–50. For economic explanations, and contrasts between the Northern and Southern Alliances as part of the Populist uprising, see Anne Mayhew, "A Reappraisal of the Causes of Farm Protest Movements in the United States, 1870–1900," *Journal of Economic History* (June 1972), 32:464–475, which concludes that it was primarily a reaction to the commercialization of agriculture rather than to specific changes in costs, prices, etc.; Robert Klepper, *The Economic Bases for Agrarian Protest Movements in the United States, 1870–1900* (New York: Arno Press, 1978), found that change in farm income was the most significant of several possible income effects on a state by state basis, and Thomas F. Cooley and Stephen J. DeCanio, "Rational Expectations in American Agriculture, 1867–1914," *Review of Economics Statistics* (February 1977), 59:9–17 examined price responsiveness of both wheat and cotton growers and found them much greater than previously supposed. Robert A. McGuire, "Economic Causes of Late Nineteenth-Century Agrarian Unrest," *Journal of Economic History* (December 1981), 41(4), pp. 835–852 isolated the same prime mover that I have suggested for earlier violent outbreaks, the threat of loss of farms through bankruptcy foreclosures and other indices of economic instability in determining the intensity and location of agrarian unrest in northern states from 1866 to 1909. For thoughtful comparisons of the Populists with analogous movements elsewhere in the world see Kenneth Barkin, "A Case Study in Comparative History: Populism in Germany and America," in Herbert Bass, ed., *The State of American History* (Chicago: Quadrangle, 1970), pp. 373–404 and Richard K. Horner, "Agrarian Movements and their Historical Conditions," *Peasant Studies* (Winter 1979), 8(1):1–16. See also James Youngdale, *Populism: A Psychological Perspective* (Port Washington, N.Y.: Kennikat Press, 1975).

39. Lyman Carrier, "The United States Agricultural Society, 1852–1860," *Agricultural History* (October 1937), 11(4):278–288; Donald R. Brown, "Jonathan Baldwin Turner and the Land-Grant Idea," *Journal of Illinois State Historical Society* (Winter 1962), 55(4):370–384; Margaret W. Rossiter, *The Emergence of Agricultural Science: Justus Liebig and the Americans, 1840–1880* (New Haven: Yale University Press, 1975).

40. Earle D. Ross, *Democracy's College: The Land Grant Movement in the Formative Stage* (Ames: Iowa State College Press, 1942); Allan G. Bogue, *The Earnest Men: Republicans of the Civil War Senate* (Ithaca: Cornell University Press, 1981).

41. Frederick Merk, *History of the Westward Movement* (New York: Knopf, 1978), pp. 457–466; W. H. Glover, *Farm and College: The College of Agriculture of the University of Wisconsin: A History* (Madison: University of Wisconsin Press, 1952), pp. 112–122; for tensions and criticisms faced in New York by the land grant institution, see Gould P. Colman, *Education and Agriculture: A History of the New York State College of Agriculture at Cornell University* (Ithaca: Cornell University Press, 1963).

42. Earl W. Hayter, *The Troubled Farmer, 1850–1900: Rural Adjustments to Industrialism* (DeKalb: Northern Illinois University Press, 1968); McMath, "Movement Culture," pp. 214–217 and Steven Hahn, *The Roots of Southern Populism: Yeoman Farmers and the Transformation of the Georgia Upcountry, 1850–1890* (New York: Oxford Press, 1983), deal with fencing problems; on irrigation "monopolies" as sources of political insurgency in the trans-Mississippi West, see James E. Wright, *The Politics of Populism: Dissent in Colorado* (New Haven: Yale University Press, 1974); Robert G. Dunbar, *Forging New Rights in Western Waters* (Lincoln: University of Nebraska Press, 1983).

43. Eric E. Lampard, *The Rise of the Dairy Industry in Wisconsin: A Study in Agricultural Change, 1820–1920* (Madison: State Historical Society of Wisconsin, 1963) pp. 228–237, 248–253; Eric Brunger, "Dairying and Urban Development in New York State, 1850–1900," *Agricultural History* (October 1955), 29(4):169–174.

44. Charles E. Rosenberg, "The Adams Act: Politics and the Cause of Scientific Research," *Agricultural History* (January 1964), 38(1):3–12 and his "Rationalization and Reality in the Shaping of American Agricultural Research, 1875–1914," *Social Studies of Science* (1977), 7:401–422; for the broader context of the interaction between research and farming improvement, see William N. Parker and Stephen J. DeCanio, "Two Hidden Sources of Productivity Growth in American Agriculture," *Agricultural History* (October 1982), 54(4):648–662.

45. In addition to the studies by Glover and Colman, cited above, see Emmett P. Fiske, "The College and its Constituency: Rural and Community Development at the University of California, 1875–1978," Ph.D. dissertation, University of California, Davis, 1979. On the bitterness of farmers after the defeat of Populism, see C. Vann Woodward, "The Populist Heritage and the Intellectual," *The Burden of Southern History* (Baton Rouge: Louisiana State University Press, 1960), pp. 141–166.

46. Charles S. Barrett, *The Mission, History, and Times of the Farmers' Union: A Narrative of the Greatest Industrial Agricultural Organization in History and Its Makers* (Nashville, Tenn.: Marshall and Bruce, 1909); William P. Tucker, "Populism Up-to-Date: The Story of the Farmers' Union," *Agricultural History* (October 1947), 21(4):198–208.

47. The rise of overt racism, and the building of a more formal, oppressive, and rigorously enforced system of segregation of blacks and whites in the South after the Populist defeat has been linked to disillusionment among whites after an earlier attempt to cooperate with those blacks, an estimated 1,200,000, who were organized in the late 1880s in a Colored Farmers' Alliance. For this and other splinter groups associated with the agrarian uprising of the 1890s, see Carl C. Taylor, "The Farmers' Movement and Larger Farmers' Organizations," in Carl C. Taylor et al., eds., *Rural Life in the United States* (New York: Knopf, 1949), pp. 510–521 and Theodore Saloutos, "Farmers' Movements," in Glenn Porter, ed., *The Encyclopedia of American Economic History* (New York: Scribners, 1980). For an engrossing portrait of one of the stronger black leaders in the Texas Alliance and the founder of the Farmers Improvement Society of Texas, a black farmers' club that lasted into the

second half of the twentieth century, see Jack Abramowitz, "John B. Rayner: Grass Roots Leader," *Journal of Negro History* (April 1951), 36:176–84. In the older plantation areas of the cotton South, decline in membership in the Colored Alliance began after an abortive cotton pickers' strike in 1891–92. See William F. Holmes, "The Demise of the Colored Farmers' Alliance," *Journal of Southern History* (May 1975), 41:187–200. On the violence against blacks in rural areas, which was a form of vigilante action distinct from the rising numbers of lynchings in the region, see William F. Holmes, "Whitecapping: Agrarian Violence in Mississippi, 1902–06," *Journal of Southern History* (May 1969), 36:165–185 and his "Whitecapping in Late Nineteenth-Century Georgia," in Walter J. Fraser, Jr. and Winfred B. Moore, Jr., eds., *From the Old South to the New: Essays on the Transitional South* (Westport, Ct.: Greenwood Press, 1981), pp. 121–132. On the dark tobacco episodes, see Dewey W. Grantham, "Black Patch War: The Story of the Kentucky and Tennessee Night Riders," *South Atlantic Quarterly* (Spring 1960), 59:225–237; Rick Gregory, "Robertson County and the Black Patch War, 1904–1909," *Tennessee Historical Quarterly* (Fall 1980), 39:341–358. Additional insights are contained in a novel based on these episodes by Robert Penn Warren, *Night Rider* (1940).

48. On the Equity movement, see Theodore Saloutos and John D. Hicks, *Agricultural Discontent in the Middle West, 1900–1939* (Madison: University of Wisconsin Press, 1951), pp. 111–148. On the Nonpartisan League, see Robert L. Morlan, *Political Prairie Fire: The Nonpartisan League, 1915–1922* (Minneapolis: University of Minnesota Press, 1955); Scott A. Ellsworth, "Origins of the Nonpartisan League," Ph.D. dissertation, Duke University, 1982; Dale Baum, "The New Day in North Dakota: The Nonpartisan League and the Politics of Negative Revolution," *North Dakota History* (Spring 1972), 40(2):5–21. On the support given the NPL by a small, but important state Farmers' Union organization between 1913 and 1921, see Larry Remele, "North Dakota's Forgotten Farmer's Union, 1913–1920," *North Dakota History* (Spring 1978), 45(2):4–21. For contemporaneous socialist movements among farmers in the Southwest, see James R. Green, *Grass-Roots Socialism: Radical Movements in the Southwest, 1895–1943* (Baton Rouge: Louisiana State University Press, 1978), pp. 23–329: and Garin Burbank, *When Farmers Voted Red: The Gospel of Socialism in the Oklahoma Countryside, 1910–1924* (Westport, Conn.: Greenwood Press, 1976); and Grady McWhiney, "Louisiana Socialism in the Early Twentieth Century: A Study of Rustic Radicalism," *Journal of Southern History* (August 1954), 20:315–336. For the failure of such movements to link forces with the national labor movement, and vice versa, see David Brody, "On the Failure of U.S. Radical Politics: A Farmer-Labor Analysis," *Industrial Relations* (Spring 1983), 22(2):141–163. For contemporaneous movements in other nations of a similar, geographically limited kind, see Tony Judt, *Socialism in Provence, 1871–1914* (Cambridge: Cambridge University Press, 1979) and Seymour Lipset, *Agrarian Socialism: The Cooperative Commonwealth Federation in Saskatchewan. A Study in Political Sociology* (Berkeley: University of California Press, 1950). For the one continuation of this tradition, fusing a cooperative movement, the remnants of the NPL, and the radical unionism of the Twin Cities and iron mines, see Millard L. Gieske, *Minnesota Farmer-Laborism: The Third Party Alternative* (Minneapolis: University of Minnesota Press, 1979). Still useful is Stuart A. Rice, *Farmers and Workers in American Politics (New York: Columbia University Press, 1924).*

49. David B. Danbom, *The Resisted Revolution: Urban America and the Industrialization of Agriculture, 1900-30* (Ames: Iowa State University Press, 1979); William L. Bowers, *The Country Life Movement in America, 1900–1920* (Port Washington, N.Y.: Kennikat Press, 1974); Paul W. Glad, *The Trumpet Soundeth: William Jennings Bryan and His*

Democracy, 1896–1912 (Lincoln: University of Nebraska Press, 1960) examine various aspects of the growing urban-rural conflict of the so-called "golden age" of agriculture. For a more general overview of the period, see Gilbert C. Fite, *American Farmers: The New Minority* (Bloomington: Indiana University Press, 1981), pp. 1–37. On the continuing interest in railroads as a solution to isolation, and in farmer-owned railroads as an essential part of utopian thought, see H. Roger Grant, "Western Utopians and the Farmers' Railroad Movement, 1890–1900," *North Dakota History* (Winter 1979), 46(1):13–18. On the manifold importance of the automobile in rural lives, see Joseph Interrante, "You Can't Go to Town in a Bathtub: Automobile Movement and the Reorganization of Rural American Space, 1900–1930," *Radical History Review* (Fall 1980), 24(2):151–168.

50. Scott, *The Reluctant Farmer*, pp. 64–311; Joseph C. Bailey, *Seaman A. Knapp: Schoolmaster of American Agriculture* (New York: Columbia University Press, 1945); Gladys L. Baker, *The County Agent* (Chicago: University of Chicago Press, 1939).

51. Orville M. Kile, *The Farm Bureau Movement* (New York: MacMillan, 1921); Robert P. Howard, *James R. Howard and the Farm Bureau* (Ames: Iowa State University Press, 1983); Grant McConnell, *The Decline of Agrarian Democracy* (Berkeley: University of California Press, 1953).

52. James H. Shideler, *Farm Crisis, 1919–1923* (Berkeley: University of California Press, 1957). On the early history of cooperatives, see H. E. Erdman, "The 'Associated Dairies' of New York as Precursors of American Agricultural Cooperation," *Agricultural History* (April 1962), 36(2):82–90, and his "The Development and Significance of California Cooperatives, 1900–1915," *ibid.* (July 1958), 32:179–184; Chelsa C. Sherlock, *The Modern Farm Cooperative Movement* (Des Moines: Homestead Company, 1922); Marin A. Abrahamsen and Claud L. Scroggs, eds., *Agricultural Cooperation* (Minneapolis: University of Minnesota Press, 1957), pp. 4–38; Knapp, *Rise of Cooperative Enterprise*, pp. 176–306.

53. Grace Larsen, "A Progressive in Agriculture: Harris Weinstock," *Agricultural History* (July 1958), 32(3):179–186; Grace H. Larsen and Henry E. Erdman, "Aaron Sapiro: Genius of Farm Cooperative Promotion," *Mississippi Valley Historical Review* (September 1962), 49(2):242–268.

54. Gilbert C. Fite, *George N. Peek and the Fight for Farm Parity* (Norman: University of Oklahoma Press, 1954); Murray R. Benedict, *Farm Policies of the United States: A Study of Their Origins and Development, 1790–1950* (New York: Twentieth Century Fund, 1953).

55. Dale Kramer, *The Wild Jackasses: The American Farmer in Revolt* (New York: Hastings House, 1956), pp. 191–251; John L. Shover, *Cornbelt Rebellion: The Farmers' Holiday Association* (Urbana: University of Illinois Press, 1965); Theodore Saloutos, *The American Farmer and the New Deal* (Ames: Iowa State University Press, 1982), pp. 3–33.

56. Allan G. Bogue, "Changes in Mechanical and Plant Technology: The Corn Belt, 1910–1940," *Journal of Economic History* (March 1983), 43(1):1–25; Daniel, *Breaking the Land*; Fite, *American Farmers*, pp. 66–79.

57. Marquis Childs, *The Farmer Takes a Hand: The Electric Power Revolution in Rural America* (Garden City, N.Y.: Doubleday, 1952); H. S. Person, "Rural Electrification Administration in Perspective," *Agricultural History* (April 1950), 24(2):70–89.

58. Saloutos, *American Farmer*, pp. 236–270; Christiana McF. Campbell, *The Farm Bureau and the New Deal: A Study in the Making of National Farm Policy* (Urbana: University of Illinois Press, 1962). On the South and the effort, belated as it often

was, to do more for the dispossessed, see Donald H. Grubbs, *Cry from the Cotton: The Southern Tenant Farmers' Union and the New Deal* (Chapel Hill: University of North Carolina Press, 1971); David E. Conrad, *The Forgotten Farmers: The Story of Sharecroppers in the New Deal* (Urbana: University of Illinois Press, 1965); Paul E. Mertz, *New Deal Policy and Southern Rural Poverty* (Baton Rouge: Louisiana State University Press, 1978); Louis Cantor, *A Prologue to the Protest Movement: The Missouri Sharecropper Roadside Demonstration of 1939* (Durham: Duke University Press, 1969).

59. Walter W. Wilcox, *The Farmer in the Second World War* (Ames: Iowa State College Press, 1947); Reo M. Christenson, *Brannan Plan: Farm Politics and Policy* (Ann Arbor: University of Michigan Press, 1959); Edward L. and Frederick H. Schapsmeier, *Ezra Taft Benson and the Politics of Agriculture* (Danville, Ill.: Interstate Printers and Publishers, 1975).

60. Among the more accessible discussions of the changes in the 1950s are Edward Higbee, *Farms and Farmers in an Urban Age* (New York: Twentieth Century Fund, 1963), which discusses "the sizzling pace" of technological change, and Lauren Soth, *An Embarrassment of Plenty: Agriculture in Affluent America* (New York: Crowell, 1965). Somewhat broader, more detailed, and plodding but useful is National Advisory Commission on Food and Fiber, *Food and Fiber for the Future* (Washington, D.C.: GPO, 1967). For a brief overview, see Wayne D. Rasmussen and Paul S. Stone, "Toward a Third Agricultural Revolution," *Proceedings of the Academy of Political Science* (1982), 24(3):174–185. For a more detailed discussion that places the entire transformation since World War II in recent perspective, and deals with fifteen different commodities as well, see U.S. Senate, Committee on Agriculture, Nutrition, and Forestry, *Farm Structure: A Historical Perspective on Changes in the Number and Size of Farms* (Washington, D.C.: GPO, 1980).

61. John T. Schlebecker, "The Great Holding Action: The N.F.O. in September, 1962," *Agricultural History* (October 1965), 39(4):204–213; George Brandsberg, *The Two Sides in NFO's Battle* (Ames: Iowa State University Press, 1964); Varden Fuller et al., "Bargaining in Agriculture and Industry: Comparisons and Contrasts," *Journal of Farm Economics* (December 1963), 45:1283–1302; David A. Carter, "The National Farmers' Organization: The Rhetoric of Institutionalization," Ph.D. dissertation, University of Iowa, 1976.

62. Don F. Hadwiger, "Farmers in Politics," *Agricultural History* (January 1976), 50(1) suggested that farmers have usually been "outsiders" in the American political system and of reduced effectiveness in proportion to their numbers in the nineteenth century because of splits along regional and ethnic lines; since then, as their numbers declined and, somewhat tardily, their political clout as well (particularly after the *Baker vs. Carr* decision that provided for "one man, one vote" reapportionment), they have split along commodity lines, so that they represent coalitions of commodity interest groups and rely on administrative cooptation rather than congressional votes to reach their goals. On the nature of farm organizations in the 1960s and 1970s, see Harold F. Breimyer, *Individual Freedom and the Economic Organization of Agriculture* (Urbana: University of Illinois Press, 1965), pp. 190–204, 261–274; Harold Guither, *The Food Lobbyists: Behind the Scenes of Food and Agriculture Politics* (Lexington, Mass.: Heath, 1980); William P. Browne, "Farm Organizations and Agribusiness," *Academy of Political Science Proceedings* (1982), 34(3):198–211.

63. Aruna N. Michie and Craig Jagger, *Why Farmers Protest: Kansas Farmers, the Farm Problem, and the American Agriculture Movement*, Kansas State University Agricultural

Experiment Station Monograph, July 1980; Gregg Easterbrook, "Making Sense of Agriculture: A Revisionist Look at Farm Policy," *The Atlantic* (July 1985), 256(1):63–84.

64. Kenneth A. Cook and Susan E. Sechler, "Agricultural Policy: Paying for our Past Mistakes," *Issues in Science and Technology* (Fall 1985) 2(1):97–110; Lee J. Alston, "Farm Foreclosure Moratorium Legislation: A Lesson from the Past," *American Economic Review* (June 1984), 74(3):445–457.

65. Luther Tweeten, "Agriculture at a Crucial Evolutionary Crossroads," in R. Goldberg, ed., *Research in Domestic and International Agribusiness Management* (1981), 2:1–16; Harold F. Breimyer, "Agriculture: Return of the Thirties?" *Challenge* (July-August 1982), pp. 35–39; Emmett Barker, "Farming Technology in Transition," *Enterprise* (June 1983), pp. 4–7; *Wall Street Journal*, November 9, 13, 15, 16, 23, 1984 and February 13, 1985; *New York Times*, January 20, 1985.

9. Technology and the Military: The Impact of Technological Change on Social Structure in the United States Navy

Derk Bruins
California State University, San Bernardino

At the birth of the U.S. Navy, its technical environment was centuries old. Wooden ships, sail, and smooth-bore cannon were the primary components of the technology familiar to merchant seamen of that day. For example, John Paul Jones' *Bonhomme Richard* had been converted from an East Indian merchantman.[1] As a result, although the rebellious colonies did obtain the services of a few former officers of the Royal Navy, officers who had served only in merchant ships also compiled creditable records in the Revolutionary Navy.[2] As for crews, the interchangeability of sailors between merchantmen and warships made feasible the practice of impressment, which seriously aggravated Anglo-American relations before the War of 1812. Despite the inheritance of an age-old technology, the United States Navy soon faced technical innovations which accumulated, accelerated, and transformed it, eventually into the organization we see today.

The Society. Almost by definition, an armed service, especially its uniformed peacetime establishment, is a social institution rather than a simple organization.[3] The U.S. Navy is such an institution, its personnel being unified by a deeply held conviction that the ability to conduct war at sea is of vital importance to the United States. The Navy is an institution not only as a whole but also in many of its subordinate components (e.g., naval aviation and the submarine service). For this reason, many of what may otherwise appear to be simply organizational changes are, in fact, changes with deep social impact for the institution or for some of its components.

In horizontal structure, the U.S. Navy, like other military services, is organized along social lines laid down in feudal times. In an analysis of military social strata, the officer corps functions as the aristocracy. Enlisted men, in turn, serve in the role of the working class, providing both skilled and unskilled labor. Within the U.S. Navy, one finds that the system of ratings used to indicate the professional development and advancement of enlisted personnel reflects its origin in the craft guild system. For example, the master craftsman in the realm of naval ordnance is the gunner. A man who has achieved this level of technical skill is honored with a grant of officership; he is made a warrant officer. Serving as apprentices to the gunner, one finds gunner's mates, arrayed in many grades of increasing mastery of the technical qualifications of the trade. At the bottom of the social structure are the seamen, the firemen, and the airmen—the unskilled laborers of the combatant naval society.[4]

In vertical structure, one finds various professional groups, typically designated as corps, which are distinguished one from another by their functional specializations within the navy. Naturally enough, the heart of the navy is formed around the skills and profession of naval combat. However, there are corps for medical, dental, legal, civil engineering, religious specialists, and even experts in land combat—the marines, all of whom support the combat naval mission. Except for the highly independent Marine Corps—the navy's army— these corps are staff or noncombatant corps. Despite their inclusion in the navy, these noncombatant specialists are functionally peripheral and socially subordinate to combatant naval society.

Because the functional specialization, for the most part, is vertically organized, one finds several corps of officers within the naval aristocracy. At the very center of this social stratum is the warrior elite, the corps of line officers, so named because of their eligibility to command ships-of-the-line-of-battle (or battleships). It is from this elite alone within the naval aristocracy that the top naval commanders are drawn.

As expected, the heart of naval society is, and the essence of the society is defined by, the corps of line officers. Thus, innovations that directly challenge the position or promise a change in the composition of this social class pose serious disturbances to the existing society. In contrast, innovations that initially affect only other corps of officers or the "working class" of the navy (i.e., the enlisted men) must be much larger in scale to alter the naval society to the degree that change is reflected back into the heart of the organization.

Technological Innovation. Change in the technology used by an organization does not necessarily cause change in the organization. This fact is captured by the distinction that Ronald J. Kurth made some years ago between "innovative departure" and "incremental innovation." According to Kurth, the innovative departure is disruptive of the existing naval society. It threatens to replace or render obsolete the technology upon which a way of life has been based. As such, innovative departures are fiercely resisted or, if the radical innovation is seen to be desirable, an attempt will be made to implement the socially disruptive change incrementally.[5]

The incremental innovation, in contrast, is a change that enhances the existing technology, the job skills of current members of the organization, and the career experience of those in management positions. Obviously, the incremental innovation is a welcome change and is accepted with little or no resistance.[6] Needless to say, Kurth's "innovative departure" and "incremental innovation" are ideal types which may be thought of as representing the end points of the spectrum of innovation. Thus, one can expect that typical innovations will have some varying mix of aspects of the two ideal types.

It is the purpose of this chapter to examine the impact that certain selected changes in naval technology may have had on social structures within the U.S. Navy. This question is approached from two directions: first, the process of introducing a technical innovation will be traced in order to observe how the social changes that do appear at that time may be linked with the change in technology; second, the precedents of large social change will be examined to discover the relative influence of those that lie in the area of technological innovation.

It must be noted that at least one major problem faces the researcher who tries to determine the nature and linkage of relationships between innovations in the technology used by a social group and changes within the social structure of that group.[7] This is because technology, according to one comprehensive definition, involves a portion of the social structure of the group. In an attempt to avoid being locked into an exclusive focus on the hardware (i.e., tools) of a group, attention has been directed also to the methods—the techniques—the group employs in using these tools and to the ways in which the group is organized to employ those tools.[8] To evade these theoretical issues, this chapter focuses on changes in the hardware used by the United States Navy.

Two Patterns of Innovation: Ordnance and Propulsion

Primary effects. During the nineteenth century, the technological environment of the U.S. Navy began to change. For example, the ordnance—the smooth-bore cannon and round shot—that had served the Revolutionary Navy became obsolete. A new concept—the built-up gun—and new techniques in building and testing cannon produced, by the time of the American Civil War, a weapon of greater power for the same or lesser weight than earlier naval ordnance. At about the same time, the introduction of rifling in the barrel allowed gunners to use a heavier, elongated shell, which not only carried more explosives than the spherical shell, but also could use a fuze that detonated on impact with a target.[9]

In defense against the more powerful guns and their exploding shells, iron was introduced, at the time of the Crimean War, as armored sheathing for warships.[10] In these cases of guns and armor, the innovations enhanced the long-accepted means of naval war—two ships dueling with cannon at short range, one trying to destroy the guns and hull of the other before the second effected such damage on the first. Although new techniques were required to manufacture the guns, shells, and armor, no radically new skills were required aboard ship to handle the new technology. Thus, this was a case of incremental innovation, a technical change that enhanced or even reinforced the existing naval society. In contrast, the shift from sail to steam was radically different.

The American effort to build the first steam-powered warship was born, purely and simply, out of desperation. After a spectacular series of successful naval engagements in the opening months of the War of 1812, the U.S. Navy was gradually swept from the sea. The Royal Navy obliterated American maritime commerce, and the British conducted amphibious raids in various coastal locations, virtually at will.[11] Although Robert Fulton had demonstrated steam propulsion only in 1807, this innovation offered the possibility of protecting American harbors against British sailing warships; a steam-powered gunboat could maneuver in restricted waters with little concern for the wind. However, Fulton's steam-powered gunboat was not completed before the war's end. Thus, it was simply tested and laid up at the Brooklyn Navy Yard without ever going into active service with the navy.[12]

Starting in the 1820s, many navies began to use steam propulsion for auxiliary vessels. For example, the U. S. Navy had two small steam-powered vessels whose primary contribution was to familiarize junior officers with the innovation. Some of these junior officers came to argue for the use of steam machinery in warships. Senior officers were resistant to the proposal, but the enthusiasm and lobbying efforts of the younger officers induced the secretary of the navy and Congress to authorize construction of three steam-powered men-of-war in the early 1840s.[13]

This commitment to steam, however tentative it appeared at the time, required specially qualified personnel to operate the novel propulsion plant aboard ship. Most personnel recruited for the U. S. Navy in the nineteenth century were hired directly from civilian life; those who were hired in significant numbers to perform noncombatant services were formed into special "staff corps," which were clearly subordinate to the fighting men. Therefore, in order to provide the technical specialists needed aboard the new warships, the Corps of Naval Engineers was created in 1842.

At the time, steam was auxiliary power, to be used only for navigation in restricted waters or in case of emergencies. American naval strategy called for patrols on distant stations during peacetime in order to protect maritime commerce, interdict the slave trade, and show the flag. In case of hostilities, the navy's experiences in both the Revolutionary War and the War of 1812 led to an expectation that the "next war" would require long-range commerce raiding against the most probable enemy, England. However, the early steam engines and their limited fuel supplies could not propel the navy's ships the thousands of miles necessary to execute that strategy.[14] Thus, engineers and the services they provided were believed to be only peripheral to the navy's mission.

Contrary to these strategic expectations, the "next war" turned out to be the American Civil War. While the Confederacy could resort to commerce raiding, the Union Navy was forced to adopt the typical British strategy of close blockade.[15] To execute this unanticipated new strategy, the blockading ships required the use of steam, first, to avoid being blown by offshore winds away from the ports and channels that blockade runners would use, and second, to avoid being blown aground by onshore winds while patrolling within effective blockading range of those same ports and channels. Finally, steam was absolutely essential to fighting in the restricted waters of southern ports and on inland rivers.

As a result, the Civil War saw a major change in the technological mix of the ships in the U.S. Navy. When President Lincoln was inaugurated in 1861, only 23 of the 42 active warships had a steam power plant onboard. In December 1864, only 112 of the 671 vessels on hand or under construction were powered by sails alone. All of the 236 vessels that had been built since the start of the war or were then under construction were steamers.[16] The secretary of the navy himself had stated: "Hereafter, every vessel-of-war must be a steam vessel."[17] Given such a pronouncement, the navy would require more engineer-officers.

By January 1864, there were 500 officers of the Engineer Corps.[18] At the same time, congressional authorization provided for 711 line officers.[19] While some senior engineer-officers were involved in shore-based tasks such as the design, procurement, and repair of steam engines, the vast majority of the engineer-officers served afloat and were responsible for keeping the Union Navy's warships moving in battle. As had happened during the earlier transition from oars to sail, a functional duality arose aboard ship: line officers, as had the sea-soldiers of earlier days, became mere combatant passengers on ships moved by engineer-officers, who were the actual masters, similar to the ancient sailors, of the new means of propulsion.[20] In order to correct this unhealthy dichotomy and to give the line officer the skills now needed to command his ship at sea, the secretary of the navy recommended that the curriculum at the Naval Academy be revised in order to "make every naval officer an engineer as well as a sailor."[21]

It became evident that the line officers rejected the need for such a change. Congress agreed to the education of prospective engineer-officers at the Naval Academy, but, as suggested by line officers, directed that separate curricula be used for cadet-midshipmen and cadet-engineers.[22] The early years of the Grant administration saw a vicious reaction of the line against the staff and the restoration of sail over steam. Pursuing a goal far more complex than a simple rejection of steam, the line officers condemned the world's fastest warship as unfit for naval service and "improved" the installed machinery to the point of inefficiency. In possible mitigation of these actions, one must recall that American naval strategy remained unchanged by the Civil War experience. For patrol on distant station, the wind was free, coal was expensive, and the United States had no overseas colonies or coaling stations.[23]

While the line officers tried to reverse the steam innovation, improvements in naval ordnance continued as before the Civil War. The interrupted screw was adopted for closing breech-loading guns, new gunpowders and other propellants were developed, and steel was employed in the manufacture of guns and shells.[24] As before, the innovations in this technology were incremental. Naval artillery remained the prime weapon for war at sea.

The American naval renaissance that occurred in the 1880s was based on steel, not on steam. For the navy, steel was an incremental innovation, completing the conversion from wood to iron. Larger, stronger hulls were now possible. Tougher, less brittle armor became available. Steel permitted the manufacture of more powerful guns, more penetrating shells, and more durable components for steam propulsion systems. Indicative of this incrementalism, the first ships of the new steel navy were rigged for full sailpower.[25] Only gradually did the demonstrated reliability of steam machinery and the wind resistance created by sails and rigging lead to the demise of sail. And in that process, the old contentious issues between line officers and engineer-officers resurfaced.

One attempt to eliminate incrementally a potential source of the friction was made in 1882. Congress directed that the two curricula at the Naval Academy—one for cadet-midshipmen, the other for cadet-engineers—be merged. But because this merging was done under the supervision of line officers, the engineering content of the new curriculum was diluted; recently graduated cadet-engineers reached the fleet with insufficient preparation to assume the duties of junior engineer-officers. As a result, Congress was persuaded, in 1890, to restore a separate course of study for the cadet-engineers in their senior year.[26]

In 1898, Assistant Secretary of the Navy Theodore Roosevelt became involved in yet another attempt to resolve the conflict between line officers and engineer-officers. He accepted the idea of amalgamating the Engineer Corps with the line and, as president of the Naval Personnel Board, drafted legislation to achieve that end. Passed in the aftermath of the Spanish-American war, the Naval Personnel Act of 1899 abolished the Engineer Corps, amalgamated its members with the line, and unified the curriculum at the Naval Academy. There were many other provisions of the act, but the primary object of restoring harmony to the wardroom was, in large part, achieved by the expedient of eliminating the Engineer Corps.[27]

The officers of the abolished Engineer Corps were divided into three groups. The most senior officers, although formally of the line, remained in their original career pattern, as if no amalgamation had occurred. The middle-ranking officers were given the choice of remaining in their original career pattern or of competing with their contemporaries of the line. The junior officers, regardless of their preferences, were thrown into the line and were required to compete for assignments and promotions. Shipboard billets that had previously been filled only by officers of the Engineer Corps were supposed to be filled by line officers, regardless of their status prior to 1899.[28]

The amalgamation of the Engineer Corps with the line demonstrates that one cannot legislate a change of attitudes and beliefs. Based on their career experiences, the senior line officers, who knew little (and saw no need to know more) about engineering, insisted that the junior ex-engineers master skills that had always led to promotion in the line; specialized knowledge in steam engineering did not enhance an officer's promotion potential. After all, the Naval Personnel Act of 1899 had provided that highly motivated and technically competent enlisted engineers could be advanced to warrant officer status. Aboard ship, these warrant machinists would assume many of the highly technical responsibilities of the former engineer-officers; line officers had more important things to do. Consequently, the service-wide result was a diminution of the marine engineering expertise that was extant in the officer corps.[29]

As the older engineer-officers retired, it became more and more difficult to fulfill competently the duties of the Bureau of Engineering. The easiest means to restore professional expertise in marine engineering was to have Congress reverse its action, as it had in 1890 when the unified curriculum at the Naval Academy led to a similar decline in engineering expertise, and bring back the Engineer Corps. However, in the early 1900s, secretaries of the navy found it impolitic to ask President Theodore Roosevelt to send Congress legislation that would undo the course of action that Assistant Secretary of the Navy Theodore Roosevelt had vigorously supported during earlier Congressional hearings.[30]

A more fundamental problem with resurrecting the Engineer Corps flowed from the widely held belief that before senior engineer-officers should be given charge of design and procurement of shipboard propulsion equipment, they should have actual experience in operating such machinery aboard ship. The dilemma arose because nobody was willing to revive the acrimony that had existed aboard ship between line officers and members of the Engineer Corps before their amalgamation in 1899. Moreover, since the advent of the warrant machinists, highly technical billets that could be filled only by engineer-specialists no longer existed in the junior ranks.

A stop-gap measure was attempted in 1909 with the establishment, at the Naval Academy, of the graduate-level School of Marine Engineering.[31] Specialized engineering knowledge was imparted to the officer-student, but this did not correct the problem of opportunities for promotion. In fact, one could argue that a line officer was wasting his time by attending the School of Marine Engineering. His contemporaries would be spending that year on career-enhancing assignments.

Finally, in a relatively obscure provision of the Naval Act of 1916—that authorized the building of a navy "second to none"—approval was obtained for a special career pattern for officers in the rank of lieutenant and above. Designated for engineering duty only (EDO), these officers could narrowly specialize in marine engineering and retain prospects for promotion. In return, the EDO-designated line officer was restricted from exercising command at sea.[32]

To close this brief account of the innovation of steam propulsion in the U.S. Navy, certain conclusions appear warranted. The reader is aware that events extrinsic to the technical development of steam propulsion played a vitally important role in its adoption. Two wars—the War of 1812 and the Civil War—demonstrated that existing naval technology was inadequate for the task at hand.[33] The initiative of European navies in adopting steam in the 1830s and steel in the 1870s provided incentives to adopt technical advances. Yet, as a social institution, the navy was unwilling to adapt its existing structure to the innovation. One can argue that the Corps of Naval Engineers was used as a mechanism for absorbing uncertainty; if the steam innovation failed at any point, the Engineer Corps could be jettisoned without inflicting damage on the corps of line officers.[34] The engineer-officers, possessors of a special knowledge, were men whom the line officers could consult on those originally rare occasions when their services were required. After the Civil War, when steam propulsion endangered the old navy, a reaction of the old believers against the innovators occurred and the new developments were sacrificed so that the old way of life could be preserved. Even when steam finally replaced sail, the line officers refused to share power with the men upon whom they had become dependent. It required the intervention of outside political authority to resolve the internal conflict.[35] And so it would appear that social groups in advanced industrial societies are as susceptible as those in today's Third World to the desire to adopt new technology without adapting the social structure to the innovation. In the end, one is forced to recognize that, despite the struggle and the bitterness, the original shipboard social organization was preserved: line officers remain in command, staff officers perform non-combatant services.

Secondary effects. If, in the long run, the introduction of steam produced no lasting change in shipboard social structures, was there any lasting impact anywhere in the navy from this salient innovative departure? Certainly, the curriculum of the Naval Academy was altered due to this innovation. One could even go back to the Academy's origins and note that the development of steam propulsion was one of the reasons given to justify the creation of an American naval academy.[36] However, there is strong reason to believe that other factors played a major role in the establishment of the institution.

Numerous political leaders had opposed the idea of a naval academy, not because education was useless, but because the institution, it was feared, would create a military class, antithetical to democratic ideals, seeking after naval appropriations, and likely to urge the prosecution of unnecessary wars.[37] But, in the early 1840s, public opinion was becoming dissatisfied with the previous mode of training prospective line officers. Naval officers, themselves, complained about a lack of training in science. As midshipmen, they served an uneven, nonstandard apprenticeship to the officers of a warship. The mutiny on the training brig USS *Somers* in late 1842 and the summary execution of a midshipman and two sailors became a *cause célèbre*, since the midshipman was the son of Secretary of War John C. Spencer. Even at this, the secretary of the navy had to resort to a subterfuge, establishing the Naval Academy in the summer of 1845, while Congress was not in session, and placing the responsibility for undoing his action, if it cared to, on the legislative body. Furthermore, subsequent events clearly demonstrated that, although the directive to the first commandant of the Naval Academy specified that instruction in "the use of steam" would be a part of the curriculum, the Academy failed to produce line officers with competence in the new technology.[38]

The steam innovation may have played a similarly peripheral role in the reorganization of the Navy Department in 1842. Harsh criticism was leveled against the previous system of organization, whereby a collegial body of three senior line officers advised the secretary of the navy on questions of naval logistics. One of the charges, that the naval commissioners were stubbornly resistant to technological change, carried more than a grain of truth. But the truth or falsity of such an assertion had little relevance to the proposed solution, the so-called bureau system, under which the overall logistic task—the provision of means for the conduct of naval operations—was disaggregated into discrete areas of responsibility and assigned to separate bureaus.[39] While the new steam engines may have been of political utility to the advocates of the bureau system, they were of no technical relevance to the replacement of collective responsibility for overall naval logistics with individual responsibility for a component of the task.

However, once the system of organization was in place, technology became relevant to shaping its content. For example, when the bureau system was expanded in 1862, the rapid shift to steam, which was required by the Civil War, led to the creation of the Bureau of Steam Engineering. After sail and rigging disappeared, the Bureau of Equipment was eliminated. The Bureau of Aeronautics was founded after World War I in order to manage the logistics of naval aviation.[40]

Actually, there are two developments directly associated with the steam innovation that have had a lasting impact on the navy. To resolve the problem of the decline of expertise in steam engineering which followed the amalgamation of the Engineer Corps with the line, the navy instituted, first, in-house graduate-level technical education for line officers and, second, the category of restricted line officer with the use of the EDO designation. Each of these innovations was expanded through its application to other areas of technology. For example, graduate-level curricula in ordnance engineering and aeronautical engineering were offered after World War I, and the designation for aeronautical engineering duty only (AEDO) was made, in 1935, to provide a new career pattern for another body of technical specialists.[41] Thus, one is led to the conclusion that although these social innovations arose from the shift from sail to steam, they could have resulted from any technological change that produced a similar problem. As in the case of the introduction of the bureau system, the existence, not the content, of a technological innovation was important.

Despite the argument that almost any innovation could have been used to trigger the introduction of, first, graduate-level technical education for line officers and, second, the designation of restricted line officers, it does not follow that the results of these innovations would have a uniform social impact on the various institutionalized groups within the navy. This proposition can be demonstrated by a brief survey of the way in which three of the navy's bureaus handled their technically trained specialists; it will show the presence of another intermediate variable—in this case, tradition.

As seen above, the Bureau of Engineering (BuEng) was a staff bureau during the nineteenth century. From its origin in 1862 until the amalgamation of the Engineer Corps with the line in 1899, BuEng was the home for that corps. The senior engineer-officers who led BuEng in the following years worked to obtain the EDO designation for their technically trained specialists. In 1937, twenty-one years after Congress authorized the EDO designation for these specialist-officers, one such restricted line officer was promoted to rear admiral and became chief of BuEng.[42]

After World War I, the Bureau of Ordnance (BuOrd) also sponsored graduate-level training in ordnance engineering. In marked contrast to BuEng, BuOrd had been a line bureau throughout its history, a factor of major importance. Although BuOrd agreed with BuEng that the men who managed logistic problems ashore had to have operating experience afloat, BuOrd held to a far more rigid interpretation. BuOrd's policy was that ordnance specialists had to serve a tour of duty in the fleet before *each* assignment to a shore-based billet that the bureau controlled. This policy, which lasted until World War II, precluded the designation of BuOrd's specialists for ordnance engineering duty only (OEDO), except for rare and special cases.[43] Even after World War II, one should note that no OEDO rose above the rank of captain while BuOrd remained in existence.[44]

Another course of graduate-level training initiated after World War I was aeronautical engineering. The Bureau of Aeronautics (BuAer), which became the sponsor of these specialists, was a hybrid bureau. Until 1943, owing to special circumstances, it was heavily dominated by naval aviation officers of the line. And yet, BuAer had staff officer and EDO-designated specialists.[45] Although none of its officers were designated for AEDO until 1935, their subsequent advancement was rapid, ten being promoted to the rank of rear admiral during World War II.[46]

It is true that each of the three bureaus managed different areas of technology. The main areas of competence were aircraft and aviation material for BuAer, naval ordnance (bombs, bullets, guns, fire control, mines, torpedoes, etc.) for BuOrd, machinery (propulsion, electric power generation and distribution, exterior and interior communication, air conditioning, refrigeration, etc.) for BuEng. But these differences are probably inconsequential to their policies toward their technical specialists. After World War II, both BuAer and BuOrd developed guided missiles, often in direct competition with each other.[47] The Bureau of Ships (BuShips), the direct successor to BuEng, developed radar and early computer systems, as did both BuAer and BuOrd. This, of course, does not prove, but merely suggests, that tradition had a stronger influence than did technology on the form of the internal social relationships between line and staff in these three bureaus. While one may argue that differences in the three bureaus' reputations for success in research and development indicates the superiority of one tradition over another,[48] such success may also be the result of yet other factors.

Procurement of Personnel

The first part of this chapter examined the effects of innovations that were initiated during a period of relative stability in the technological environment of the U.S. Navy. In fact, the introduction of steam, even as it replaced wind, began the substitution of mechanical energy for human energy aboard ship. This process, accelerated by the development of electrical machinery and electric-powered devices, marks the beginning of an initially slow, but accelerating, chain of seemingly ceaseless changes in naval technologies. Since there was subsequently a major shift, at about the start of the twentieth century, in the recruiting and training policies with regard to the naval work force, the navy's enlisted men, one might suppose that this change was a *direct* result of the industrial revolution in the navy. such an assumption, however, is premature.

Throughout most of the nineteenth century, the navy recruited its enlisted men from among the international seafaring population which could be found in the nation's seaports. Men who had no previous shipboard training were consigned to the landsman rating (a specific naval occupation for unskilled workers) with little or no hope for advancement. Although certain ratings—seaman gunner, for example—were restricted to American citizens, warship crews were typically cosmopolitan and multilingual.[49]

Starting slightly before the time of the Spanish-American War, about fourteen years after Congress authorized construction of the first four steel-hulled warships of the new navy, a transformation occurred in American naval recruiting and training policies. The Great Lakes Naval Training Center is the best symbol of that change. Its mission—to train the raw recruit—signifies the abandonment of dependence upon previously trained manpower. Its location—inland and relatively remote from the sea—demonstrates the shift to recruitment of native-born Americans from inland areas. Instead of remaining a parasite on the international pool of trained seafaring men, the navy has developed a gigantic network of trade schools.[50]

In view of the technological complexity of weapons in the late twentieth century, such a development seems natural. But, given the lower degree of technical sophistication at the turn of the century, that judgment does not seem warranted.[51] Except in the areas of ordnance and armor, naval and merchant marine technology were not seriously divergent. Even in the area of gunnery, demands for enlisted technical expertise were not very great. Continuous aim gunnery, which permitted the development of integrated fire control systems, was just beginning to be introduced.[52] And, at least until recently, it was widely understood that "gunner's mate repairs" were effected with a sledge-hammer.

Dismissing changes in naval hardware as a direct explanation of the shift in the navy's training and recruiting policies, one also cannot rely entirely on the widely expressed desire to "Americanize" the navy's crews.[53] Instead one can refer to the demand for and supply of maritime personnel, an intermediate variable itself affected by innovations in marine engineering and the foreign policy of imperialism followed by industrialized states.

As stated above, the introduction of steel late in the nineteenth century made feasible the building of not only larger ships but also more dependable steam propulsion plants. Larger merchant ships, of course, could carry heavier cargoes for a given cost. Dependable power plants made transport by sea both safer and more reliable; they also made the arrival time of commercial vessels more predictable. This reliability, in turn, made it feasible to ship perishable agricultural products over longer distances or to increase the passenger load for a given amount of food and water. As a result, international seaborne commerce increased dramatically.[54]

One can argue, therefore, that these innovations made profitable the particular course of European imperialism, oriented as it was to the sea. There was, of course, a consequent need to defend the gains and the maritime lines of communication which provided access to overseas colonies. Not surprisingly then, the turn of the century also saw general increases in the size of various navies.[55] Statistics indicate that a growing proportion of crews in the British merchant marine were non-European; this suggests a general decline in the international availability of ethnically desirable (i.e., white) seamen.[56] At the same time, one notes an increase in the U.S. Navy's enlisted strength from approximately 8,000 (1875–1893) to 10,000 (1894–1897), to between 15,000 and 20,000 (1898–1902), and on up to roughly 50,000 prior to World War I.[57] One can trace through these data an indirect chain which is associated with technology, but a direct causal connection between the changes in naval hardware and the change in the social origins of the enlisted force is missing.

In a much clearer manner, one can associate the demand for numbers with the changes that were made after World War II in the procurement of officers for the regular navy. Historically, the navy had protected the vital core of the institution, the line officers of the regular navy, from adulteration. In the nineteenth century, emergencies were met by the acceptance of volunteers.[58] In the twentieth century, a naval reserve was created in an attempt to assure a modicum of naval indoctrination of personnel who might be called to wartime duty.[59] After World War II, it became apparent that the Naval Academy could not supply enough officers to meet the needs of the world's most powerful navy. Rather than overexpand the Naval Academy and dilute its traditions, the naval high command determined to procure one-quarter of its annual input of new line officers from the Naval Academy and three-quarters from Naval Reserve Officer Training Corps (NROTC) units which were associated with major universities and colleges.[60] Although officers with NROTC origins are not yet represented in the flag ranks in proportion to the inputs, the officer corps of the regular navy has been altered irrevocably.[61]

Four Other Cases

Having made major caveats on claims that changes in naval organization and social structure are basically a direct result of changes in naval technology, it is appropriate to turn to instances where that judgment can be more easily supported. In 1879, the navy sent two recently graduated cadet-engineers to the Royal Naval College at Greenwich, England to study naval architecture.[62] This action, which anticipated by four years Congress's authorization of the first four steel ships of the new navy, most probably was taken in response to advances in the techniques used in Europe in shipbuilding and the use of steel in warships. What is fascinating about the navy's first sponsorship of graduate-level technical education is that the men so trained became not line officers, but naval constructors, members of a shore-based staff corps.

The training of the two cadet-engineers and their designation as naval constructors began the militarization of the Construction Corps. Since the navy had obtained its staff corps officers, even the steam engineers until 1864, from civilian professions, one may ask why the navy began to train its own naval constructors in 1879. Clearly, the new technology of working with steel was a factor. But, except in the limited case of armor, the use of steel in shipbuilding was not restricted to warships. Had the navy been willing to pay the necessary salary, or to wait until more shipwrights were trained and qualified in the use of steel, it could have relied on its traditional source for obtaining naval constructors. But the navy was sufficiently embarrassed by the antiques that passed for warships that it was unwilling to wait for civilian shipwrights to obtain the requisite skills.[63]

A second instance of technological change impacting on naval society is in the area of job skills and the level of expertise possessed by the navy's enlisted force. In the beginning, there were a limited number of ratings, and the bulk of the enlisted men were in the lowest pay grades, thereby forming a socioeconomic pyramid. In subsequent years, certain ratings have completely disappeared. Besides those associated with sail and wooden hulls, some—such as bugler, printer, turret captain, and airship rigger—have been eliminated during the shift to new or newer technologies. More important has been the increase, during the twentieth century, in the total number of ratings. One must also recognize that the technical skills needed for some of the old ratings have changed considerably. Furthermore, the distribution of enlisted personnel within today's rating structure—no longer a pyramid, more like a flat-bottomed egg—indicates that personnel are much more highly skilled than the enlisted force in 1900.[64]

A third example of technology's impact is in the expansion of the numbers and types of specializations recognized within the community of restricted line officers. To those engineer-specialists designed for EDO and AEDO, one can add the officers designated for ordnance engineering duty only (OEDO). Another category, officers designated for special duty only (SDO), consists of specialists in the fields of cryptology, intelligence, and public affairs.[65] While the specialties in cryptology and intelligence analysis respond to developments in military technologies, the public affairs officer is one of the clearest examples of the impact of civilian technology upon the Navy. But beyond these groups is that category of officers designated for limited duty only (LDO).

The development of the LDO program is the result of agitation by vocal members of the warrant officer community before World War II.[66] In the old days, warrant officers were those master craftsmen, such as gunners and boatswains, to whom the enlisted men were apprenticed as gunner's mates and boatswain's mates. The modern warrant officers are the technical experts in the use, maintenance, and repair of naval equipment. But the modern warrant officer resides in an increasingly anomalous position between enlisted men and officers—superior in rank to the enlisted man, often inferior in education to the officer.[67]

Well before World War II, it was possible for the bright, hard-working and ambitious man who had enlisted at age seventeen to reach the rank of chief warrant officer at age thirty-three. Unfortunately, all he had to look forward to within his specialty was thirty years of service at the very same rank, until he reached retirement age.[68] For thirty years, this man would rank "with, but behind" ensigns, principally because he did not have the educational background which might have allowed him to compete with those who attended the Naval Academy. At age sixty-two, the chief warrant officer was legally subordinate to the brand-new twenty-two-year-old ensign. Consequently, the warrant officers wanted Congress to provide a grade and category that would allow them not only to rank with the three junior grades of unrestricted line officers, but also to remain specialists within their occupations.[69]

In keeping with a desire to move almost all of the restricted line officers into staff corps, the naval high command stoutly refused the warrant officers' plan, adamantly arguing that specialization was antithetical to the concept of a line officer. A line officer was a warrior; specialists were noncombatants.[70] During World War II, when warrant officers were temporarily promoted to officer status, the Navy Department assigned these men to billets as though they were Academy graduates. In the fleet, however, commanding officers followed their instincts. Only if the ex-warrants were used in their area of specialization could one reliably expect excellent performance. Based on this experience, the navy, after the war, decided to provide a new career pattern for the enlisted man who wished to assume greatly increased responsibility, but also to remain within his limited area of expertise.[71] Starting with twelve specialty areas in the late 1940s, thirty-one occupational specialties for LDO-designated officers were officially recognized in 1980.[72]

A fourth area that must be mentioned before ending this survey is the impact that the introduction of two new combat vehicles—the airplane and the submarine—has had on the navy since their appearance in the first decade of the twentieth century. The airplane, of course, led to the creation of the Bureau of Aeronautics in 1921. However, no new bureau was founded for the submarine, for at least three reasons. First, the submarine was not a radically different machine; until nuclear power became available, it was only a submersible torpedo boat. Second, this new weapons system fell under a singularly dark cloud, i.e., the legal objections that the United States government had raised during World War I against the German strategy of unrestricted submarine warfare, until the United States itself used unrestricted submarine warfare against Japan in World War II. And, third, with respect to the military use of submarine technology, the navy had no domestic competitor comparable to General Billy Mitchell, who had threatened to monopolize aviation to the exclusion of the navy.

During World War II, naval aviation came to dominate the navy, and the carrier replaced the battleship as the capital ship of the fleet. Therefore, assignment policies were altered in order to place naval aviators in important command and staff positions in the fleet. Even in Washington, D.C., a new post, the deputy chief of naval operations for air, DCNO(Air), was created at naval headquarters.[73] To fill all the newly available billets, large numbers of naval aviators were promoted to flag rank.[74]

In 1947, proportionately more submarine-qualified officers were in the navy's flag ranks than there had been in 1940.[75] But relative to the aviators, fewer submariners had received these promotions.[76] In part, this was due to the relatively smaller number of submarine-related billets which were available to these officers after they had commanded a submarine.[77] They also enjoyed less political support; an effort to create, parallel to the DCNO(Air), a DCNO billet expressly for the submariners failed in 1946.[78] Moreover, the number of submariners on the navy's active list of admirals dropped in the late 1940s.[79] No submarine-qualified officer served as chief of naval operations (CNO) between 1949 and 1982.[80]

In the mid-1950s, nuclear propulsion radically improved the operating characteristics of submarines. The larger, more capable, and much more expensive attack submarines called for a commanding officer with greater experience than before.[81] The subsequent innovation of the submarine-launched ballistic missile gave the navy an undisputed role in strategic nuclear affairs. It also resulted in ships whose commanding officer had to be a submariner in the rank of captain. Moreover, the innovative concept of assigning two crews to each ballistic missile submarine, in order to keep the missiles at sea for a greater proportion of time, instantly doubled the number of commanding officer billets. The introduction of, first, the nuclear-powered attack submarine and, second, the ballistic missile submarine, therefore, completed a career pattern for submariners to rise from ensign to flag rank within their own specialty. Gradually, the number of submariners in the flag ranks has increased.[82]

Since World War II, the aircraft carrier and naval aviators have dominated the navy. Although *Polaris*, the first submarine-launched ballistic missile, was deployed during Admiral Arleigh Burke's tenure as CNO, in the twenty years following Burke's departure, only one nonaviation admiral had held the navy's highest post.[83] Then, at the end of June 1982, Admiral James D. Watkins, a submariner, was sworn in as CNO.[84]

Whether Admiral Watkin's tenure as CNO opens an era of dominance by submariners or of power-sharing among the three principal warfare specialties—air, surface, and submarine—within the unrestricted line, only the future will tell. But the old concept that the aviator or the submariner was a naval officer first and a specialist second has passed into history. In 1971, the billets of DCNO (submarine warfare) and DCNO (surface warfare) were created.[85] At about the same time, the four-digit "1100" designator, which for about thirty years had indicated "an unrestricted line officer not a member of the aeronautical organization," was abandoned and left to the navy's female officers. Now submariners (1120) and surface officers (1110) possess separate designators, just as the aviators (1310) had from the beginning.[86] In the mid-1970s, this division was reinforced when several warrant officer and LDO specialties were divided between surface and submarine.[87] The final step would be for the secretary of the navy to establish, for purposes of promotion, separate categories for officers of the three principal warfare specialties.[88]

Of course, it is possible that such an irrevocable step may not be taken, if only out of courtesy to the traditional values associated with the historic meaning of the phrase "unrestricted line officer." Should the warfare specialties be discriminated against for promotion purposes, the term "line officer" will cease to be much more than an administrative category. Nevertheless, the development to date of completely distinct career patterns within the unrestricted line is so antithetical to naval mythology that one tongue-in-cheek suggestion for unification of the armed services is to merge the army and the air force into the navy. After all, the navy is already a multiservice organization.

Conclusion

In the course of approximately two centuries, the organization of the U.S. Navy has grown in both size and complexity. Of course, some of that complexity, especially the growth in the number of ranks and pay grades—horizontal strata—is directly linked to the greater size of the navy and of its components and to the consequent need for further layers of supervision. Another part of the complexity is due to the growing bureaucratization which is so evident in modern governmental agencies. However, it seems certain that most of the complexity in the organization of the naval service, particularly the proliferation of professional groups—vertical structures—is a result, both directly and indirectly, of the increased variety and sophistication of the technology applied to naval warfare.

As indicated above, the number of job specializations among enlisted men and warrant officers has expanded and their character, of course, has shifted. Moreover, the level of technical competence required to operate the modern navy has so increased that the distribution of the numbers of personnel among the enlisted ranks has shifted upwards. Within the officer corps, the number of noncombatant categories has greatly increased. Even the previously privileged caste of line officers has been subdivided between restricted and unrestricted line officers. And within the elite of unrestricted line officers—the warrior class of the modern navy—specializations in air, surface, and submarine warfare are openly acknowledged.

Of course, this extension of complexity has not been unilinear. In the introduction of steam propulsion, we saw not only the creation, but also the final demise of a staff corps, the Engineer Corps, as the effect of this organizational change crossed the spectrum from incidental to critical with regard to the combat operations of a warship. Even though the adoption of steam propulsion plants was not smooth and continuous, there was an even greater discontinuity in the acceptance of the technology of steam engineering as a body of technical knowledge that was essential to the line officer's retaining a legitimate claim to command the new steam-propelled warships. Here, the battle-tested, traditional understanding of the need for unity of command dominated the question of shipboard organization. In such an environment, the Engineer Corps could not survive aboard ship.

However, it is clear that in the case of the introduction of two new combat vehicles—the airplane and the submarine—the navy has undergone fundamental changes in its internal structure. Distinct career patterns exist for aviators, submariners, and surface officers, from ensign to flag rank. Within the enlisted ranks, recruits seeking careers in aviation specializations are clearly distinguished by uniform markings from their fellow recruits who will be trained in job categories associated with surface and subsurface ships. And, as noted above, recent developments within the warrant officer and LDO communities distinguish between those specialists who have gained their expertise in surface ships and their contemporaries in the same technical field who have served in submarines.

Besides social changes which seem directly linked to growing technical complexity, technical innovation has also been a "trigger" for change. In the case of the establishment of the Naval Academy and the bureau system, technical change seems to have been useful, but not essential, to the arguments of the proponents. In cases such as graduate-level technical education for line officers, the innovation of steam propulsion did "trigger" a response, but any similar technological change could have performed the same function. To support this view, one need merely recall the variations in status that were accorded to the restricted line technical specialists in the three principal material bureaus—BuAer, BuOrd, and BuShips. And, finally, with regard to the changing social origins and means of educating the enlisted force and, more recently, the officer corps, the increasing size of the navy has played a vital role, perhaps one more important than technological change.

Notes

1. Elmer B. Potter, ed., *The United States and World Sea Power* (Englewood Cliffs, N.J.: Prentice-Hall, 1955), p. 105.
2. Nicholas Biddle had served in the Royal Navy. John Paul Jones and Gustavus Conyngham had been masters of merchant vessels only. *Dictionary of American Biography* (1930), s.v. "Nicholas Biddle," "Gustavus Conyngham," and "John Paul Jones."
3. An organization becomes an institution when its members cease to view it as an expendable tool for the achievement of specific, concrete goals. Instead, they begin to value the organization itself as a source of personal satisfaction and as a vehicle for group identity. Philip Selznick, *Leadership in Administration* (Evanston, Ill.: Row, Peterson, 1957), p. 17.
4. There are also noncombatant unskilled "workers." Here one finds constructionmen, hospitalmen, and dentalmen.
5. Ronald J. Kurth, " The Politics of Technological Innovation in the United States Navy," Ph.D. dissertation, Harvard University, 1970, pp. 3–4, 45, 47.
6. *Ibid.*, pp. 2–3, 61–62.
7. One discussion of these issues is found in Dennis S. Mileti, David F. Gillespie, and Elizabeth Morrissey, "Technology and Organizations: Methodological Deficiencies and Lacunae," *Technology and Culture* (January 1978); 19:83–92.
8. *Ibid.*, p. 84.
9. Potter, *The United States and World Sea Power*, pp. 264–267. Prior to this time, exploding shells used very dangerous and crudely timed, burning fuzes.
10. *Ibid.*, pp. 262, 268–269.
11. Nathan Miller, *The U.S. Navy* (New York: American Heritage; and Annapolis, Md.: Naval Institute Press, 1977), pp. 89–95. The raids included operations against Washington, Baltimore, and New Orleans.
12. *Ibid.*, pp. 109–110. Harold Sprout and Margaret Sprout, *The Rise of American Naval Power, 1776–1918* (Princeton: Princeton University Press, 1967), pp. 111–112.
13. Potter, *The United States and World Sea Power*, p. 259; Charles Oscar Paullin, *Paullin's History of Naval Administration, 1775–1911* (Annapolis, Md.: U.S. Naval Institute, 1968), pp. 178–180.
14. Paullin, *History of Naval Administration*, pp. 197, 220; Sprout and Sprout, *The Rise of American Naval Power*, pp. 86–87, 94.
15. Sprout and Sprout, *The Rise of American Naval Power*, pp. 154–157.

16. U.S. Navy, *Report of the Secretary of the Navy, with an Appendix Containing Reports from Officers, December 1862* (Washington, D.C.: GPO, 1863), pp. 24, 26; and similarly titled reports for December 1863 (p. xii) and December 1864 (pp. xxiii-xxiv).

17. *Report of the Secretary of the Navy, December 1864*, p. xxxvi.

18. U.S. Navy, *Navy Register of the United States for the Year 1864* (Washington, D.C.: 1864), pp. 62–79. Hereafter, this publication data: (GPO, year).

19. Paullin, *History of Naval Administration*, p. 301.

20. Edward W. Sloan, III, *Benjamin Franklin Isherwood, Naval Engineer* (USNI, 1965), p. 191; Paullin, *History of Naval Administration*, pp. 459–460.

21. *Report of the Secretary of the Navy, December 1963*, p. xix.

22. *Report of the Secretary of the Navy, December 1864*, p. xxxvi.

23. Paullin, *History of Naval Administration*, pp. 312–314, 318–323; Sloan, *Isherwood*, pp. 228–234; Sprout and Sprout, *Rise of American Naval Power*, pp. 165–170.

24. Potter, *The United States and World Sea Power*, pp. 387–388.

25. Paullin, *History of Naval Administration*, pp. 387–402; Sprout and Sprout, *Rise of American Naval Power*, pp. 188–195.

26. Rear Admiral Philip W. Snyder, "Bring Back the Corps," *United States Naval Institute Proceedings* (February 1979), 105:50. Hereafter, this journal: *USNIP*.

27. Paullin, *History of Naval Administration*, pp. 458–462.

28. *Ibid.*, pp. 461–463.

29. *Ibid.* Snyder, "Bring Back the Corps," p. 50.

30. Paullin, *History of Naval Administration*, p. 463.

31. Robert W. McNitt, "The Naval Postgraduate School: Sixty Years Young," *USNIP* (June 1970), 96:69.

32. This was the beginning of the corps of restricted line officers. Julius A. Furer, *Administration of the Navy Department in World War II* (Washington, D.C.: GPO, 1957), pp. 236–237; Snyder, "Bring Back the Corps," pp. 50–51.

33. On the role of "trigger events" in innovation, see Samuel P. Huntington, *The Common Defense: Strategic Programs in National Politics* (New York: Columbia University Press, 1961), p. 291; and Michael H. Armacost, *The Politics of Weapons Innovation: The Thor-Jupiter Controversy* (New York: Columbia University Press, 1969), p. 256. On the role of dissatisfaction with the status quo in regard to innovation, see James G. March and Herbert A. Simon, *Organizations* (New York: Wiley, 1958), p. 48.

34. Donald Schon argues that compartmentalization is one response of business firms to innovation. Not only does the corporation reduce the systemic shock which failure might produce in a centralized organization, but it also isolates the social effects of innovation. Donald Schon, *Technology and Change: The New Heraclitus* (New York: Delacorte, 1967), pp. 71, 119–122.

35. Ronald Kurth argues that this is typical for "innovative departures." Kurth, "Politics of Technological Innovation in the United States Navy," p. 4.

36. John Crane and James F. Kieley, *United States Naval Academy: The First Hundred Years* (New York: Whittlesey House, McGraw-Hill, 1945), p. 18; Jack Sweetman, *The U.S. Naval Academy* (Annapolis, Md.: Naval Institute Press, 1979), p. 13.

37. Sprout and Sprout, *Rise of American Naval Power*, pp. 102–103.

38. Crane and Kieley, *United States Naval Academy*, pp. 8–11, 17, 20–25; Sweetman, *U.S. Naval Academy*, pp. 3–6, 12. For a slightly different emphasis on the mutiny, see Miller, *U.S. Navy*, pp. 128–131.

39. Furer, *Administration of the Navy Department*, pp. 195–198. Cf. Paullin, *History of Naval Administration*, pp. 201–203, 209–210. The argument that the steam engine was merely the first of a series of technical innovations that required management

by individual specialists must be acknowledged. However, the bureau system was expanded to its greatest diversity in 1862—from five to eight—well in advance of the vast increase of complexity in naval technologies seen in the twentieth century. The number of bureaus remained fairly stable over the next century—between six and eight, until the system was abolished in 1966.

40. Furer, *Administration of the Navy Department,* pp. 199–201.

41. McNitt, "The Naval Postgraduate School," pp. 71–72; "Navy Picks Officers for Flying Branch," *New York Times,* October 4, 1935, p. 16.

42. Harold G. Bowen, *Ships, Machinery, and Mossbacks: The Autobiography of a Naval Engineer* (Princeton: Princeton University Press, 1954), ch. 2 *passim.*

43. Albert B. Christman, "Untaped Interview: Rear Admiral Malcolm Schoeffel: 1966," p. 10. China Lake Oral History Project; Operational Archives, Naval Historical Center, Washington Navy Yard, Washington, D.C. In 1940, there were three OEDO-designated officers out of 348 restricted line officers and more than 7,000 line officers total. U.S. House Committee on Naval Affairs, *Sundry Legislation Affecting the Naval Establishment, 1941, Hearings,* 77th Cong., 1st sess., 1941, p. 174. Hereafter, sources in this series: HCNA, *Sundry Legislation* (year).

44. Telephone conversation, Dr. Wm. F. Whitmore, August 7, 1980. Dr. Whitmore was a civilian mathematician with the navy's Operations Evaluation Group and the Special Projects Office, which developed *Polaris.*

   The first OEDO to reach flag rank was Levering Smith who worked on the *Polaris* project.

45. I.e., naval constructors, who were trained in aeronautical engineering and EDO-designated officers who were trained on aircraft engines.

46. U.S. Bureau of Naval Personnel, *Register of Commissioned and Warrant Officers of the United States Navy and Marine Corps, 1 July 1947* (GPO, 1947), pp. 14–17. Hereafter, this corporate author: BuPers. Hereafter, volumes of this series: *Register* (year).

47. BuAer's *Rigel* and BuOrd's *Triton* both were projects for the development of a ramjet-powered cruise missile. Berend D. Bruins, "U.S. Naval Bombardment Missiles, 1940–1958," Ph.D. dissertation, Columbia University, 1981, pp. 234–239.

48. One witness suggested that there was an inverse relationship between the status of the restricted duty technical officers and the quality of the bureau's laboratories. Telephone Conversation, Dr. Wm. F. Whitmore, August 7, 1980.

49. Frederick S. Harrod, *Manning the New Navy: The Development of a Modern Naval Enlisted Force, 1899–1940,* Contributions in American History no. 68 (Westport, Conn.: Greenwood, 1978), pp. 8–10, 15–17, 74. Blacks were invariably assigned to the landsman rating.

50. *Ibid.,* pp. 79–80, 89–92.

51. This judgment contradicts Harrod, e.g., p. 5.

52. In 1901, Lieutenant Wm. S. Sims learned of the British innovation of continuous aim gunnery. Only in 1905 had the navy's gunnery improved sufficiently to warrant development of central fire control systems. Elting E. Morison, *Admiral Sims and the Modern American Navy* (Boston: Houghton Mifflin, 1942), pp. 81–84, 145–147.

53. The navy's "mongrel crews" were the despair of the officer corps and civilian administrators; the crews were considered to be "the dregs of all countries." Harrod, *Manning the New Navy,* pp. 15–17. In 1889, the navy's enlisted force consisted of 3,668 native-born men and 4,278 foreign-born men from some fifty-seven countries. Paullin, *History of Naval Administration,* p. 424.

54. The numbers and tonnage of steam ships registered by the principal European states uniformly increased between 1880 and 1914. B. R. Mitchell, *European Historical Statistics, 1750–1970* (New York: Columbia University Press, 1975), pp. 619–623.

In 1909, the tonnage of vessels engaged in foreign trade that entered and cleared ports of the United Kingdom was more than twice that of 1880. Similar figures for the United States for the same period likewise show that commercial maritime tonnages more than doubled. Between 1888 and 1900, there was an 8 percent increase in the number of persons employed on registered vessels of the United Kingdom. No similar figures were found for the United States. Augustus D. Webb, *The New Dictionary of Statistics* (London: Routledge, 1911), p. 564, U.S. Bureau of the Census, *Historical Statistics of the United States; Colonial Times to 1970* (GPO, 1975), pp. 759–760.

55. Potter, *The United States and World Sea Power*, pp. 450–458. American naval expenditures rose 150 percent between 1890 and 1900.

56. Between 1888 and 1907, the proportion of "Lascars and Asiatics" increased from 9 percent to 16 percent. Webb, *New Dictionary of Statistics*, p. 567.

57. U.S. Bureau of the Census, *Historical Statistics of the United States*, pp. 1141–42.

58. E.g., Paullin, *History of Naval Administration*, pp. 298–299, 451–452.

59. Furer, *Administration of the Navy Department*, pp. 272–273.

60. U.S. House, Committee on Armed Services, *Sundry Legislation Affecting the Naval and Military Establishments, Hearings*, 80th Cong., 1st sess., 1947, p. 2475. Hereafter, this source: HCAS, *Sundry Legislation* (1947).

61. Between August 7, 1955, and June 15, 1956, 1,579 unrestricted line (URL) officers were commissioned in the rank of ensign. Of these, 405 (25.6 percent) were graduates of the Naval Academy. In 1979, 129 of 192 (67.2 percent) of the navy's URL flag officers were graduates of the Naval Academy. This included 8 of 8 admirals, 23 of 29 (79.3 percent) vice-admirals, but only 98 of 155 (63.2 percent) rear admirals. BuPers, *Annual Register of the United States Naval Academy, Annapolis, Md.: One Hundred and Twelfth Academic Year, 1956–1957* (GPO, 1956), p. 22, BuPers, *Register* (1957), pp. 280–296, 299; U.S. Naval Military Personnel Command, *Register* (1979), pp. 1–2. Hereafter, this corporate author: NMPC.

62. Furer, *Administration of the Navy Department*, p. 234. Snyder, "Bring Back the Corps," p. 51.

63. "In one of Oscar Wilde's satirical stories, an American girl who said that there were no ruins or curiosities in her country was told by the Canterville Ghost: 'No ruins! No curiosities! You have your navy and your manners.' " Miller, *U.S. Navy*, p. 192.

64. "Changing Jobs of the U.S. Navyman," *All Hands* (August 1958), no. 499, pp. 32–37; NMPC, *Naval Military Personnel Statistics, Third Quarter FY-81*, NAVPERS 15658 of June 30, 1981, p. iv. The gunner's mate rating was established in 1797. One career group under this rating now has responsibilities for nuclear weapons.

In 1918, there were about thirty identifiable ratings; today, there are some ninety separate categories in the rating structure. Colonel Dion Williams, USMC, *Army and Navy Uniforms and Insignia*, rev. and enlarged ed., (New York: Stokes, 1918), pp. 139–40. U.S. Senate, Committee on Armed Services, *Department of Defense Authorization for Appropriations for Fiscal Year 1982, Hearings on S. 815*, 97th Cong., 1st sess., 1981, pp. 3735–3736.

In 1904, slightly less than 30 percent of the enlisted men were petty officers. In 1978, slightly more than 60 percent were petty officers. U.S. Navy, *Annual Reports of the Navy Department for the Year 1904* (GPO, 1904), p. 501. U.S. Senate, Committee on Armed Services, *Department of Defense Authorization for Appropriations for Fiscal Year 1980, Hearings on S. 428*, 96th Cong., 1st sess., 1979, p. 1931.

65. NMPC, *Register* 1979, p. vii.

66. HCNA, *Sundry Legislation* (1941), pp. 1165–1305; HCNA, *Sundry Legislation* (1942), pp. 2295–2392.

67. Chief Warrant Officer J. B. Hart, "Warrant Officers: Use Them or Lose Them," *USNIP* (April 1982), 108:59–61.

68. HCNA, *Sundry Legislation* (1941), pp. 1239, 1276.

69. *Ibid.*, pp. 1165–1166.

70. *Ibid.*, pp. 176–179, 719–720, 1177–1183, 1278.

71. HCAS, *Sundry Legislation* (1947), pp. 2475–2477.

72. BuPers, *Register* (1949), p. xii; NMPC, *Register* (1980), p. viii.

73. Thomas B. Buell, *Master of Sea Power; A Biography of Fleet Admiral Ernest J. King* (Boston: Little, Brown, 1980), pp. 366–368, 371.

74. In 1940, 10 of 70 (14.3 percent) flag officers of the unrestricted line (URL) wore navy wings. In 1947, 68 of 220 (30.9 percent) URL flag officers were naval aviators. U.S. Bureau of Navigation, *Register* (1940), pp. 14–17; BuPers, *Register* (1947), pp. 14–17. Of the ten aviation flag officers in 1940, two were not pilots, but only naval aviation observers. Of the eight remaining pilots, only one had earned his wings before 1926, the year in which Congressional legislation induced the navy to have older URL officers undergo flight training. Regarding this "Morrow Board" legislation, see Clark G. Reynolds, *The Fast Carriers: The Forging of an Air Navy* (New York: McGraw-Hill, 1968), pp. 15–16.

75. In 1940, 6 of 70 (8.6 percent) URL flag officers wore the submariner's dolphins. In 1947, 48 of 220 (21.8 percent) URL flag officers were submariners. U.S. Bureau of Navigation, *Register* (1940), pp. 14–17; BuPers, *Register*, (1947), pp. 14–17. Of this latter figure, four wore both wings and dolphins.

76. Sixty-three of the aviation flag officers in 1947 had been promoted from a pool of 141 aviation captains and commanders in 1940. Forty-five of the submarine-qualified flag officers in 1947 had been promoted from a pool of 199 submarine-qualified captains and commanders. Thus, the promotion rates were 45 percent for naval aviators and 23 percent for submariners. U.S. Bureau of Navigation, *Register* (1940), pp. 18–33; BuPers, *Register* (1947), pp. 14–17.

77. In the early (nonnuclear) submarines, the rank of the commanding officer was that of lieutenant commander. Since sea duty and especially command at sea are essential to promotion, this meant that the officer would have to serve in surface ships in the ranks of commander and captain before he could be eligible for selection to flag rank.

78. Chief of Naval Operations memo to Secretary of the Navy, serial 62P00 of 15 May 1946, "Establishment of a Deputy Chief of Naval Operations for Sub-surface Warfare." Records of Secretary of the Navy James Forrestal, Record Group 80, General Records of the Department of Navy, 1798–1947, National Archives, Washington, D.C.

79. In 1950, only 30 of 180 (16.7 percent) URL admirals were submariners, while 64 (35.5 percent) were naval aviators. BuPers, *Register* (1950), pp. 1–3.

80. Admiral Louis E. Denfeld, a submariner, was fired by Secretary of Defense Louis Johnson in 1949 in a political dispute on behalf of naval aviation. Ironically, his replacement as CNO was Admiral Forrest P. Sherman, a naval aviator. Miller, *U.S. Navy*, pp. 382–383.

81. The rank of the commanding officer of nuclear-powered attack submarines is that of commnander.

82. Submariners as a percentage of URL flag officers have increased from 18.4 percent in 1960, to 21.0 percent in 1970, to 22.5 percent in 1980. BuPers, *Register* (1960), pp. 1–3; BuPers, *Register* (1970), pp. 1–3; NMPC, *Register* (1980), pp. 1–2.

83. Admiral Elmo R. Zumwalt, Jr. (1970–1974).

84. Cover photo, *USNIP* (August 1982), and caption 108:3.

85. Orr Kelly, "New Submarine Head Seeks Five Attack Craft Yearly," *Washington Star*, April 29, 1971, reprinted in *USNIP* (October 1971), 97:110–111.
86. BuPers, *Register* (1952), p. xii; BuPers, *Register* (1971), p. xiii.
87. BuPers, *Register* (1976), pp. viii–ix.
88. Reportedly, this is an option available under the Defense Officer Personnel Management Act of 1980, as amended. Captain Brayton Harris, "At Long Last: DOPMA . . . How Long Will It Last?" *USNIP* (September 1981), 107:129.

10. The Impact of Technology on American Education, 1880–1980

Geraldine Joncich Clifford
University of California, Berkeley

William F. Ogburn likens technology to a great mountain: "From one vantage point . . . the outlook is clouded: yet we may get a clear view from another side."[1] Technology's relationship to American education is like Mount Rainier's to Seattle—dominating but usually invisible. This essay takes several vantage points, considering technology to incorporate both material and procedural innovation, machine culture and managerial culture, hardware and software. There are direct interventions in classrooms through instructional technologies. Schools and colleges are also reshaped by technology's indirect, culturally mediated effects on population, communication, transportation, industrial and agricultural production, and business operations.

Technology's impact cannot be disentangled from other forces; it does not act unassisted.[2] Technology created the buses that daily transport 48,000 pupils to schools in Charlotte-Mecklenburg County, North Carolina; but many ride because of a federal court order representing the civil rights movement. New varieties of tomatoes and mechanical pickers converge with political processes to get farm workers' children into the education system. The vaccine for poliomyelitis loosened parental restraints on children's movements; so did courts prodded by civil libertarians. Authorized by the Morrill Act of 1862, land grant colleges made room in higher education for agricultural research and engineering education, but their acceptance profited from anti-intellectualism in the culture. (John Purdue specified that the new technical university would lose his bequest if a Greek or Latin book appeared in its library).[3] A plummeting birth rate that owed little to modern contraceptive technology, when combined with schools' traditional emphasis on paper, punctuality, and accepting instruction, opened office work to women more than did the invention of the typewriter.[4]

At least in the short run, technology's effects may be conservative, and contradictory tendencies flourish together. Printing encouraged both dogmatism and tolerance, faith and skepticism.[5] The science curriculum reforms after Sputnik represented "a refinement of the status quo."[6] So far school computers are used mainly for drill. As Braudel notes, the history of technology consists of both the accelerator and the brake.[7] The reverse gear also operates. Dead ends and unanticipated consequences litter the historical record. Because aviation and the radio altered man's conception of place and promoted "world-mindedness," school geography was expected to flourish. Instead, in the elementary grades it was buried in "social studies" and a leading state university recently closed its geography department. Smaller proportions of American high school students were studying science, mathematics, and foreign languages in 1980 than before the expensive new curricula and language laboratories spurred by Sputnik.

Yet, the consequences of technology continue to invite educational remedies. Technological unemployment, industrial competition among nations, the human control of technology, and ecological concerns—these are present-day versions of the challenges to schools and colleges that earlier generations of educators met, moderated, or evaded. After a review of major changes in American education in the past one hundred years, we will see, in turn, how educational institutions were affected by the technologies of management, the revolutions in transport and communications, demographic shifts, and occupational changes. In addition to these culturally mediated influences, I will examine how schools interpreted "vocational education" and adapted instructional technologies to their daily lives. In the conclusion, an interactive conception of the relations of technology and education will be suggested.

A Century of Change in Education

America's ability to exploit early British industrial technology probably relied on widespread literacy. By 1830 the United States had achieved rough parity with Western Europe in school participation rates.[8] There was precedent, then, for the surpassing story of this century: increasing school and college enrollments, larger institutional numbers and sizes, more educational employment, money and manpower devoted to education. School expansions that vastly exceeded population growth also triggered or shaped other educational changes.

"In 1890 our America was still a land of little things—little farms, little towns, little factories, little houses, little schools, little colleges," recalled a leading educational reform theorist.[9] As early as 1894, however, the United States outdistanced Europe's leading nations in industrial and educational output. Its emergence raised German and English alarms at "the American menace."[10] Europe's response to the widely claimed linkage of education to economic productivity did not, however, stimulate a comparable expansion of its secondary and tertiary education until after World War II, when new arenas of technological competition beckoned.[11]

The enlargement of America's own secondary schooling was startling. The equivalent of one public high school a day was opened between 1890 and 1920. "For economic efficiency, as well as for intelligent citizenship, responsible parenthood, and personal fulfillment, industrial civilization demands a radical extension of the period of general education."[12] This educator's understanding of that demand anticipated subsequent developments in higher education. In 1940, 14.5 percent of the eighteen-to-twenty-one age group was enrolled in colleges and universities; by 1970 that figure was 47.6 percent.[13] Economic depressions increased high school attendance in the 1890s and high school and college growth in the 1930s. Veterans' preference policies and military deferments stimulated male enrollments and the feminist movement had its effects on attendance and persistence rates.

As colleges, elite and specialized, reached downward for more students, and as the mass, general education, elementary school system held higher proportions of students for secondary schools, new institutions emerged and old ones changed to accommodate their more diverse clients. The junior high school was designed to keep early adolescents in school and introduce some vocational preparation through multiple curricula, when universal high school attendance was not yet envisioned. Junior colleges added new options at the other end of secondary education; by the early 1960s, 30 percent of first-time higher education enrollments were in this sector, with its unique mix of "transfer" (degree) programs, occupational training, and adult education.[14]

Costs rose with increased numbers and upward expansions. The Cornersville, Indiana High School had, around 1910, 18 percent of the district's students but captured 30 percent of the educational budget. "It has been the thought of the school authorities for the last few years that the High School course should be broadened so as to appeal to as many of the community as possible," the superintendent acknowledged. "The purpose of the High School should be to educate all boys and girls of the community rather than a select few who may want to go to college. This necessarily means great freedom of selection of subjects, and the doing away with hard and fast lines beyond certain necessary limitations."[15] A nationwide movement emerged to redress inequities by varying the curriculum to retain more students. In 1910, 8.8 percent of the nation's seventeen-year-old population graduated from high school; in 1975, graduates were 75 percent of that age group.[16] The high school was remade in the process; in courses offered, teaching styles, textbooks, and "school climate." Despite certain economies of scale gained in the popularization of high school attendance, the bill for education mounted. In 1889–1890, high school students were 1.6 percent of public school enrollments; in 1975–76, they were 31.9 percent.[17] Between 1950 and 1980, alone, school expenditures grew by over 500 percent in constant dollars.[18] Analogous changes in higher education enrollments and program accretions had similar fiscal implications except that the costs there were better shared between public and private sources.

Schooling has been and remains a labor-intensive activity. In 1891, when the United States Post Office Department had the highest number of public employees (95,440, two-thirds of them political appointees), there were already 368,338 public school classroom teachers and other nonsupervisory staff.[19] Throughout this century teachers remained more numerous than civilian (nonschool) employees at the federal, state, or local government levels. As schools and school systems became larger, more differentiated and resource-using, as state and local requirements became complex and insistent in matters of facilities, health and safety, curriculum, instructional materials, record keeping, purchasing, personnel policies, and finance, educators and public officials more frequently asserted their readiness for a science of efficient administration.

Technologies of Management

To friend and foe alike technology is less its products than its essence as a process, "a way of working, a method of attacking problems," emphasizing precision and planning; *technique* "converts spontaneous and unreflective behavior into behavior that is deliberate and rationalized."[20] As immigrants flooded into the nation, raising fears of social unpredictability, and as schools and colleges became large institutions or parts of massive systems, their managers borrowed what they knew of the technologies of people- and paper-processing invented by American business. "The factory was the cradle in which modern management was born, and the multi-unit business is the environment in which it has taken its place among the major technologies of the present era."[21] In the interests of order and efficiency, school superintendents applied business methods and interpreted the principles of scientific management—so much so that, to a modern critic, "by 1925 the position had more of the characteristics of a managerial job in business or industry than it did of an educational one."[22]

Educational institutions readily adopted some part of business methods, from filing and manual record systems to computers. The lead pencil, telephone, typewriter, mimeograph, dictaphone, and photocopier moved, in turn, into school offices.[23] The *material culture* associated with business had, however, still farther-reaching effects on education, as on the culture generally. The social uses of the telephone took time from homework. Like the typewriter it led to a deterioration in handwriting standards, to which schools responded by giving penmanship's place in the curriculum to other subjects. Reductions in the costs of paper with the shift from hand to machine manufacture and from rags to wood pulp stimulated newspaper, magazine, and book production, as it had earlier promoted personal correspondence, diary-keeping, and copybooks.[24] Nineteenth-century school slates gave way to paper, encouraging "creative writing" in all the grades, as well as consumable workbooks for drill purposes.

It is the impersonal writing of business—the memo, the form, the directive—that we associate with bureaucracy in large organizations. They are, however, mere instruments of management science: the organizing of human activity to some given end, with optimal economy and efficiency. Businessmen and business culture heavily influenced large educational systems between 1910 and 1930, because of evident parallels in the organizational development of the two sectors. As the apprentice or journeyman who lived and worked in the workshop-home of the owner-manager-master had ceased to be of economic importance, the teacher no longer boarded in the homes of her patrons or labored in a schoolroom open to the community. Like business and industrial sites, schooling moved from scattered, independent, often temporary operations by "owners" (proprietors or trustees) to become merged, coordinated, and "permanent" systems managed by salaried professionals in administrative hierarchies. The diversified, multiunit modern business enterprise, already mature by 1920, had a counterpart in the multisite and multifunction school system.[25] Its "products" expanded to school lunch programs, transportation, sports and recreation, education of the handicapped, vocational education, adult education, child care, and (until divestiture) the junior colleges. In support of the regular educational program, administrative units emerged in finance, personnel, testing, counseling, school psychology, "resource specialists," and, recently, legal affairs and government programs. The technologies of management grew to coordinate and rationalize such complexities.

As schoolhouses became "educational plants" and college presidents and school superintendents became "executives," their relationships to their governing bodies changed—in part, with the latter's differing composition as business and professional men replaced ministers, tradesmen, and farmers on many boards. Moreover, the delegation of responsibility to a growing class of expert career managers seems inevitable considering the society-wide movement toward professionalism and its appurtenances: professional courses in universities, journals and societies, funded research, and access to the knowledge that legitimates the expert and disarms the layman. If a du Pont could not enter the middle management of his family's firm without an engineering degree, no responsible school board member or university regent should presume to meddle in a modern educational organization.[26]

"A city engages an expert to study its water supply before making changes," argued a proponent of the school survey movement that generated hundreds of local studies between 1910 and 1925. "Why should it not have an expert educational engineer's report on the matter of intended educational changes?"[27] Superintendents and their "educational engineers" hired consultants who belonged to the same interest group, presenting themselves as the surest guides to a rational future for schooling. In education and business the proliferation of statistics gathering and research bureaus, the invention of psychological testing, research on human dynamics, systems analysis, and management by objectives successively represented the movement to apply the scientific method, at last, "to the Man-Man relationships as well as the Man-Thing relationships," wrote a prominent educator, textbook author, and former civil engineer.[28]

The Transportation Revolution

Around 1910 the school superintendent was likened to the "conductor on the educational railroad"; the better analogue would have been the manager of a trunk line.[29] While ordinary Americans appreciated the railroad for ending the isolation of their communities, transporting themselves and their goods with speed, comfort, and regularity, historians know such innovations as railroads to be more broadly revolutionary. Associated changes in transportation and communication "brought into being entirely new outlooks, have quickened the pace of living, and have made advisable or necessary many important social adjustments."[30] The wheel and seagoing ships were invented five thousand years ago but transportation progressed very slowly. Napoleon moved no faster than Caesar.[31] In the past one hundred and fifty years, however, steamships, railroads, automobiles, airplanes, and rockets were invented and accepted; compared with the two thousand years required for the acceptance of paper, the pace of recent transportation change seems unprecedented.[32]

In 1880 America still knew "the tyranny of distance." Towns were separated by many miles of bad roads. The rural share of the total population remained large: 72 percent in 1880, 51 percent in 1920.

Rural teachers still outnumbered their urban counterparts in 1941–42, when rural children were 46 percent of the nation's students.[33] The automobile affected school directly and was considered a particular godsend by rural educators. *The Journal of Rural Education* published an article a month, on average, between 1921 and 1926, discussing the transportation of country children.[34] Although schools had sometimes moved students in wagons, effective school transportation required the faster, all-weather bus. Urban areas adopted school buses with city growth by annexation and the building of central high schools drawing children citywide. The discovery that free transportation improved attendance and retention rates encouraged authorities to lease buses and negotiate student passes with public bus and streetcar lines. In 1961–62, before desegregation pressures, 28 percent of all public school children already rode school buses; by 1967–68, the figure was 42 percent.[35]

The automobile also facilitated the work of agricultural extension agents, increasing public acceptance of agricultural education and the land grant colleges; more farmers' sons went to high school and college, and the votes of rural-dominated state legislatures followed. It became less common to hear farm organizations dismiss state universities as "a cold storage institution of dead languages and useless learning which costs several billion bushels of wheat each year."[36] Rural school supervisors, school nurses, and traveling libraries brought rural schools closer to rising urban standards and probably increased rural residents' sense of well-being.

Without economies of scale, to add or expand programs uses greater proportions of district budgets in rural than in urban systems. Therefore, many innovations were not implemented.[37] Nevertheless, consolidated rural schools and school districts exposed rural children to a broader curriculum and permitted them to live at home while attending high school.[38] School consolidation depended heavily on automobile use and the attendant building and maintaining of paved roads. There were, perhaps, 200,000 school districts in 1900, many of them operating a single one-room school. By 1945 consolidation left 100,000 districts nationwide, and 16,000 by 1980. As in the automobile industry, the building phase was succeeded, under the influence of technological change, by the consolidation phase.[39]

Before modern technology existed Americans were a mobile people. Yankees moved from New England to Ohio and Oregon, spreading their schools and other institutions ahead of the railroads. Surveying expeditions, wagon trains, the postal system, news of gold strikes, and plain restlessness encouraged those transfers that can transform.[40] An exodus of population closed schools—from the abandoned farm lands of Aroostook County, Maine to the deserted gold fields of Plumas County, California. Assisted by rapid and easy transportation, migration continues to affect education. Movement from the rural South to the urban North and West, and from central cities to suburbs, created more racially and class-segregated schools.[41] Retirements to Florida put pensioners' needs in competition with those of school children in the struggle over tax revenues. The technologies of air conditioning and water transfer, combined with political events like the OPEC oil embargo, stimulated population resettlement and institution building in previously inhospitable regions. Geographically distant university faculties climbed into airplanes to attend scholarly meetings and consult with government officials, maintaining their membership in the peer group.

Moving to the city put more work, and more varied work, within reach of women and children. Employment opportunities might cause students to drop out of schools or to stay in school to qualify better for "city jobs." Adding courses in driver education and auto mechanics inclined youth toward the second alternative—and was a fitting tribute to the revolution in transportation which brought so many to cities and city schools.

The Communications Revolution

"Before the day of the automobile and consolidated school, it was almost impossible to find a group of rural boys of approximately the same age who got together often enough to make . . . organized games possible. . . ."[42] What improved transportation did for strengthening the face-to-face society of the peer group the electronic media of communication extended into a national and international youth culture. Although schools and colleges hesitated in adopting the new techniques of film, recording, and television, they encountered their indirect effects. Moviegoing became a mania. Between 1952 and 1962, 90 percent of homes acquired television sets. The cultural referees for many youth became characters in television programs and music and sports stars, rather than the characters in books, or the teachers, preachers, and parents who, presumably, once so functioned.

Colleges and universities have served the West as the custodians of culture, of esoteric as distinct from common knowledge, since the invention of print when the scriptoria of the monasteries surrendered their role in the preservation of knowledge. The common schools and everyday preaching, however, have been in closer touch with the whole society. As I have written elsewhere about the popular character of schools in the United States, "the press of the whole culture has been greater upon schoolmen, the points of interaction with mass society more numerous."[43] In the face-to-face society of nineteenth-century America, which Coleman calls "experience rich and information poor," books read at home or in school represented windows onto the larger world. "Throughout their history schools have been the community's gateway for information," as "a source of, and guide to books." Because reading is a slow means of acquiring information, and home and school libraries were small, and not everyone read much, vicarious experience grew slowly.[44] This altered with the advent of mass publishing and, especially, the inventions of radio, television, and film. Instant communications annihilated provincialism even more than did the automobile. Schools lost much of their virtual monopoly on dispensing information to youth, as the scribes long ago lost theirs on teaching writing. Schools could no longer exclude knowledge by virtue of what they did *not* teach; the sources of information became too pluralistic and competitive.

It is one thing to lose a monopoly. For educational institutions it is a far worse thing to lose authority. That happened, however. A culture of play and consumption was spread efficiently by the electronic media through programming and advertising. It offered a counter-culture to school culture, treating all work and discipline as a "middle class hang up." Drugs are another technology popularized by the electronic media that affects schools. Spread through the peer group and hardened to dogma, the lessons of the media weakened or denied outright the claims to authority of traditional educators. Some teachers decided to "go with the flow," thereby opening schools to the same charges of irresponsibility leveled at the curriculum of the electronic educators.

Although television watching does not confer competence, "it is the cheapest way of spending time that the human race has ever devised . . . a thousand times cheaper than a teacher."[45] Teachers worried about competing with this highly visual, rapid-fire entertainment medium. The effects of television on cognitive styles concerned educators as much as the fact that the fourteen-year-old had already viewed 18,000 homicides.[46] There was slender evidence that schools were succeeding any better than were parents in teaching youth discriminating taste or critical consumption of the to them now familiar and established media of communications.[47] Perhaps the youthful protests against the Vietnam War, and the consumer and environmental protection movements, may count here, but could educators take credit?

Demographic Shifts

During the "baby boom" years, there was an unprecedented entry into schools of thousands of young, undersocialized teachers, themselves nourished on the popular culture of the mass media. One theory holds that *they* undermined schools' and colleges' resistance to a dysfunctional media culture. True or not, demographic shifts clearly figure in education's history. Modern contraceptives have already affected schools and colleges. Despite high birth rates following World War II, the secular trend in America has been towards an older population, resulting from declining fertility and longer life expectancies.[48] The 1790 Census reported a median age of 15; in 1980 it was 30. The steady growth of urbanization reduced incentives for large families and increased the cost and difficulties of raising children. The declining demand for farm labor also encouraged reductions in family size in rural America.[49] A reduction by half in household size between 1800 and 1900 promoted school attendance among girls who had fewer child care and housekeeping responsibilities. By 1900 females were two-thirds of high school graduates and nearly 40 percent of college undergraduates. These trends also encouraged women to become teachers.[50] Since their employment lowered costs, schools proliferated, their terms lengthened, and schools became universal child care institutions for youth below employment age.

For several centuries in the West slowly improving technologies of disease control and family limitation were changing children's status and increasing investment in their educations. Technological change helped divert mothers' time to childrearing, especially preparing children for school and monitoring their progress throughout.[51] In the most education-conscious segment of society, mothers enlisted as "education strategists" for their children. In the general population a rising educational level and smaller families spread this phenomenon, escalating expectations and intensifying pressures on institutions.

Demographic changes in the past half century had roller-coaster effects on education. The depressed birth rates of the 1930s caused unprecedented declines, in the period 1946–1955, in numbers of high school graduates.[52] It left schools ill prepared for the extreme teacher shortages caused by postwar birth rates. "Emergency credentials," double sessions, temporary buildings, and the spread of junior colleges resulted. The birth rate since the mid-1960s had different consequences: collapse of the market for teachers, causing a rise in median teacher age and experience, with consequent increases in salaries; teacher layoffs, despite smaller class size and without teacher displacement by machines; closed programs in colleges, with institutions advertising for students; universities eager to exploit the commercial possibilities of research; discouragement of "open university" experiments by over-built higher education.[53] Education's share of the GNP began declining with the fact that the under-eighteen population was 20 percent smaller in 1980 than in 1970. Political support eroded since only 23 percent of eligible voters now have children in public schools.[54] The needs of the more numerous older Americans ensured struggles over resources.

Changes in Social Security legislation and mandatory retirement policies, economists' discussions of "over-investment" in schooling, proposals to begin lower education at four and end it at age sixteen— all reflect recent population shifts. Potential labor shortages and falling productivity should have the opposite effect on education's future that labor surplus and high productivity had earlier. We might expect deemphasis on extended schooling for the masses, more job-driven educational remedies, stress on retraining older workers, and relaxation of barriers before young workers. If support of vocational education grows as a function of having to fit a large youth cohort into the economy, then youth's declining share of the population should be accompanied by reduced interest in schools' explicit preparation of youth for employment.[55]

The Occupational Structure and Vocationalism in Education

In 1853 a new, two-room schoolhouse was dedicated in the town of Beverly, Massachusetts. Robert Rantoul, member of the School Committee from 1818 to 1854, recorded the thinking of one of the speakers:

> R. Putnam advanced the idea that the introduction of machinery in the arts had increased the demand for education inasmuch as there was more mind required in the use of machinery than without it . . . and an increase in a greater proportion of mental power to produce the increased results calls for more education. This remark he strengthened by his own observation in the High School of Salem. When he first took charge of the school parents found it difficult to procure suitable places for the boys who had gone through the regular course of study but lately he found that there was such an increase in demand for well-educated boys that some were induced to leave school before they had completed their regular course of study.[56]

Although free education was recognized in the English Poor Laws as an element in creating workmen, nineteenth-century industrial development increasingly joined schooling to qualifications for work: literacy, numeracy, and work discipline. Male literacy was promoted in New England, where schooling was more available as a result of population density, commercial agriculture, and trade. The female workforce in the early textile mills was literate and functional literacy was required to read the Montgomery Ward catalogue; its appearance in 1872, encouraged by Granger support, evidences widespread reading capacity.[57] Although the Massachusetts legislature made drawing a required study in public schools in 1870, answering a petition from manufacturers decrying the lack of design skills among workmen, most contemporary opinion did not rank high vocational objectives for schooling.[58]

In 1913 Indiana's state superintendent for public instruction characteristically described vocational education: "Nature study, agriculture, drawing, handwork, manual training, domestic science, and a study of the household arts, help to overcome the isolation which at present exists between school and life."[59] The next year a teacher at Washington Irving High School in New York City, where girls could learn dressmaking, millinery, bookbinding, stenography, and designing, reported that "the girls and their parents are willing to make sacrifices for the sake of the one or two or even three years of education that will fit a girl to earn her living, when they would by no means think it worthwhile to struggle for a like amount of general training."[60]

Popular perceptions that schooling, general or vocational, was becoming economically decisive reflected employment shifts in the technological society, from primary to secondary to service industries. Between 1820 and 1950, agricultural workers declined from 72 percent to 12 percent of the American labor force, while manufacturing employees grew from 12 percent to 36 percent, and service workers from 16 percent to 51 percent; after 1950 a fourth sector, the producers of ideas and technological innovations, spurred Ph.D. output.[61]

By 1900 only one American in three still worked in agriculture; technology had revolutionized the industry. The farm boys who formerly attended district schools only in slack seasons and the farm daughters who cooked and laundered for farm hands both had to find other employment. Federally supported vocational agriculture in country high schools gained adherents; but so did the academic and commercial courses that pointed away from the land.[62]

Industrial development created the wealth that endowed many schools and universities. Modern business and industry also made jobs that had not existed before, diminishing the ability of families and the apprenticeship system to train and socialize for new work. The opinion grew that schools should teach trade skills or, at least, familiarize students with occupations. Manual arts, industrial arts, and specific occupational training appeared in many schools. Despite the founding of some trade, vocational and technical high schools, public school educators determined that vocational education should be combined with college preparatory and general curricula to create the comprehensive high school. They succeeded, supported by labor's fears that employers would gain control of vocational public schools and by a generalized anxiety about the undemocratic consequences if parallel schools emerged.[63]

Vocational classes reproduced the sexual division of labor in the economy and the cultural preference that women be full-time home-makers. For decades the largest enrollments supported by the Smith-Hughes Act for Vocational Education were in home economics classes in secondary schools, and were without employment potential. In the formative years home economics was advocated for immigrant girls and the rest who dropped out of school, worked in shops and factories, or married early; "unless the school supplies the training these enter upon their duties without adequate preparation for home-keeping."[64] Being unconnected with the labor market, home economics enroll-ments rose during the Great Depression unlike trade and industrial training.[65]

Although more women moved into the labor force, sex typing in employment remained strong and unchallenged by vocational edu-cation. However, in the expectation that 90 percent of women would hold a paying job at some time in their lives, the 1976 Education Amendments charged vocational educators to overcome gender ster-eotyping. But a recent study of one city still found girls comprising 49 percent of enrollment in vocational courses in grades ten to twelve; over half were in Office Occupations, while their male counterparts were in Trades and Industries. Although, nationwide, females enrolled in programs with better employment prospects than did males, these uniformly offered much lower wages than did male-enrolled programs.[66]

Offices, telephone companies, and retail stores became women's workplaces. When nineteenth-century schools taught bookkeeping and shorthand, it was for personal, not occupational use. But the demand for low-paid white-collar employees, like that for teachers, grew such that only females could supply the need. High school typing and stenography classes and, later, "distributive education" courses, gave some training, although private secretarial and business "col-leges" flourished and employers provided on-the-job training. The bulk of the qualifications was not, however, gained in the vocational education curriculum, for either sex, but in the schools' general cur-riculum and socialization to people and paperwork. For females, "by being unspecialized and inexpensive, the academic curriculum was 'practical,' given the near-universal expectation that women wanted and would have short careers as paid workers."[67]

Vocational curricula were intended primarily to keep fourteen-to sixteen-year-olds in school. Child labor, once considered desirable, lost out in an industrializing society; child-welfare reformers, union spokesmen, and educators joined in condemning it. Those who left school early worked as stock boys or cash girls and wrappers in department stores, as delivery boys or telegraph messengers, and did odd jobs in factories. Recent immigrants' children made artificial flowers in home manufacture or were domestic servants.[68]

"There are not jobs for children under 16 which they ought to take," warned a federal official.[69] Not only were children's jobs called "dead-end," exploitative, and morally and physically dangerous, but they were also scarcer because of union opposition to young workers and their wage-lowering effects on adult workers, and because of large immigrations that filled the economy's need for unskilled labor. Such technology as the cash register, pneumatic tube, telephone, paper folder, conveyor belt, and typewriter also eliminated many jobs and demanded higher skills of those remaining.[70] Given the decline in work opportunities, it was not surprising that reports proliferated that the majority of those who left school early did so because they were dissatisfied with school, not because they were forced to work.

The out-of-school, out-of-work adolescent was a danger to himself and society. Idle children, "street arabs," in nineteenth-century parlance, were potential juvenile delinquents in twentieth-century minds. "Prevention is peculiarly the province of the school," a teacher wrote[71]—prevention through adding vocational classes, vocational guidance, even job placement bureaus in the regular public schools. Some thought schools should teach job skills. More agreed that they should teach about available jobs and their requirements. Still more saw schools as shelters, protecting youth from the miseducation of the workplace.[72] Manual experience was called natural, especially for boys, who "burn to test the strength of materials and the magnitude of forces."[73] Vocational educators sought a bridge between "the old American work-world values—and the changing and threatening present."[74].

Schools did improve their "holding power." High school enrollments rose steadily, although graduation first became an experience of the majority of adolescents only in 1940. Vocational subjects kept some youngsters in school voluntarily. Successful child labor laws and the better enforcement of compulsory school attendance legislation confirmed what had become reality: most children *were* in school. Their percentage of the labor force plummeted between 1910 and 1930. Was it because the economy became unable to utilize their labor efficiently? Lebergott thinks not, looking instead at changes in family income and social attitudes.[75] From 1900 to 1950 real family income doubled in the United States. This allowed more families to patronize education, turning the high school from an elite to a mass institution, guaranteeing that steadily smaller proportions of their students were college bound—until the great reversal after 1950, when college attendance soared. Schools were required to adjust to a more diverse student body. Discretionary income also permitted more Americans the luxury of using educational institutions for their historic function of conferring status. The middle classes had wanted their children to associate with the social elite in the high schools; the irony is that these schools and, later, the colleges and universities were becoming less elite. Nonetheless, the process could not be stopped: to refuse to climb the education ladder was to sink in the American social structure.[76] The fact that occupational growth *was* in white-collar work for the high-school educated, and in professional, technical, and managerial careers for the college bound, retained a measure of rationality in the system. But education's prosperity also permitted some decoupling of the education and work worlds.

The Technologies of Instruction

Sputnik-inspired innovations in science, mathematics, and foreign language education were aimed at high aptitude, college-bound students and suburban high schools. Failures in implementation hurt these programs. So did their elitist image when educational policy abruptly shifted its focus from "excellence" to "equality." The current interest in computer technology in education is being promoted as a mass movement consistent with this technology's probable broad impact on human activities. Nonetheless, the fear is being voiced that these newer technologies will widen the gaps between social groups. While males study programming in mathematics departments, females learn word processing in clerical programs. Initial reports on children enrolling in summer computer camps confirm still greater male, white, and upper-middle-class dominance.[77]

These examples illustrate that education is, foremost, a social and political system; its problems are not primarily technical. If a new technique is adopted *and* implemented, the results may surprise, since an innovation must be "superimposed on, or merged or nested with ongoing practices, structures, ideologies, and ways of doing things."[78] Programmed instruction, for example, orients teachers' relationships to individuals rather than groups. Their predictable effort to "domesticate" the innovation entails trying to turn its use into accustomed channels; failing this, a new technology gathers dust. Teachers' bottom drawers are filled with curriculum "frameworks" and model courses of study, as are classroom cupboards with "adopted" textbooks and school storerooms with successive generations of artifacts from stereopticons to teaching machines.

This century offers many examples of anticipated revolutions premised on new technologies. Moreover, progressive educational theory favored diversified instructional approaches "to make teaching more creative and learning more self-directive as well as insightful." This same observer went on to rejoice that "elementary, high school, or college teachers . . . who rely exclusively upon the teacher-centered lecture . . . now find themselves virtually expendable with the advent of television teaching."[79] This prediction ranks with the whopper about a helicopter in every garage.

In 1910 Rochester, New York became the first system to adopt films for instructional use, while Boston barred projectors from schools as a fire menace.[80] The fragility, undependability, and logistical problems of storage, maintenance, and distribution, and the difficulties of darkening and ventilating classrooms, dogged this "reform." It did not simplify teaching classroom management. Hence, only 25,000 16-mm sound projectors were reported in 1948, for over 200,000 school buildings and their 700,000 classrooms.[81] Insufficient markets kept film costs high. Moreover, audio-visual aids represented "add-ons" in cost and time; they could not replace books, chalkboards, and flash cards. Despite state requirements that prospective teachers learn to use these aids, most did not acquire competence. The majority of public school teachers were women, trained to be "antitechnocrats."

Yet, in the overwhelmingly male faculties of colleges, equipment was also generally ignored or actively resisted. In fact, variations in instructional "technologies" were greater in the elementary schools and declined sharply as one went up in the grades.[82]

Extravagant claims are now being made about computer-assisted instruction, its flexibility, cost effectiveness, and qualitative differences from the audio-visual tradition. Simon Ramo, in 1957, observed that the television set or motion picture permits the student to look out the window as much as does the human teacher; not so the machine that engages the student and fits instruction precisely to the responses made.[83] "The computer is the Proteus of machines," wrote another enthusiast.[84] Although the dangers of overpromising are present, and many educators still see computers as "a solution in search of problems," theirs may not be the "same old story" of misapplied enthusiasm for technological solutions to educational realities. Because computers are economic or work tools as well as an instructional technology, the computer appears more analogous to the typewriter or sewing machine in school than to leisure-oriented films or television. As such it is reasonable to suppose that computer *use* will be widely taught and learned, although it is less certain, perhaps, that cybernetics will revolutionize school teaching and learning.

Educators often perceive innovations as "scratching where it isn't itching,"[85] but when they know that the system is seriously amiss, computers would be welcomed. The junior high school is an obvious case—being the most violence- and vandalism-plagued sector, a Siberia for teachers that is already undergoing reorganization into "middle schools."[86]

Once established, subsequent innovations in a technology become acceptable as refinements, even improvements. The book is an example. Eventually established as a successor to the oral tradition of educating, its catechetical pedagogy was supported by scarcity. Memorization, rather than reading, was expected—first, because of the theory of mental discipline, and second, because educated persons were sufficiently uncommon as to be on display; and third, because there was so little reading material and so much school time to fill. In the nineteenth century, well ahead of the paperback's contribution, books "once dear" began to become comparatively "cheap and plenty." Memorization, "mastery," and reading aloud fell before the goals of comprehension and wide, silent reading. Where the entire six-year elementary school curriculum of the 1890s reportedly could be *read* in forty-six hours, by 1936 ten times as much reading material was introduced in school.[87] No other instructional technology has approached, in its actual effects on schooling, the yet unfinished revolution of print.

Afterword

Radical historiography depicts schools and colleges as virtual captives of technological society. Jacques Ellul conceives progressive education as not liberating from or transcending technology but as social adaptation to it. Such assessments, being extreme, are suspect, although it would also be unwarranted to think that educational institutions could remain impervious. But schools and colleges are social systems in their own right, as well as public utilities, and have developed strategies by which to accept what is acceptable.

Schools and colleges did not have to "pull out all the stops" in response to technology's many challenges. The students came, and stayed longer, because the competition from employment was weakened, because the jobs were lost, or because employers' attitudes put them out of reach of those who left school "prematurely." With their friends in school, with the extracurriculum and a more relaxed academic culture to "sweeten the deal," the high school was a tolerable place for many, probably most, youth—without there being an unambiguous accommodation of the course of study to many students' presumed narrow occupational interests.

Parents were satisfied since schooling itself conferred status without much regard to what was studied. University graduates gained employment less for what they studied than for having been university students, with all that implied about background, intelligence, and ambition. The majority of industrial, white-collar, and service workers learned on the job. Increased purchasing power was achieved through the economy's high productivity, which came with capital investment and better technology and management. Employers of entry level workers were interested in work experience but not in high school vocational education, which was dominated by prevocational "industrial arts" courses that were as academic as possible—"roads to wisdom and culture"—and by enrollments in vocational agriculture and home economics that had nothing to do with the mass-production industries.[88] Of the high-school-educated blue-collar workers in this century, Drucker writes, no wonder he was "willing to settle for a school that was 'caring' rather than demanding."[89] As persisting youth unemployment lessened some students' incentives to do their best in school, educational institutions lost their incentives for maintaining academic quality when they ceased to be elite institutions answerable only to a knowledgeable clientele. "Holding power" was more important when the prevailing ideology stressed democratic inclusiveness.

Higher education did add professional schools and vocational curricula. Largely underwritten by government, research universities pursued research that the private sector would not risk but from which it might profit. Yet these diverse institutions shared internally derived values, and the "best managed" of them exploit external pressures, like the "high-tech emergency" in manpower, to sustain unmarketable "academic" programs. As engineering and business training moved out of the shop and storeroom and into the university, the liberal arts grabbed a share of their students' time. Even in the more narrowly conceived vocational programs of the community colleges, general academic requirements are common.[90] In bringing itself into secondary and higher education, then, technology, business, and vocationalism were subjected to academic influence. If they were not "humanized" in the process, the institutions of formal education were nonetheless aggrandized. Education became, perhaps, the most remarkable of all examples of a "growth industry."

Notes

1. William F. Ogburn, "The Meaning of Technology," in Francis R. Allen et al., eds., *Technology and Social Change* (New York: Appleton, 1957), p. 3.
2. George H. Daniels, "The Big Questions in the History of American Technology," *Technology and Culture* (1970), 2:1–21.
3. Herbert J. Muller, *The Children of Frankenstein: A Primer on Modern Technology and Human Values* (Bloomington: Indiana University Press, 1970), p. 212.
4. Elizabeth Faulkner Baker, *Technology and Woman's Work* (New York: Columbia University Press, 1964); Ruth Schwartz Cowan, "From Virginia Dare to Virginia Slims: Women and Technology in American Life." *Technology and Culture* (1979), 20:51–63.
5. Elizabeth L. Eisenstein, *The Printing Press as an Agent of Change: Communications and Cultural Transformations in Early Modern Europe* (Cambridge: Cambridge University

Press, 1979), 2 vols.: Charles A. Thrall, "The Conservative Use of Modern Household Technology," *Technology and Culture* (1982), 23:175–194.

6. Jennifer A. Mundy, "Science and Technology in Schools and Working Life: Are We Aiming in the Right Direction?" *Comparative Education* (1978), 14:117.

7. Fernand Braudel, *The Structures of Everyday Life* (New York: Harper and Row, 1981), p. 430.

8. Nathan Rosenberg, *Technology and American Economic Growth* (White Plains, N.Y.: Sharpe, 1972), p. 84.

9. Harold Rugg, *Foundations for American Education* (Yonkers, N.Y.: World, 1947), p. 237.

10. David B. Tyack, *The One Best System: A History of American Urban Education* (Cambridge, Mass.: Harvard University Press, 1974), p. 29; Sol Cohen, "The Industrial Education Movement, 1906–1917," *American Quarterly* (1968), 20:100.

11. Alexander King, "The Role of Government," in Trevor I. Williams, ed., *A History of Technology* (Oxford: Oxford University Press, 1978), 6:126–127.

12. George C. Counts, *Education and American Civilization* (New York: Greenwood, 1952), p. 374.

13. Carnegie Commission on Higher Education, *New Students and New Places* (New York: Carnegie Foundation, 1971), p. 127.

14. Abbott L. Ferriss, *Indicators of Trends in American Education* (New York: Russell Sage, 1969), pp. 44–49.

15. G. M. Wilson, *Cornersville [Indiana] Public Schools, Report of the Superintendent, 1907–1912* (1912), pp. 19, 28. The annual per-pupil costs were $18 in the grade schools and $45 in the high school.

16. U.S. Bureau of the Census, *Historical Statistics of the United States, Colonial Times to 1957* (Washington, D.C.: Bureau of Census, 1960), p. 207.

17. National Center of Education Statistics, *Digest of American Statistics, 1981* (Washington, D.C.: GPO, 1981), p. 38.

18. James W. Guthrie, "Emerging Political Economy of Educational Policy," in Kathryn Cirincioni-Coles, ed., *The Future of Education: Policy Issues and Challenges* (Beverly Hills: Sage, 1981), p. 114.

19. *Historical Statistics*, p. 208; Alfred D. Chandler, Jr., *The Visible Hand: The Managerial Revolution in American Business* (Cambridge, Mass.: Harvard University Press, 1977), pp. 204–205. The Pennsylvania Railroad alone employed 110,000 workers, railroads being the largest management systems in the economy. Shortly after 1950 teachers surpassed the total number of railroad workers for the first time since 1870: Stanley Lebergott, *Manpower in Economic Growth: The American Record Since 1800* (New York: McGraw-Hill, 1964), p. 510.

20. Counts, *Education and American Civilization*, pp. 139–140; John Wilkinson, introduction to Jacques Ellul, *The Technological Society* (New York: Knopf, 1964), p. vi.

21. Glenn Porter, "Management," in Williams, *A History of Technology*, 6:89.

22. Raymond E. Callahan, *Education and the Cult of Efficiency* (Chicago: University of Chicago Press, 1962), p. 148.

23. The Bell Telephone patent is often described as the most valuable ever issued in the United States. Because of high costs, business had a virtual monopoly on telephone usage for several decades. Of the three hundred telephone subscribers in the 1879 Pittsburgh directory, only six were not businesses: Ithiel de Sola Pool, *The Social Impact of the Telephone* (Cambridge, Mass.: Harvard University Press, 1977), p. 27.

24. E. Haylock, "Paper," in Williams, *A History of Technology*, 6:607–621; Thomas M. Smith, "Late Nineteenth-Century Communications: Techniques and Machines," in Melvin Kranzberg and Carroll W. Pursell, Jr., eds., *Technology in Western Civili-*

zation (New York: Oxford University Press, 1967), 1:636–648; Eisenstein, *The Printing Press*, p. 217.

25. Chandler, *The Visible Hand;* Porter, "Management," esp. 6:87–90. See also Tyack, *The One Best System*, pp. 41–42, and David Tyack and Elizabeth Hansot, *Managers of Virtue: Public School Leadership in America, 1820–1980* (New York: Basic Books, 1982), p. 110 et passim.

26. Chandler, *The Visible Hand*, p. 452.

27. Leonard Righter, "The Educational Survey Preparatory to the Organization of Vocational Education," *Teachers College Record* (1913), 14:3.

28. Harold Rugg, *The Great Technology: Social Chaos and the Public Mind* (New York: Day, 1933), p. v.

29. A. E. Winship, "What the Superintendent is Not," *Journal Proceedings and Addresses*, National Education Association, 38th Annual Meeting, Chicago, 1899, p. 309. Editor of the *Journal of Education*, Winship concluded his address to the Department of Superintendence: "Your word alone is law. . . . The president of the road is a mere passenger on your train. The school system of the town, city, county, state, and nation is to be conducted into the great union station of this imperial nation by men and women of this department."

30. Francis R. Allen, "Influence of Technology on Communications and Transportation," in Allen et al., *Technology and Social Change*, p. 278. On the rail and telegraphic companies as America's first modern business enterprises, pioneers in the managerial revolution, see Chandler, *The Visible Hand*, pp. 81–121.

31. Paul Valéry, quoted in Braudel, *The Structures of Everyday Life*, p. 429.

32. John Platt, "Eight Major Evolutionary Jumps Today," in Andrei Markovits and Karl W. Deutsch, eds., *Fear of Science, Trust in Science* (Cambridge, Mass.: Harvard University Press, 1980), pp. 149–155; A. Rupert Hall, "Early Modern Technology to 1600," in Kranzberg and Pursell, *Technology in Western Civilization*, 1:101.

33. David T. Blose, *Statistics on Schools in Urban and Rural Areas, 1941–42*, U.S. Office of Education Circular no. 231 (Washington, D.C.: GPO, 1945).

34. Michael Louis Berger, "The Social Impact of the Automobile on Rural America, 1893–1929: A Documentary History," Ed.D. dissertation, Teachers College, Columbia University, 1972, p. 4.

35. Joseph Froomkin et al., *A Report to the President's Commission on School Finance: Population, Enrollment, and Costs of Public Elementary and Secondary Education, 1975–76 and 1980–81* (n.p., May 1971), p. 21.

36. Quoted in Theodore Saloutos and John D. Hicks, *Agricultural Discontent in the Middle West, 1900–1930* (Madison: University of Wisconsin Press, 1951), p. 128.

37. A study of vocational education programs found 100 percent of central cities, 57 percent of cities with a population of over 100,000, and 16 percent of rural towns making recent changes: Charles Benson et al., *Descriptive Study of the Distribution of Federal, State, and Local Funds for Vocational Education*, final report of the Project on National Vocational Education Resources, National Institute of Education Contract no. 400-78-0039 (Berkeley: University of California Press, 1981), p. 215.

38. For a review of the perceived advantages of consolidated schools, see Berger, *The Social Impact of the Automobile*, pp. 264–272.

39. There were once 1,400 auto companies in the United States: Reynold Millard Wik, "Henry Ford's Science and Technology for Rural America," in Melvin Kranzberg and William H. Davenport, eds., *Technology and Culture: An Anthology* (New York: Schocken, 1972), p. 252.

40. George W. Pierson, "A Restless Temper," *American Historical Review* (1964), 69:969–989.

41. Sam B. Warner, Jr., "Population Movements and Urbanization," in Kranzberg and Pursell, *Technology in Western Civilization,* 1:544–545.

42. Carl C. Taylor, *Rural Sociology: In Its Economic, Historical, and Psychological Aspects,* rev. ed. (New York: Harper, 1933), p. 507.

43. Geraldine J. Clifford, "A History of the Impact of Research on Teaching," in Robert M.W. Travers, ed., *Second Handbook of Research on Teaching* (Chicago: Rand McNally, 1973), p. 25.

44. James S. Coleman, "The Children Have Outgrown the Schools," *Psychology Today* (1972), 5:72.

45. Platt, "Eight Major Evolutionary Jumps," p. 153

46. For example, Neil Postman, "Engaging Students in the Great Conversation," *Phi Delta Kappan* (1983), 64:310–316.

47. See the optimism in Edgar Dale, "Teaching Discrimination in Motion Pictures," in Nelson B. Henry, ed., *Mass Media and Education,* Fifty-Third Yearbook, National Society for the Study of Education. (Chicago: University of Chicago Press, 1954), part 2, p. 259; and Frank G. Jennings, "Mass Media, Mass Mind, and Makeshift: Comments on Educational Innovation in the Public Weal," in Matthew B. Miles, ed., *Innovation in Education* (New York: Teachers College Press, 1964), pp. 583–584.

48. The live birth rate for women (ages 15–44) in the United States was 3.7 in 1957; in 1982 it was 1.8.

49. Mark A. Rozenzweig, "The Demand for Children in Farm Households," *Journal of Political Economy* (1977), 85:123–146.

50. Geraldine J. Clifford, "Daughters into Teachers: Educational and Demographic Influences on the Transformation of Teaching into Women's Work," *History of Education Review* (1983), 12:15–28.

51. Ruth Schwartz Cowan, "The 'Industrial Revolution' in the Home: Household Technology and Social Change in the Twentieth Century," *Technology and Culture* (1976), 17:1–23, and "From Virginia Dare to Virginia Slims"; Thrall, "The Conservative Use of Modern Household Technology," pp. 175–194.

52. *Historical Statistics,* p. 207; Ferriss, *Indicators of Trends,* pp. 20, 69, 103.

53. Indicative was the ending of "Sunrise Semester," after a quarter-century partnership of CBS and New York Univerity, and the University of Mid-America, an off-campus adult education consortium of twenty-five universities: Fred Hechinger, "Hard Times for Video Colleges," *This World* (August 19, 1982), p. 16.

54. Guthrie, "Emerging Political Economy," p. 112.

55. The former proposition is argued in C. H. Edison, "Schooling for Work and Working-Class Education in Urban America, 1880–1920," unpublished paper, University of Oregon, n.d., p. 47.

56. Manuscript autobiography, Robert Rantoul Papers, Beverly (Massachusetts) Historical Society, p. 229.

57. Kenneth Lockridge, *Literacy in Colonial New England* (New York: Norton, 1974); Chandler, *The Visible Hand,* esp. pp. 23–28; Theodore F. Marburg, "The Organization of Distribution and Marketing," in Kranzberg and Pursell, *Technology in Western Civilization,* 2:82.

58. Arthur G. Wirth, *Education in a Technological Society* (Scranton, Pa.: INTEXT, 1972), p. 69.

59. Charles Greathouse, *Tentative Course of Study in Industrial Subjects for the Public Schools of Indiana,* Department of Public Instruction Bulletin No. 2 (Indianapolis: 1913), p. 5.

60. Edith M. Tuttle, "Vocational Education for Girls," *Education* (1914), 34:449–450.
61. Burton R. Clark, *Educating the Expert Society* (San Francisco: Chandler, 1962), esp. pp. 44–51.
62. For a complain about rural schools' city orientations, see Will Carson Ryan, Jr., *Vocational Guidance and the Public Schools*, U.S. Bureau of Education Bulletin No. 24, 1918 (Washington, D.C.: GPO, 1919), pp. 15–16. The female share in vocational agriculture enrollments in all-day school programs averaged 3 percent between the passage of the Smith Hughes Act (1917) and 1937; it was 7 percent in evening classes: Roy W. Roberts, *Vocational and Practical Arts Education: History, Development, and Principles* (New York: Harper and Row, 1957), p. 196.
63. In 1978–79, 17.3 million students were enrolled in vocational education programs, excluding enrollments in apprenticeship programs, the military, and private firms; 60 percent of these were in secondary schools' courses, almost all in comprehensive high schools: Alan Weisberg, "What Research Has to Say About Vocational Education and the High Schools," *Phi Delta Kappan* (1983), 64:355.
64. Frank F. Bunker, *Reorganization of the Public School System*, U.S. Bureau of Education Bulletin No. 8, 1916 (Washington, D.C.: GPO, 1916), p. 127.
65. Federal Board for Vocational Education, *Sixteenth Annual Report to Congress* (Washington, D.C.: GPO, 1932), pp. 5, 37.
66. Edward Gross, "Plus Ça Change . . . ? The Sexual Structure of Occupations Over Time," *Social Problems* (1968), 16:198–208; Benson et al., *Descriptive Study of the Distribution of . . . Funds*, pp. 226, 255–277, 290–293; NAACP Legal Defense and Education Fund, *Vocational Education: Cause or Cure for Youth Unemployment? A Report to the Citizens of Oakland, California* (Oakland: 1981), p. 22.
67. Geraldine Joncich Clifford, " 'Marry, Stitch, Die, or Do Worse': Educating Women for Work," in Harvey Kantor and David B. Tyack, eds., *Work, Youth, and Schooling: Historical Perspectives on Vocationalism in American Education* (Stanford, Calif.: Stanford University Press, 1982), p. 268.
68. Susan J. Kleinberg, "Technology's Stepdaughters: The Impact of Industrialization upon Working Class Women, Pittsburgh, 1865-1890," Ph.D. dissertation, University of Pittsburgh, 1973, esp. pp. 203–219.
69. Ryan, *Vocational Guidance*, p. 49.
70. Selwyn K. Troen, "The Discovery of the Adolescent by American Educational Reformers, 1900–1920: An Economic Perspective," in Lawrence Stone, ed., *Schooling and Society* (Baltimore: John Hopkins University Press, 1976), esp. pp. 241–243.
71. J. Edward Mayman, "The Evolution of the Continuation School in New York City," *The School Review* (1933), 41:198.
72. "While the girl is getting her vocational training she cannot help getting the culture that comes from associating with other [more privileged] girls in a school community [with] a chance for fresh air and freedom which a factory or shop life, begun at fourteen, does not give." Tuttle, "Vocational Education for Girls," p. 450.
73. Quoted in Troen, "Discovery of the Adolescent," p. 244.
74. Berenice M. Fisher, *Industrial Education: American Ideals and Institutions* (Madison: University of Wisconsin Press, 1967), p. 48.
75. Lebergott, *Manpower in Economic Growth*, pp. 53*ff*.
76. Robert Church and Michael W. Sedlak, *Education in the United States; An Interpretive History* (New York: Free Press, 1976), pp. 181–186, 288–315; Edward Krug, *The Shaping of the American High School*, 2 vols. (vol. 1, New York: Harper and Row, 1964; vol. 2, Madison: University of Wisconsin Press, 1972).

77. Robert Hess and Irene Niura, "Sex and Class Affect Summer-Camp Enrollment," *InfoWorld* (1983), 5:52–55.

78. Richard O. Carlson, *Adoption of Educational Innovations* (Eugene; University of Oregon Press, 1965), pp. 74–75. Educators are not unique here. One of the reported obstacles to adopting teleconferencing in business is the tradition of doing business face to face: Stanley Pogrow, *Technological Change: Policy Implications for Funding and Delivering Educational Services in the 80s*, National Institute of Education School Finance Project, Contract No. NIE-P-81-0139, unpublished paper, 1982, p. 28. On the selective nature of the general transfer of technology, see Rosenberg, *Technology and American Economic Growth*, esp. pp. 83–86.

79. Lindley J. Stiles, "Revolution in Instruction," in *A Decade of Thought on Teacher Education: The Charles W. Hunt Lectures, 1960–1969*, compiled by Esther D. Hemsing (Washington, D.C.: 1969), pp. 35–36, 44.

80. Paul Saettler, *A History of Instructional Technology* (New York: McGraw-Hill, 1968), p. 98.

81. Floyd E. Brooker, "Communication in the Modern World," in Nelson B. Henry, ed., *Audiovisual Materials of Instruction*, Forty-Eighth Yearbook, National Society for the Study of Education. (Chicago: 1949), part 1, p. 18.

82. Henry, *Audiovisual Materials*, pp. 28–71; Saettler, *History of Instructional Technology;* Jennings *"Mass Media, Mind, and Makeshift,"* pp. 566–568; Michael Scriven, "Breakthroughs in Educational Technology," in Cirincioni-Coles, *The Future of Education*, esp. pp. 234–240; Cowan, "From Virginia Dare to Virginia Slims," pp. 61–63; T. R. Ide, "The Potentials and Limitations of Television as an Educational Medium," in David R. Olson, ed., *Media and Symbols: The Forms of Expression, Communication, and Education*, Seventy-Third Yearbook, National Society for the Study of Education (Chicago: University of Chicago Press, 1974), part 1, pp. 330–356; Richard I. Evans et al., *The University Faculty and Educational Television: Hostility, Resistance, and Change* (Houston: 1962); Wailand Bessant et al., *Adoption and Utilization of Instructional Television* (Austin: University of Texas Press, 1968).

83. Simon Ramo, "A New Technique in Education," in Morris Philipson, ed., *Automation: Implications for the Future* (New York: Vintage, 1962), p. 434. See also Tom Whiston et al., *An Annotated Bibliography on the Relationship Between Technological Change and Educational Development* (Paris: 1980), pp. 117–134; Anthony G. Oettinger, *Run, Computer, Run: The Mythology of Educational Innovation* (Cambridge, Mass.: Harvard University Press, 1969).

84. Seymour Papert, *Mindstorms: Children, Computers, and Powerful Ideas* (New York: Basic Books, 1980), p. viii. On the conservative uses of computers in instruction to date he contends that this is a natural but temporary response. "It took years before designers of automobiles accepted the idea that they were cars, not 'horseless carriages.' " (p. 36).

85. Henry F. Wolcott, *Teachers Versus Technocrats* (Eugene: Center of Educational Policy Management, 1977), p. 245.

86. Greater use was made of programmed instruction in junior high schools, especially in mathematics and English: Saettler, *A History of Instructional Technology*, p. 225. Current newspaper accounts report more computers available in junior high schools than in other schools.

87. Charles H. Judd, "The Significance for Textbook-Making of the Newer Concepts in Education," *Elementary School Journal* (1936), 36:575.

88. Donald F. Hackett, "Industrial Arts Leads the Way," *Man/Society/Technology* (1971), 31:35.

89. Peter F. Drucker, "Quality Education: The New Growth Area," *Wall Street Journal,* July 19, 1983.

90. The American Society of Engineering Education's Committee on Goals recommended, in 1968, "an increase of emphasis upon professionally oriented liberal education in a lengthened program": W. E. Howland, "The Argument: Engineering Education for Social Leadership," *Technology and Culture* (1969), 10:3. Also, Charles S. Benson et al., *An Assessment of the the Reliability and Consistency in Reporting of Vocational Education Data Available from National Information Systems,* Project on National Vocational Education Resources, unpublished paper, University of California, Berkeley, December 1980, p. 41.

11. The Impact of Technology on American Religion

Martin E. Marty
University of Chicago

What many have regarded as the most searching critiques of the technological order were issued in 1954 from the pen of a French lay Protestant who has had enormous influence in American religion, Jacques Ellul. In *La Technique* he spoke of technology as "the ensemble of practices by which one uses available resources in order to achieve certain valued ends." For the Ellulians in America, this has meant that an autonomous and artifical "envelope" or milieu has been created by humans and now threatens to engulf them, to determine virtually all aspects of their existence. While the rise of technology, related as it is to tool making, begins with the wheel and the oldest weapons, the acceleration in technological invention and the exponential increase in energies devoted to its order and milieu in modern times—the term "technology" was first needed and invented as recently as 1829—have issued in reflections upon both the positive and negative aspects of technology in the domain of the spirit, of religion. The response has been profoundly ambiguous.

Technology, Participation, Privatization

If we see the development of technology as a main feature of or a parallel element in the late stages of the Industrial Revolution, it is natural to apply characteristic sociological modes of understanding and expectation and thus to project and observe certain almost inevitable trends. Sociologists like Thomas Luckmann, for example, observe how in Western Europe the coming of industrialization helped lead to a drastic decline in religious participation.

For a complex of reasons, this decline has been less characteristic of the United States. If we take 1829 as a symbolic year, the year in which "technology" was coined and when more goods were first produced in factories than at home, we would find that perhaps 10 to 20 percent of the population was religiously affiliated. It may be that the terms of affiliation became cheaper as time passed, or that the culture bore fewer religious meanings and differentiated institutions had to take over. In any case, the coming of technological industrialization was accompanied by an almost consistent rise in church membership (to over 60 percent) from the 1870s into the 1960s. Somehow, Americans blended technological mastery with religious search and identification.

At the same time the "privatization" that Luckmann and others observed, in which religion becomes "a private affair," and can be taken à la carte, on a pick and choose basis, has been enhanced by the technology of modern publishing and broadcasting. These make it easier for a consumers' market to develop and for people to resist or neglect community and come into command of religious signals that appeal to them in privacy.

The Technology of Worship

Gathered and incorporated American religion converges on worship. While religious institutions may possess mimeograph machines, television recorders, committees, mailing lists, and computers just as other institutions do, they see themselves primarily as communities of praise and prayer or contemplation. Worship and liturgy, usually in a sanctuary, is the concentrated and peak experience of those who come together.

Technology has made many kinds of impact on American congregations gathered for worship. While the sanctuaries evoke pretechnological instrumentalities, often in the form of candle flames and tracker-action pipe organs (as if these marvellous instruments were not the highest technology of their day), the "artificial" has largely taken over. The electronic organ, the electric candle, the neon cross, the air conditioner, do not seem jarring to people who use imagery from natural and anciently historical worlds.

The satirist of religion can find fair fields here. In Baptist traditions, for example, where a tank must be provided for adult baptism by immersion, various companies vie to produce more efficient filling, emptying, and safety devices. There are "drive-in" viewing chambers for people to pay last respects to a corpse. Yet if there is some contradiction and pathos in these displays, there is also confirmation of the thesis that churches and synagogues (with their electric doors opening and closing before the sacred scrolls) house people who are at least ambiguous and often affirmative about technology right at the center of their corporate lives.

Technology and the Spiritual Search

For all the celebration of the mixed blessings of technology during industrialization and urbanization, it cannot be said that on any extensive scale the religious groups of America have been able to find or fabricate an extensive symbolic network for liturgical appreciation of technology. In many, but still the minority, of cases, stained glass windows will rely on the symbolism of spacecraft, aircraft, and skyscraper. Yet these are not easily seen as primal symbols and often become dated while bread, wine, water, circles, lambs, and the like from pastoral or archaic realms remain dominant.

When Americans celebrate their "operative" worlds, they are ready to see technology as somehow inside the divine order of human expansiveness. When they converge on their "passional" sides, somehow the primal wins out and either through nostalgia or conscious and calculated endeavor, efforts are made to connect the spiritual with the rural. One goes on retreats into the countryside. The Catholic seminary until Vatican II was addressed R.F.D., though Catholicism is largely an urban movement in America. The Thomas Mertons in remote Gethsemanes have been more frequently seen as spiritual leaders, while the Dorothy Days in New York are practical activists—though both of them can also be seen in reversed roles and situations. "Seek a city saint!" a book title enjoined, in its effort to encourage spirituality and sanctity in the technological order. Yet the psalmic language of tree and brook and natural experience still dominate imagery for the soul.

The Engineering Mentality

Many theologians of recent decades have tried to make distinctions between types of reasoning as a result of the technological impact. Paul Tillich, notably, spoke of "technical reason" as but one way of reflecting. Many religious thinkers have come to a fundamental distinction between the types of reason which Pascal spoke of as "the heart's reasons, which reason does not know" and technical reasoning of a problem-solving sort.

The engineering mentality, to take but one illustration, is pervasive in the religious laity in an age of engineering. Such an outlook is heavily empirical: it deals with classification, enumeration, and easily documentable fact. Either a truss is strong enough to hold a certain weight or it is not; which is the case can easily be tested. Such practical and calculable reason can come to dominate thinking at the expense of modes that relate to philosophical idealism, religious experientialism, and the like.

It has often been noted that religious fundamentalism is often attractive to certain kinds of scientists while the social sciences and humanities, where other modes of reasoning prevail, are avoided. The practical, technical, statistical, and engineering mentalities have led some religious groups to measure their truth by their success, their attractiveness, their efficiency. Other, not necessarily superior but still religiously valid modes, are then on the defensive, cherished apologetically by a minority.

Technology and the Application of Ethics

Most religious groups assert both that their ethical systems draw on "absolute," timeless, or universal mandates *and* that they can be somehow situational. Thus "thou shalt not kill" is qualified by the permission or injunction to kill if one is a policeman involved in preventing crime or a military person in a "just war." Yet the situational is usually secondary to the universal or timeless features. Modern technology, however, has created greater strain than ever before

on such ethical systems. The best illustration is technological weaponry. In the Christian case, which has analogues elsewhere, between
the ethics of mere violence in the name of God on one hand and pure
passivity and pacifism on the other, churches generated "just war"
theories. These were more easily applied in eras when one could more
easily differentiate between civilian and military populations and targets. Chemical warfare and nuclear weapons, however, have made
these distinctions largely invalid.

For these reasons leaders like the U.S. Catholic bishops in 1983 in
their pastoral letter on the nuclear weapon showed the need to struggle with new ethical formulations. They might insist that the "just
war" belongs to permanent Catholic teaching but that its norms cannot be applied in the indiscriminate potential of weaponry in the
nuclear age. This assault on old ethical traditions shows up in the
moral fields of communication, commerce, and the like—all altered
by technology.

The Natural Order

For the most part, American religionists welcomed the tools and
instruments technology made available. These were seen as extensions
of the domain of God. In biblical faith, which shaped much of the
American ethos through Christianity, Judaism, and the Enlightenment (which rationalized the processes and entered the mainstream
through the nation's founders), there has always been a strong impulse to use technology to transform and reshape the natural world
toward human ends.

If there have all along been critics who feared technology as a rival
to the divine Creator, as a beguiling world of artifact which seduced
humans to hubris, a fundamental sin, or to the apotheosis of the
human, these have been countered by celebrators of technology. So
while religious leadership can be portrayed as a grudging acceptant
of scientific dominion, another side of religious expression has encouraged technology.

Some critics of Christian impulses to dominate nature complain
that page one of the Bible, with its command to have dominion over
nature, is at the root of the western impulse to pollute and destroy. It
cannot be doubted that some religious forces have worked to such

ends. At the same time, from Native Americans through Transcendentalists to psalmists and poets, people with a concern for the spiritual have also worked to preserve, conserve, celebrate, and be stewards of nature over technology—in the name of faith.

The Biological Revolutions

Religion has always had a great stake in understandings of *bios,* the body, physical and biological existence. Native American, Jewish-Christian, African, and Asian religions of the sort that have been at home in the American landscape, were all born with rich ties to concepts of wellness and wholeness. Any changes in the understandings and uses of the body through technology therefore necessarily produce threat and opportunity to traditional faiths.

Nowhere has the impact of technology on religious systems of understanding been more profound than where it collides with historic interpretations and employments of the cycle of human development. When technology produced "the pill" it gave people instruments to plan population and control birth. Originally most religions resisted all the technological or "artificial" forms of birth control. Today only Catholicism among the larger faith clusters in America officially resists, and opinion polls reveal that in practice even such resistance has become routine.

Yet technological medicine as it relates to abortion, *in vitro* fertilization, organ transplants, the production of instruments for prolonging or shortening biological existence, "genetic tampering," and the like in every case has called forth "bioethical" responses. These are not all specifically religious, since ethics has many bases. Yet very frequently theological comprehensions are at stake, and almost all religious groups have seen the medical milieu to be one of decisive challenge and opportunity to belief and practice systems.

What Is the Human?

Religions of America like all complex systems possess anthropological insights. What is man, or, nowadays, what is the human or what is humane is a root question in religion, taken up as it ordinarily is with a divine/human dialectic. While spiritual Luddites have asked "How can we prevent the development of a technological order?" the majority of religionists have, without using precisely such terms, asked "How can a *humane* technological order emerge?"

Since the technological envelope alters almost all the circumstances of life for the human, it is natural that leadership in partly rival systems, and this includes most religions, should see themselves as custodians of that which is distinctively human. Technological understandings of brain and mind have many kinds of impacts on religion, most of them reductionist. The human is "nothing but" this or that—a behaviorist mechanism, for example—or, in most recent probes, characterized by interest in artificial intelligence, the brain is "nothing but" a most sophisticated and well-programmed computer.

Religious forces have tended to resist such reductionism and made claims, not all of them easily demonstrated empirically, that the human is "something more." Most American religions have had a kind of dualistic outlook on the human, seeing humankind as open to orders of transcendence, sacrality, and the divine, to "more than" what appears in the laboratory or engineering center. Exactly how the rationale for the distinctively human "image of God" motif is argued depends upon the particular faiths and articulators.

What Is Valuable to the Person?

Not only definitions of humanness matter to those who cope with technology. They also are preoccupied with the ways to guard personhood in the face of what even the most enthusiastic celebrators of technology know can be a threat: the loss of appreciation for the individual person or the person-in-community, in the face of the values that more readily accompany life in the technological milieu.

There is no doubt that technology has made it possible and sometimes necessary to treat people more manifestly as "things" than before. Religious prophets protest what one has called this "thingification" of persons. They become numbers, part of statistical composites, subjects transferred from personal identity to computer cards, automated potential constituents and clients, elements of a market.

Religion sees itself as custodian of the person. The founders of most faiths came to disrupt existing stultifying systems and replace them by forms in which the human counts more than the system. So their heirs are troubled when secular systems overwhelm the person. It must also be said, however, that religious leadership on many occasions notes that technology can also aid personhood. The telephone, for instance, promotes human communication and warmth in the case of people who would otherwise be isolated and alienated. The automobile makes possible more convenient access to gathering and thus to personal life in community.

Technology and Instrumentality: an Irony

When the larger implications of the industrial revolution and technological refinements impressed themselves on American psyches late in the nineteenth century, American Protestantism and, to a lesser extent, other faith clusters, generated "modernist" theologies. These embraced progressivism, liberalism, and human creativity. Theology came to be adapted to meet the new age, not only in the embrace of evolutionary development but also in the encouragement of the scientific Zeitgeist. In precisely the same period most of the modern conservatisms and antiprogressivisms developed, forms characterized by the term "fundamentalism."

Ironically, the modernist and liberal forces have been relatively slow and maladept at using many technological instruments. Meanwhile the fundamentalists, who had little rationale for embracing technology, put it to work almost uncritically. When radio came on the scene in the 1920s, characteristically, the Old Fashioned Revival Hour, the conservative Lutheran Hour, and the like were born. The modern "electronic church" on television is almost entirely in the hands of people who mistrusted science. The fundamentalists are ready to use the instrumentalities of mass mailing, opinion formation, printing, and the like, all in the name of "spreading the Gospel," while the liberals are the worriers about the encroachments of technology on the vital meaning and message of religion. In sum: protechnology cannot be tied to liberal and antitechnology to conservative practice, no matter how their competing belief systems would lead one to expect the two kinds of forces to think and act.

The Mission of the Religious Organizations: Humanitarianism

American religions have seen themselves as decisively moral agencies. Not all religions elsewhere have ethical and moral impulses near their centers: they concentrate more on how people locate themselves in the sacral realm, how they find meaning in the face of chaos. The biblical prophetic faith impels people to works of justice and mercy. The privileged place that religious organizations hold in America as cherished and tax-exempt institutions goads them into advertising themselves as being of service in ethical and humanitarian ways.

To fill these ends, most religious organizations have taken advantage of technology to promote their causes. To take but one example: whereas once religious groups saw their mission to be one chiefly of converting people around the world, more recently many of them have justified their work and carried out their mandates by building schools, clinics, hospitals, and relief centers. Most notably, they have promoted Third World development. This has led them not so much to "send food" as to send Ph.D.s in agronomy, to encourage the "green revolution," to lend engineers and engineering, and the like.

Whoever studies twentieth-century mission literature, then, will see that very close to its fundamental justification is the way American religious involvement can lead to the enhancement of life for suffering people in underdeveloped nations. The relief agencies welcome rapid transportation, high-quality packaging, and electronic instruments for staying in touch with their outposts. There is little criticism of technology in these circumstances.

Summary

Religious institutions in a technological world are less able than before to segregate themselves from cultural shifts. Mount Athos or Mt. St. Michel and the desert are ever harder to preserve or turn into creative alternatives for significant minorities in modern populations. What happens around them happens also to believers. They may create spiritual cocoons that shelter them from some changes, or build greenhouses of faith to protect and nurture the young. It is possible to produce a para-society inside the larger one in the case of strenuous cognitive minorities like the Jehovah's Witnesses.

Yet technology is pervasive. The television set and the radio penetrate the monasteries and rectories. The Jehovah's Witnesses turn on fluorescent lights and go into computerized printing. What Ellul saw as a "milieu" is present on all hands. Yet somehow individuals grow a kind of psychic cuticle, which means that technology reaches only some aspects of their life, or all aspects but only in some ways. While religious thinkers and other concerned people have served as critics and work to help protect what they see to be the distinctively human and thus spiritual, it cannot be said that in America technology is seen only as *la technique,* as a threat. Too many religious people have incorporated its modalities into their thinking and doing, have used its means to spread their message, and have celebrated its physical and, more ambiguously, its spiritual potential. The question for them remains, then, not how to resist or worship technology but how to make the technological order more open to humaneness.